EXERCISES in ENGLISH

Teacher Guide

LEVEL H

LoyolaPress.

CHICAGO

The Workout That Brings Mastery in Grammar, Usage, and Mechanics

Exercises in English is the perfect teaching tool for educators who want their students to be educationally fit and READY—ready to communicate effectively when writing or speaking, ready for everyday language arts tasks, ready for accelerated English-language learning, and ready for assessment. Here are some ways that a workout with Exercises in English helps students become READY for any language arts task that they encounter:

RIGOROUS PRACTICE

Students are provided with a multitude of exercises on each page. With so many opportunities for learning, "practice makes perfect" is achievable!

EXAMPLES AND DEFINITIONS

Success comes with systematic instruction. Each new grammar, usage, or mechanics concept is clearly explained through examples and definitions.

ASSESSMENT

GUM scores increase as students are assessed and master their work with sentences, verbal agreement, and punctuation.

DIAGRAMMING FOR IN-DEPTH LANGUAGE STUDY

When students diagram sentences, they create visual representations of their learning—they can actually see how words work together to make correctly constructed sentences.

YEARLONG REINFORCEMENT FOR LEARNERS AT EVERY LEVEL

With six books of varying levels and a multitude of lessons in each book, students are provided with learning opportunities that last a full school year and beyond.

Grammar Workbook

EXERCISES in ENGLISH
LEVEL G

EXERCISES in ENGLISH
LEVEL G

Name _____

85. Reviewing Adverbs

A. Underline each adverb. On the line write its type—time, place, degree, manner, affirmation, negation.

[place] 1. Christopher Columbus sailed westward from Spain in 1492.

[affirmation] 2. He was actually looking for Asia when he landed in America.

[time] 3. Christopher Columbus is often credited with America's discovery.

[time] 4. But civilizations were already here when he arrived.

[degree] 5. Many were highly developed cultures.

... with an appropriate interrogative adverb. [Answers may vary.]

... reach America come from?

... water?

D. Write on the line whether each *italicized* word is an adjective or an adverb.

[adjective] 16. Most Native American cultures had developed agriculture by 2000 BC.

[adverb] 17. Maize was the most commonly grown grain.

[adverb] 18. Livestock was less important to Native American cultures.

[adverb] 19. Protein was obtained primarily from plants.

[adjective] 20. Additional protein was acquired through hunting and fishing.

E. Underline each adverb phrase once and each adverb clause twice. A sentence may have a phrase, a clause, or both. Circle the word(s) the phrase or the clause modifies.

21. Astronauts float in space, our science teacher said, because there is no gravity.

22. Gravity is what holds people down; if there wasn't any gravity, they would float everywhere.

23. Yesterday our class performed a gravity experiment in the lab.

24. Although we were careful, it did not work.

25. We should have read the lab manual before we started.

26. I repeated the experiment several times by myself.

27. Unfortunately, I failed in every attempt.

28. Even though I didn't succeed, I may try again.

29. Since there is gravity everywhere on Earth, my experiments are probably permanently doomed.

30. Eventually, as an astronaut, I'll fly to the Moon and personally experience the lack of gravity.

... It Yourself

... sheet of paper, write five or six sentences about something ... recently. Be sure to use adverbs correctly.

... journal, a work in progress, ... applying the skills you have

... and adverbs?

... correctly?

Name _____

58. Reviewing Verbs

A. Underline the verb in each sentence. On the first line write **T** if the verb is transitive or **I** if it is intransitive. On the second line write **A** if the verb is active or **P** if it is passive.

[I] [A] 1. Some animals migrate every year.

[T] [P] 2. Monarch butterflies are found in Canada and the United States in the summer and in Mexico in the winter.

[I] [A] 3. Many birds fly to new homes every spring and fall.

[T] [P] 4. Pacific salmon complete their migration over their lifetimes.

[T] [P] 5. These migratory patterns are studied by U.S. and Canadian scientists

B. Underline the linking verb in each sentence. Circle the subject complement.

6. Irruption is an unpredictable form of migration.

7. Lemmings are an example of an animal that migrates in this manner.

8. Another migratory pattern is remigration, which occurs across generations.

9. Many scientists are intent on studying irruption.

10. Animal migration is hard for scientists to track.

C. Complete each sentence with the correct form of the verb.

study–present progressive, active

taught–present perfect, passive

visit–future, active

migrate–future progressive, active

travels–present, active

place–present perfect, passive

hatch–present, active

swim–future, active

11. June's class [is studying] _____ animal migration.

12. It [has been taught] _____ many interesting facts.

13. The students _____ the Columbia River next semester. [will visit]

14. The Chinook salmon _____ then. [will be migrating]

15. This salmon [travels] _____ more than 2,000 miles to spawn.

16. These fish [have been placed] _____ on the threatened species list.

17. Baby salmon [hatch] _____ in rivers and streams.

18. After spending their adult lives in the ocean, they [will swim] _____ back to the same river to spawn.

CONTINUED

Name _____

prevent–present perfect, active

work–present perfect progressive, active

19. Dams across the rivers _____ some salmon from reaching their spawning grounds. [have prevented]

20. Many people _____ to save the salmon. [have been working]

D. Write on the line the mood of the *italicized* verb. Use **A** for indicative, **B** for imperative, and **C** for subjunctive.

[B] 21. *Return* these books to the library.

[C] 22. Lamont wishes he *were* already on vacation.

[A] 23. My sister *is reading* a scary book.

[C] 24. If Emily *were* here, she would know what to do.

[A] 25. Nathan *can walk* to school if he chooses.

E. Circle the correct verb in parentheses.

26. The team (is are) meeting before the game.

27. The team (has have) to win to advance in the tournament.

28. Each of the players (want wants) to do well.

29. Neither of the captains (know knows) which team is playing today.

30. After the game was over, everyone (raised rose) to leave.

Try It Yourself
On a separate sheet of paper write five sentences about something you and your friends do. Be sure to use verbs correctly.

Check Your Own Work
Choose a selection from your writing portfolio, your journal, a work in progress, an assignment from school, or a letter. Revise it, applying the skills you have learned in this chapter. This checklist will help you.

✔ Have you conveyed the meaning clearly and accurately by using the correct form of the verb?

✔ Have you written the correct form of the troublesome verbs?

✔ Have you used verb tense correctly?

Inside Exercises in English

RIGOROUS PRACTICE

Focused skills are practiced in a variety of ways.

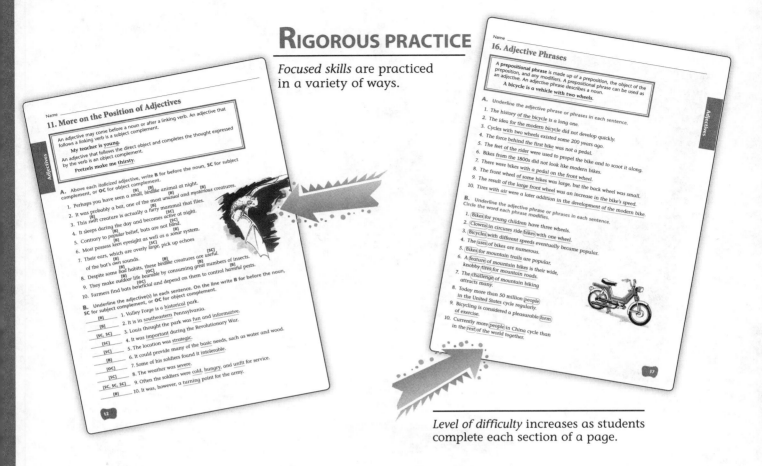

Level of difficulty increases as students complete each section of a page.

EXAMPLES AND DEFINITIONS

Clear definitions and numerous examples guide instruction.

Name ____

11. More on the Position of Adjectives

An adjective may come before a noun or after a linking verb. An adjective that follows a linking verb is a subject complement.

My teacher is young.

An adjective that follows the direct object and completes the thought expressed by the verb is an object complement.

Pretzels make me thirsty.

A. Above each italicized adjective, write **B** for before the noun, **SC** for subject complement, or **OC** for object complement.

1. Perhaps you have seen a *small, birdlike* animal at night.
2. It was probably a bat, one of the most *unusual* and *mysterious* creatures.
3. This *swift* creature is actually a *furry* mammal that flies.
4. It sleeps during the day and becomes *active* at night.
5. Contrary to *popular* belief, bats are not *blind.*
6. Most possess *keen* eyesight as well as a *sonar* system.
7. Their ears, which are overly *large,* pick up echoes of the bat's own sounds.
8. Despite some bad habits, these *birdlike* creatures are *useful.*
9. They make *outdoor* life *bearable* by consuming *great* numbers of insects.
10. Farmers find bats *beneficial* and depend on them to control *harmful* pests.

B. Underline the adjective(s) in each sentence. On the line write **B** for before the noun, **SC** for subject complement, or **OC** for object complement.

___ 1. Valley Forge is a historical park.
___ 2. It is in southeastern Pennsylvania.
___ 3. Louis thought the park was fun and informative.
___ 4. It was important during the Revolutionary War.
___ 5. The location was strategic.
___ 6. It could provide many of the basic needs, such as water and wood.
___ 7. Some of his soldiers found it intolerable.
___ 8. The weather was severe.
___ 9. Often the soldiers were cold, hungry, and unfit for service.
___ 10. It was, however, a turning point for the army.

Name ____

16. Adjective Phrases

A prepositional phrase is made up of a preposition, the object of the preposition, and any modifiers. A prepositional phrase can be used as an adjective. An adjective phrase describes a noun.

A bicycle is a vehicle with two wheels.

A. Underline the adjective phrase or phrases in each sentence.

1. The history of the bicycle is a long one.
2. The idea for the modern bicycle did not develop quickly.
3. Cycles with two wheels existed some 200 years ago.
4. The force behind the first bike was not a pedal.
5. The feet of the rider were used to propel the bike and to scoot it along.
6. Bikes from the 1800s did not look like modern bikes.
7. There were bikes with a pedal on the front wheel.
8. The front wheel of some bikes was large, but the back wheel was small.
9. The result of the large front wheel was an increase in the bike's speed.
10. Tires with air were a later addition in the development of the modern bike.

B. Underline the adjective phrase or phrases in each sentence. Circle the word each phrase modifies.

1. Bikes for young children have three wheels.
2. Clowns in circuses ride bikes with one wheel.
3. Bicycles with different speeds eventually became popular.
4. The uses of bikes are numerous.
5. Bikes for mountain trails are popular.
6. A feature of mountain bikes is their wide, knobby tires for mountain roads.
7. The challenge of mountain biking attracts many.
8. Today more than 50 million people in the United States cycle regularly.
9. Bicycling is considered a pleasurable form of exercise.
10. Currently more people in China cycle than in the rest of the world together.

Name ____

67. Possessives with Gerunds; Using *-ing* Verb Forms

Gerunds may be preceded by a possessive noun or a possessive adjective. These possessives describe the doer of action of the gerund.

My deciding to go on the camping trip surprised my family.

A verb with an *-ing* ending may be a gerund (a noun), a participle (an adjective), or a part of a verb phrase in the progressive tense.

Exciting adults as well as children was the aim of the trapeze artist. (gerund)

Meanwhile, exciting the audience in the arena, acrobats performed their acts. (participial adjective before a noun)

Their performances, exciting and courageous, left us in awe. (participial adjective after a noun)

Every act was exciting. (participial adjective after a linking verb)

Large elephants were exciting children in a nearby tent. (part of a progressive verb)

A. Underline the correct form.

1. (Our Us) choosing a camping trip proved to be a good idea.
2. My brother agreed to (my me) taking his sleeping bag.
3. The scout leader was surprised at (me my) volunteering to put up the tent.
4. He watched (my me), wearing a pleased expression, as I did the job efficiently.
5. (Him His) praising me for my work made me feel good.
6. (Joe Joe's) cooking the supper was a surprise to us.
7. (Him His) making pioneer stew was a good idea—we loved the meal.
8. The (animals animals') chattering far into the night kept us awake.
9. On the second night we again heard (them their), noting that they had moved closer to our camp.
10. (Them Their) enjoying the outdoor experience so wholeheartedly meant that the scouts would make a similar trip soon.

B. Identify each italicized word ending in *-ing* as a gerund, a participial adjective, or part of a progressive verb.

[gerund] 1. *Singing* around the campfire was a fun part of the trip.
[participial adjective] 2. Our *singing* voices filled the night air.
[participial adjective] 3. *Singing* the entire campfire song, James proved to us that he knew all the verses.
[part of a progressive verb] 4. We were *singing* old songs into the night.
[gerund] 5. After the *singing* ended, we returned to our tents.
[participial adjective] 6. *Hiking* in the woods, we learned to identify certain trees and wildlife.
[part of a progressive verb] 7. I was *hiking* in the woods when I saw a dappled fawn.
[gerund] 8. *Hiking* in the woods was the highlight of the trip for me.
[participial adjective] 9. It is a good thing I had brought good *hiking* boots.
[participial adjective] 10. This *hiking* experience made me appreciate the outdoors.

ASSESSMENT

Comprehensive reviews allow for classroom assessment or preparation for standardized tests.

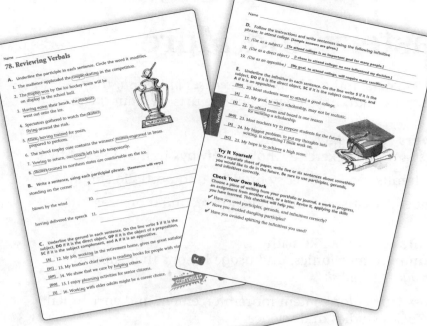

DIAGRAMMING FOR IN-DEPTH LANGUAGE STUDY

Sentence diagramming helps students better understand and remember concepts.

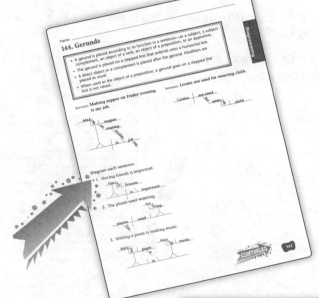

YEARLONG REINFORCEMENT FOR LEARNERS AT EVERY LEVEL

Leveled books allow for differentiated instruction. Determine which books to use based on individual student achievement rather than grade level.

Handbook of Terms invites all learners to refresh and expand their knowledge.

Handbook of Terms

ADJECTIVES

An **adjective** points out or describes a noun.

An **article** points out a noun. *A, an,* and *the* are articles: *a game, an apple, the rules.*

A **demonstrative adjective** points out a specific person, place, or thing. *This, that, these,* and *those* are demonstrative adjectives: *this book, those pencils.*

A **descriptive adjective** tells about age, size, shape, color, origin, or another quality of a noun. A descriptive adjective usually comes before the noun it describes, but it may follow the noun. It may also follow a linking verb: It was a *sunny* morning. The popcorn, *crunchy* and *salty,* tasted great.

An **indefinite adjective** refers to any or all members of a group. Indefinite adjectives include *all, another, any, both, each, either, few, many, more, most, much, neither, other, several,* and *some: both* boys, *either* girl.

An **interrogative adjective** is used in questions. *What, which,* and *whose* are interrogative adjectives: *Whose* book is this?

A **possessive adjective** shows possession or ownership. The possessive adjectives are *my, your, his, her, its, our, your,* and *their: my* car, *your* motorcycle.

A **proper adjective** is formed from a proper noun. A proper adjective begins with a capital letter: *American* history.

See also **antecedents, clauses, comparisons, participles, prepositions, sentences, subject-verb agreement.**

ADVERBS

An **adverb** modifies a verb, an adjective, or another adverb.

- An **adverb of affirmation** tells that something is positive or gives consent or approval: The music is *certainly* beautiful.
- An **adverb of degree** answers the question *how much* or *how little:* The boy is *very* tall.
- An **adverb of manner** answers the question *how,* or *in what manner:* Jason draws *well.*

Mastery and More

When teachers and students use *Exercises in English,* they receive more than any other language arts workout offers.

Teachers receive MORE with

- easy-to-grade exercises that are always in multiples of five.

- perforated pages for easy grading and portfolio storage.

- embedded answers that make correcting a breeze.

Students receive MORE with

- grammar, mechanics, and usage lessons that support *Voyages in English.*

- cross-curricular content for reinforcement and enrichment in social studies and science.

- character-education lessons with positive role models as examples.

- practice in context for authentic writing opportunities and self-assessment.

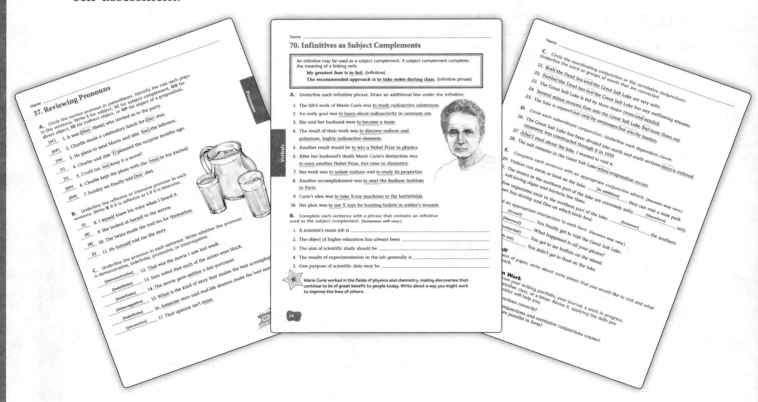

Comprehensive Scope and Sequence

Review the Scope and Sequence on pages T7–T11 to note how skill instruction is scaffolded across levels. Use the level or levels that best meet your students' needs.

Exercises in English—Scope and Sequence

SENTENCES	C	D	E	F	G	H
The Four Kinds of Sentences	✔	✔	✔	✔	✔	✔
Subjects and Predicates	✔	✔	✔	✔	✔	✔
Simple Subjects and Predicates		✔		✔	✔	✔
Compound Subjects and Predicates		✔	✔	✔	✔	✔
Direct Objects		✔	✔	✔	✔	✔
Complete Subjects and Predicates			✔	✔	✔	✔
Natural and Inverted Order in Sentences			✔	✔	✔	✔
Indirect Objects				✔	✔	✔
Compound Sentences				✔	✔	✔
Complex Sentences					✔	✔
Compound Complex Sentences						✔
NOUNS	**C**	**D**	**E**	**F**	**G**	**H**
Proper and Common Nouns	✔	✔	✔	✔	✔	
Singular and Plural Nouns	✔	✔	✔	✔	✔	✔
Possessive Nouns	✔	✔	✔	✔	✔	✔
Nouns Used as Subjects		✔	✔	✔		✔
Nouns Used as Objects		✔	✔	✔	✔	✔
Count and Noncount Nouns		✔	✔	✔		✔
Nouns Used as Subject Complements			✔	✔	✔	✔
Nouns Used in Direct Address			✔	✔		
Nouns Used as Objects of Prepositions			✔	✔	✔	✔
Appositives				✔	✔	✔
Collective Nouns				✔	✔	
Concrete and Abstract Nouns				✔	✔	
Words Used as Nouns and Verbs				✔		
Nouns Used as Object Complements						✔
VERBS	**C**	**D**	**E**	**F**	**G**	**H**
Regular and Irregular Verbs	✔	✔	✔	✔	✔	✔
Present Tense	✔	✔	✔	✔	✔	✔
Progressive Tenses	✔	✔	✔	✔	✔	✔
Past Tense	✔	✔	✔	✔	✔	✔
Future Tenses	✔	✔	✔	✔	✔	✔
Action Verbs	✔	✔	✔			
Verbs of Being	✔	✔	✔			
Helping Verbs	✔	✔				
Forms of *Bring*	✔					

Forms of *Buy*	✔					
Forms of *Come*	✔					
Forms of *Eat*	✔					
Forms of *Go*	✔		✔			
Forms of *See*	✔		✔			
Forms of *Sit* and *Set*	✔		✔	✔		
Forms of *Take*	✔		✔			
Forms of *Write*	✔					
Forms of *To Be*	✔	✔	✔			
Forms of *Begin*		✔				
Forms of *Break*		✔	✔			
Forms of *Choose*		✔	✔			
Forms of *Do*		✔				
Verb Phrases		✔	✔	✔	✔	
Intransitive Verbs (Linking Verbs)		✔	✔	✔	✔	✔
There Is and *There Are*		✔		✔	✔	
Subject-Verb Agreement			✔	✔	✔	✔
Transitive Verbs			✔	✔	✔	✔
Doesn't and *Don't*			✔	✔	✔	✔
Let and *Leave*			✔	✔		
Teach and *Learn*			✔			
Lie and *Lay*			✔	✔		
Rise and *Raise*				✔		
Perfect Tenses				✔	✔	
Words Used as Nouns and Verbs					✔	
Active and Passive Voice					✔	✔
Modal Auxiliary Verbs					✔	✔
You Are and *You Were*					✔	
Compound Tenses						✔
Emphatic Verb Forms						✔
PRONOUNS	**C**	**D**	**E**	**F**	**G**	**H**
Singular and Plural Pronouns	✔	✔	✔			
Subject Pronouns	✔	✔	✔	✔	✔	✔
Possessive Pronouns	✔	✔	✔	✔	✔	✔
I and *Me*	✔	✔				
Pronouns Used as Subject Complements	✔		✔	✔	✔	✔
Pronouns Used as Direct Objects		✔	✔	✔	✔	✔
The Person of Pronouns		✔	✔	✔		
The Gender of Pronouns			✔			

	C	D	E	F	G	H
We and *Us*		✔				
Pronouns Used as Objects of Prepositions			✔	✔		
Pronouns Used in Contractions			✔	✔		
Reflexive Pronouns			✔	✔	✔	
Interrogative Pronouns				✔	✔	✔
Indefinite Pronouns				✔	✔	✔
Double Negatives				✔		
Pronouns Used as Indirect Objects					✔	✔
Who and *Whom*					✔	✔
Pronouns Used After *Than* and *As*					✔	✔
Relative Pronouns					✔	✔
Demonstrative Pronouns					✔	✔
Nothing and *Anything*					✔	
Pronouns Used as Objects of Prepositions						✔
Intensive Pronouns			✔			✔
ADJECTIVES	**C**	**D**	**E**	**F**	**G**	**H**
Descriptive Adjectives	✔			✔	✔	✔
Adjectives That Tell How Many	✔	✔	✔	✔		
Indefinite and Definite Articles	✔	✔	✔	✔	✔	
Demonstrative Adjectives	✔	✔	✔	✔	✔	✔
Comparative Forms of Adjectives	✔	✔	✔	✔	✔	✔
Possessive Adjectives		✔	✔	✔		
Common and Proper Adjectives		✔	✔			✔
Good and *Bad*		✔				
The Position of Adjectives			✔	✔	✔	✔
Superlative Forms of Adjectives			✔	✔	✔	✔
Adjectives Used as Subject Complements				✔		
Words Used as Adjectives or Nouns				✔	✔	✔
Those and *Them*				✔		
Interrogative Adjectives				✔		✔
Few and *Little*					✔	✔
ADVERBS	**C**	**D**	**E**	**F**	**G**	**H**
Adverbs of Time	✔	✔	✔	✔		
Adverbs of Place	✔	✔	✔	✔		
Good and *Well*	✔	✔	✔			
Comparative Adverbs		✔	✔	✔		✔
Adverbs of Manner		✔	✔	✔		
No, Not, and *Never*		✔	✔	✔		
Superlative Adverbs			✔	✔		
Real and *Very*			✔			

Their and *There*			✔	✔		
To, *Too*, and *Two*			✔	✔		
Adverbs and Adjectives				✔	✔	✔
There, *Their*, and *They're*					✔	
Farther and *Further*					✔	✔
Interrogative Adverbs					✔	✔
Adverbial Nouns					✔	✔
As . . . As, *So . . . As*, and *Equally*						✔
PUNCTUATION, CAPITALIZATION, ABBREVIATIONS	C	D	E	F	G	H
End Punctuation	✔	✔	✔	✔	✔	✔
Periods After Abbreviations, Titles, and Initials	✔	✔				
Capital Letters	✔	✔	✔	✔	✔	
Titles of Books and Poems	✔		✔	✔	✔	
Commas Used in Direct Address	✔	✔	✔	✔		
Punctuation in Direct Quotations	✔	✔	✔	✔		
Apostrophes		✔	✔			
Commas After *Yes* and *No*		✔	✔	✔		
Commas Separating Words in a Series		✔	✔	✔		
Commas After Parts of a Letter			✔	✔		
Commas in Dates and Addresses			✔	✔		
Commas in Geographical Names			✔			
Commas Used with Appositives				✔		
Commas Used in Compound Sentences				✔		
Semicolons and Colons				✔	✔	✔
Apostrophes, Hyphens, and Dashes				✔	✔	✔
Commas and Semicolons						✔
PREPOSITIONS, CONJUNCTIONS, INTERJECTIONS	C	D	E	F	G	H
Prepositions and Prepositional Phrases			✔	✔	✔	✔
Interjections			✔	✔	✔	✔
Between and *Among*			✔	✔		
From and *Off*			✔			
Adjectival Phrases			✔			
Adverbial Phrases			✔			
Coordinate Conjunctions			✔			
Words Used as Prepositions and Adverbs				✔	✔	✔
At and *To*				✔		
Beside and *Besides*, *In* and *Into*				✔		
Coordinate and Correlative Conjunctions					✔	

	C	D	E	F	G	H
Conjunctive Adverbs					✔	
Subordinate Conjunctions					✔	✔
Without and *Unless, Like, As,* and *As If*					✔	✔
PHRASES, CLAUSES	C	D	E	F	G	H
Adjectival Phrases				✔	✔	
Adverbial Phrases				✔	✔	
Adjectival Clauses					✔	✔
Adverbial Clauses					✔	✔
Restrictive and Nonrestrictive Clauses					✔	
Noun Clauses						✔
PARTICIPLES, GERUNDS, INFINITIVES	C	D	E	F	G	H
Participles						✔
Dangling Participles						✔
Gerunds						✔
Infinitives						✔
Hidden and Split Infinitives						✔
WORD STUDY SKILLS	C	D	E	F	G	H
Synonyms	✔	✔	✔	✔		
Antonyms	✔	✔				
Homophones	✔	✔	✔			
Contractions	✔	✔				
Compound Words		✔				

Correlation of Grade 8 *Voyages in English, 2006,* and Level H *Exercises in English, 2008*

Exercises in English, 2008

- Grammar is arranged in the same order as in *Voyages*, 2006, allowing students to work through the books simultaneously.

- Each grammar section in *Voyages* is supported by at least one lesson in *Exercises*.

- Some grammar sections in *Voyages* are supported by two or more lessons in *Exercises*. For example, Section 1.6 of *Voyages*, Grade 6, treats nouns used as objects. This section is supported by three lessons in *Exercises* that treat separately nouns used as direct objects, nouns used as indirect objects, and nouns used as objects of prepositions. This gives students extra practice in discrete grammar points.

- The grammar explanations in *Exercises* were rewritten to match those in *Voyages*, making it easy to move back and forth between books.

- An entire chapter of diagramming was added to *Exercises* to match that in *Voyages*. (This replaces the old Research Skills section. Research skills are taught in *Voyages* as part of the writing process, not as part of the grammar.)

- The Handbook of Terms for each level was rewritten to match that of *Voyages*.

- The TE front matter now contains a correlation of *Exercises* with the appropriate grade level of *Voyages*. (This replaces the old Sentence Analysis section.)

Features that were retained from the old *Exercises* include:

- Each exercise is based on grade-level science, social studies, or language arts content.

- The items in each exercise are divisible by 5 for easy grading.

- Character education lessons appear throughout each book.

- Section reviews provide regular assessment.

- Writing in context and self-assessment allow students to practice what they learn and to evaluate their own work.

- The TE contains overprinted answers.

- The TE front matter contains a scope and sequence chart of the entire program.

EXERCISES in ENGLISH

LOYOLAPRESS.

CHICAGO

Consultants

Therese Elizabeth Bauer
Martina Anne Erdlen
Anita Patrick Gallagher
Patricia Healey
Irene Kervick
Susan Platt

Linguistics Advisor

Timothy G. Collins
National-Louis University

Series Design: Loyola Press
Interior Art:
Jim Mitchell: 3, 26, 52, 74, 90, 96, 104, 110, 131.
Greg Phillips: 2, 14, 144.
All interior illustrations not listed above are by Dan Hatala/munrocampagna.com

ISBN-10: 0-8294-2346-X; ISBN-13: 978-0-8294-2346-4

ISBN-10: 0-8294-2340-0; ISBN-13: 978-0-8294-2340-2

Exercises in English® is a registered trademark of Loyola Press.

Manufactured in the United States of America.

06 07 08 09 10 11 12 VonH 10 9 8 7 6 5 4 3 2 1

06 07 08 09 10 11 12 VonH 10 9 8 7 6 5 4 3 2 1

Contents

1. Singular and Plural Nouns

A noun is a name word. A **singular noun** names one person, place, thing, or idea. A **plural noun** names more than one. The plural of most nouns is formed by adding *-s* or *-es* to the singular form. For nouns ending in *y* after a consonant, change the *y* to *i* and add *-es*. Some singular nouns use a different word to show the plural. Some nouns use the same word for the singular and the plural.

A. Write the plural form for each noun.

1. ranch _____[ranches]_____
2. berry _____[berries]_____
3. mouse _____[mice]_____
4. barrel _____[barrels]_____
5. fish _____[fish]_____

6. journey _____[journeys]_____
7. class _____[classes]_____
8. tooth _____[teeth]_____
9. bus _____[buses]_____
10. species _____[species]_____

B. Complete each sentence with the plural form of the noun. Use a dictionary to check your answers.

medium
1. Students can work in a number of _____[media]_____ in a science lab.

inquiry
2. They have a wide range of tools for their scientific _____[inquiries]_____.

Computer
3. _____[Computers]_____ are used to tabulate data and to compare results.

change
4. In the lab, students can manipulate _____[changes]_____ in materials.

series
5. Students can study _____[series]_____ of changes in physical systems.

process
6. Complicated scientific _____[processes]_____ can be simulated in a lab.

instrument
7. Students have access to sophisticated _____[instruments]_____.

dish
8. Biology students can grow cultures in petri _____[dishes]_____.

microscope
9. They can observe cells with high-powered _____[microscopes]_____.

technology
10. The _____[technologies]_____ in labs have improved science education.

Nouns

2. More Singular and Plural Nouns

For nouns ending in *o* after a vowel, form the plural by adding -*s* to the singular form. For some nouns ending in *o* after a consonant, form the plural by adding -*es* to the singular. For some nouns ending in *f* or *fe*, change the *f* or *fe* to *v* and add -*es*. For most compound words, form the plural by adding -*s*. For some compounds, make the principal word plural.

A. Write the plural form for each noun.

1. sister-in-law ___[sisters-in-law]___   6. hero ___[heroes]___

2. potato ___[potatoes]___   7. scarf ___[scarves]___

3. cell phone ___[cell phones]___   8. mouthful ___[mouthfuls]___

4. leaf ___[leaves]___   9. safe ___[safes]___

5. tie-in ___[tie-ins]___   10. attorney general ___[attorneys general]___

B. Complete each sentence with the plural form of the noun. Use a dictionary to check your answers.

Cliff swallow   1. ___[Cliff swallows]___ often live close to people.

gourd   2. Their nests are made of mud and are shaped like ___[gourds]___.

entrance   3. The ___[entrances]___ to the nests face downward.

cliff   4. The nests are usually built under bridges or on ___[cliffs]___.

roof   5. Sometimes they are built under the eaves of ___[roofs]___.

colony   6. Some cliff swallow ___[colonies]___ contain more than 35,000 nests.

mosquito   7. These birds eat flies, ___[mosquitoes]___, and beetles.

clutch   8. The mother birds lay ___[clutches]___ of three or four eggs.

bull snake   9. Predators such as ___[bull snakes]___ eat many of the eggs.

migrant   10. Every spring these ___[migrants]___ return to San Juan Capistrano.

Name _____

3. Nouns as Subjects and Subject Complements

> A noun can be the subject of a sentence. The **subject** tells whom or what the sentence is about.
>
> **Colonists** waged war against the British.
>
> A noun can be the **subject complement** of a sentence. A subject complement follows a linking verb and renames the subject.
>
> **The war was the beginning of a new nation.**

Write **S** if the underlined noun is the subject of the sentence. Write **SC** if it is the subject complement.

[S] 1. Benjamin Franklin had a fascinating career.

[SC] 2. He was a man who was interested in many topics.

[SC] 3. Though born in Boston, Franklin became a printer in Philadelphia.

[S] 4. His newspaper, the *Philadelphia Gazette,* became quite popular.

[S] 5. His wise sayings, published in *Poor Richard's Almanac,* are still popular.

[SC] 6. A library and a fire department were two improvements he instituted for Philadelphia.

[S] 7. Passionate about exploring unanswered questions, Franklin joined the Leather Apron Club.

[S] 8. By experimenting with a kite, Franklin discovered that electricity and lightning are the same thing.

[SC] 9. The Franklin stove was his invention.

[SC] 10. Franklin was a deep thinker who became interested in the politics of our young nation.

[SC] 11. Franklin was a writer and a signer of the Declaration of Independence.

[S] 12. After the Revolutionary War began, Franklin went abroad to forge an alliance with France.

[SC] 13. Many people he met at the French court became his friends.

[SC] 14. At the age of 81, Franklin was one of the authors of the U.S. Constitution.

[S] 15. What an interesting life Benjamin Franklin had!

Benjamin Franklin shared his talents by inventing things that helped people in daily life and by participating in civic life. Give an example of how you can help others by sharing your talents.

4. Nouns as Objects

> A noun can be used as the direct object or the indirect object of a verb or as the object of a preposition. The **direct object** answers the question *whom* or *what* after a verb. The **indirect object** tells to *whom, for whom, to what,* or *for what* the action was done. A noun that follows a preposition in a prepositional phrase is called the **object of the preposition.**

A. Underline the nouns that are used as objects. Above each, write **DO** if it is a direct object, **IO** if it is an indirect object, and **OP** if it is the object of a preposition.

          [DO]   [OP]
1. History gives us many puzzles, such as the disappearance of Amelia Earhart.

    [OP]   [DO]   [OP] [OP]
2. Even at an early age, Amelia experienced excitement at the thought of flight.

    [IO]   [DO]   [OP]
3. Flying offered Amelia unique opportunities with new challenges.

    [DO]   [OP]
4. She set many records for solo and nonstop flights before she attempted a

  [DO]   [OP]
flight around the world.

         [OP]   [IO]   [DO]
5. Her tragic disappearance during that trip gives historians a true mystery to solve.

B. Underline each noun used as an object. Above each, write **DO** if it is a direct object, **IO** if it is an indirect object, and **OP** if it is the object of a preposition.

     [DO]   [OP]   [OP]
1. Dad's company produces parts for automobiles and for mopeds.

  [OP]   [IO]   [DO]
2. Over the years car designers have given customers some great designs.

    [DO]   [DO]   [OP]
3. Designers specify the size and other features of each new design.

    [DO]   [OP]   [OP]   [OP]
4. I'm awaiting the arrival of a car with built-in video games and a snack bar.

    [DO]   [OP]
5. My dream car has fenders that become wings in traffic jams so it can fly.

    [IO]   [DO]   [OP]   [OP]   [OP]
6. Instruction manuals give buyers information about the operation and care of their cars.

    [OP]   [DO]
7. When shopping for a car, a person should consider safety features.

    [DO]   [OP]   [OP]   [OP]
8. Many people search the Internet for information on prices and models.

    [IO]   [DO]   [DO]
9. Driver education instructors teach students traffic laws and proper driving procedures.

    [DO]   [OP]   [OP]
10. Have you seen the announcement about the auto show at the coliseum?

Nouns

5. Nouns as Object Complements

> A noun can be used as an object complement. An **object complement** follows a direct object. The object complement renames or describes the direct object.
>
> **They elected George W. Bush <u>president</u>.**

A. If the *italicized* word is an object complement, write **OC** above it. If it is not an object complement, write **N.**

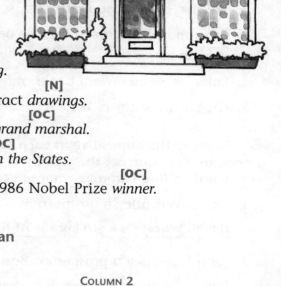

1. They considered the evening meal a *disaster*. [OC]
2. The sun is about 93 million *miles* from Earth. [N]
3. Sharon and Hamad named their daughter *Grace*. [OC]
4. Sue calls her floral shop *Love in Bloom*. [OC]
5. Christine and Mari completed a 10-mile *hike*. [N]
6. At the memorial service Arturo gave the first *reading*. [N]
7. In art class the students made black-and-white abstract *drawings*. [N]
8. The organizers of the parade appointed the mayor *grand marshal*. [OC]
9. Many Southerners call the Civil War *the War Between the States*. [OC]
10. The physics committee named Dr. Ernst Ruska the 1986 Nobel Prize *winner*. [OC]

B. Use an appropriate noun phrase from Column 2 as an object complement to complete each sentence.

Column 1	Column 2
The school board designated the first Monday in April	the Fun Run
The organizing committee called our fund-raising event	a good sport
Once again the principal named Neil	Activity Day
Because she tries so hard, the other athletes consider May	the official score keeper
Neil appointed Harry	chairperson for the event

1. ___[The school board designated the first Monday in April Activity Day.]___

2. ___[The organizing committee called our fund-raising event the Fun Run.]___

3. ___[Once again the principal named Neil chairperson for the event.]___

4. ___[Because she tries so hard, the other athletes consider May a good sport.]___

5. ___[Neil appointed Harry the official score keeper.]___

6. Appositives

An **appositive** is a word that follows a noun and renames it. An **appositive phrase** is an appositive and its modifiers. A **nonrestrictive appositive** is not necessary in order to understand the sentence; it is set off by commas. A **restrictive appositive** is necessary to understand the sentence; it is not set off by commas.

NONRESTRICTIVE APPOSITIVE   **George Washington, our first <u>president</u>, was a surveyor.**

RESTRICTIVE APPOSITIVE   **The 18th-century printer <u>Parson Weems</u> wrote a biography of George Washington.**

A. Circle the appositive in each sentence. Underline the noun it renames.

1. <u>Mason Locke Weems</u>, an early (historian,) was born in Dumfries, Virginia, in 1759.

2. <u>Weems</u>, an Episcopal (minister,) served as the rector of a parish in Virginia.

3. To support his large family, he became a book agent for <u>Matthew Carey</u>, a Philadelphia (publisher.)

4. Later he wrote several <u>books</u>, mostly political and moral (works.)

5. His <u>book</u> (*The Life of Washington*) tells the tale of George chopping down a cherry tree.

B. Identify the appositive in each sentence and decide whether it is restrictive or nonrestrictive. Correct the sentences with nonrestrictive appositives by rewriting them and adding commas where necessary.

1. Phillis Wheatley a girl born in Africa in about 1753 was sold into slavery in 1761.

   [Phillis Wheatley, a girl born in Africa in about 1753, was sold into slavery in 1761.]

2. John Wheatley a prosperous Boston merchant bought her as a servant for his wife.

   [John Wheatley, a prosperous Boston merchant, bought her as a servant for his wife.]

3. Phillis a sickly girl was encouraged by the Wheatleys to study literature.

   [Phillis, a sickly girl, was encouraged by the Wheatleys to study literature.]

4. Her book *Poems on Various Subjects* was the first book of poetry ever published by an African American.

   _____

5. John Wheatley emancipated Phillis in 1767, and in 1778 she married John Peters a free black Bostonian.

   [John Wheatley emancipated Phillis in 1767, and in 1778 she married John Peters, a free black Bostonian.]

7. Possessive Nouns

> The possessive form of a noun expresses possession or ownership. Add -'s to singular nouns and to irregular plural nouns to form the possessives.
>
> <u>cat's</u> paws   <u>women's</u> shoes
>
> Add only an apostrophe (') to plural nouns that end in s.
>
> <u>students'</u> papers   <u>hostesses'</u> jobs

A. Write the singular possessive and the plural possessive of each word.

	SINGULAR POSSESSIVE	PLURAL POSSESSIVE
1. child	[child's]	[children's]
2. hero	[hero's]	[heroes']
3. man	[man's]	[men's]
4. pilot	[pilot's]	[pilots']
5. writer	[writer's]	[writers']
6. secretary	[secretary's]	[secretaries']
7. son-in-law	[son-in-law's]	[sons-in-law's]
8. judge	[judge's]	[judges']
9. actress	[actress's]	[actresses']
10. officer	[officer's]	[officers']

B. Complete each sentence with the possessive of the noun at the left.

sister-in-law   1. My __[sister-in-law's]__ watch is very valuable.

David   2. What happened to __[David's]__ pen?

Mr. Enley   3. __[Mr. Enley's]__ explanation about the lost items was clear.

police officers   4. The __[police officers']__ opinion was different.

men   5. All the __[men's]__ jewelry was gone.

Sally   6. We looked in the drawer for __[Sally's]__ silver.

weeks   7. Mr. King donated two __[weeks']__ free ad space for the notice.

readers   8. The __[readers']__ papers carried news of the thefts.

culprit   9. The __[culprit's]__ motive was uncovered.

Ms. Alexis   10. __[Ms. Alexis's]__ detective work paid off.

Nouns

8. Separate or Joint Possession

Separate possession exists when two or more people own things independently of each other. To show separate possession, add -'s to each noun.

John's and Jack's tools

Joint possession exists when two or more people own something together. To show joint possession, add -'s to the last noun only.

John and Jack's hardware store

A. Write whether the possessive nouns express separate or joint ownership.

[separate] 1. Arthur's and Henry's songs were well-performed.

[joint] 2. It was a good start to North High and South High's art fair.

[separate] 3. Julia's and Roy's sculptures both used found objects this year.

[separate] 4. We visited the art exhibit at North's and South's art rooms.

[separate] 5. Consuela's and her sister's paintings received awards.

[separate] 6. We always look forward to Jane's and Ann's performances.

[joint] 7. Tomorrow we will hear Gilbert and Sullivan's opera *The Mikado*.

[joint] 8. Margo and Anthony's sets really portrayed the mood.

[separate] 9. A group performed a choral reading of Longfellow's and Whittier's poems.

[joint] 10. This year awards were given by Thompson and Moreno's Art Emporium.

B. For each phrase write a sentence that shows separate ownership. **[Sample answers are given.]**

Rembrandt and Leonardo 1. ___[Rembrandt's and Leonardo's art is well known.]___

Jupiter and Saturn 2. ___[Jupiter's and Saturn's orbits differ.]___

Canada and Mexico 3. ___[Canada's and Mexico's citizens visit the United States.]___

Sara and Eddie 4. ___[Sara's and Eddie's talents go well together.]___

car and truck 5. ___[The car's and the truck's brakes were replaced.]___

C. For each phrase write a sentence that shows joint ownership. **[Sample answers are given.]**

Mom and Dad 1. ___[Mom and Dad's rules usually are not harsh.]___

Lewis and Clark 2. ___[Lewis and Clark's explorations were far-reaching.]___

Jim and Bev 3. ___[Jim and Bev's store will open soon.]___

Lennon and McCartney 4. ___[Lennon and McCartney's music will live forever.]___

freshmen and sophomores 5. ___[The freshmen and sophomores' scores have gone up.]___

Name _____

9. Reviewing Nouns

A. Write the number of the *italicized* noun in each sentence. Write **S** for singular or **P** for plural.

___[S]___ 1. Astronomers are discovering much about the *planet.*

___[P]___ 2. We, the *scientists,* are thrilled with the news.

___[S]___ 3. *Mars* might have had life forms.

___[P]___ 4. *Women* have played an important part in space travel.

___[S]___ 5. *Water* has been shown to be trapped between the rocks on Mars.

B. Write the plural of each of the following singular nouns.

6. hoof ___[hooves]___   11. sheep ___[sheep]___

7. freeman ___[freemen]___   12. chocolate chip ___[chocolate chips]___

8. patio ___[patios]___   13. poppy ___[poppies]___

9. crossroad ___[crossroads]___   14. commander in chief ___[commanders in chief]___

10. wharf ___[wharves]___   15. earful ___[earfuls]___

C. Identify the way each *italicized* noun is used. Use **S** for subject, **SC** for subject complement, and **App** for appositive.

___[S]___ 16. At least 50 times a year the *Empire State Building* is struck by lightning.

___[App]___ 17. Hippocrates, the *Father of Medicine,* applied logic to medicine.

___[SC]___ 18. A major improvement in health care was the *development* of vaccines.

___[S]___ 19. *Triskaidekaphobia* is the fear of the number 13.

___[SC]___ 20. One major tourist attraction is the *Great Wall of China.*

___[App]___ 21. Robinson Crusoe, a marooned *sailor,* was on an island 28 years.

D. Write whether the possessive nouns express separate or joint ownership.

___[joint]___ 22. Last week we celebrated Joan and Henry's wedding anniversary.

___[separate]___ 23. Michael's and Dan's gifts were the same.

___[separate]___ 24. Celia Cruz's and Louis Armstrong's CDs are still popular.

___[joint]___ 25. We watched Ann and Jack's dance steps at the reception.

Name _____

E. Write the singular possessive and the plural possessive of each word.

	SINGULAR POSSESSIVE	PLURAL POSSESSIVE
26. brother-in-law	[brother-in-law's]	[brothers-in-law's]
27. deer	[deer's]	[deer's]
28. woman	[woman's]	[women's]
29. hostess	[hostess's]	[hostesses']
30. goose	[goose's]	[geese's]

F. The *italicized* nouns are used as objects. Write whether each is a direct object (**DO**), an indirect object (**IO**), or the object of a preposition (**OP**).

[DO] 31. Henry Ford began his motor *company* in 1903.

[OP] 32. He employed 12 workers and made his cars in a *factory*.

[OP] 33. Soon Ford ran out of *money*.

[IO] 34. A friend's sister gave *Ford* a loan.

[DO] 35. Soon many people wanted *Model Ts*.

[IO] 36. The company offered *Ford* a way to become wealthy.

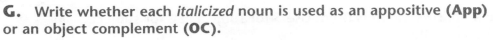

G. Write whether each *italicized* noun is used as an appositive (**App**) or an object complement (**OC**).

[OC] 37. The basketball team chose Patrick *captain*.

[App] 38. Have you seen Christie's new horse, *Midnight?*

[App] 39. I cheered for my favorite team, *the Yankees*.

[OC] 40. The Bulls called their mascot *Benny*.

Try It Yourself
On a separate sheet of paper, write four sentences about a person or a place. Be sure to use nouns correctly.

Check Your Own Work
Choose a piece of writing from your portfolio or journal, a work in progress, an assignment from another class, or a letter. Revise it, applying the skills you have learned. This checklist will help you.

✔ Have you used the correct spellings of plural nouns?

✔ Have you used nouns in a variety of ways?

✔ Have you used possessive nouns correctly?

10. Descriptive Adjectives, Position of Adjectives

> A **descriptive adjective** describes a noun's or a pronoun's number, color, size, type, or other qualities.
>
> <u>Beautiful</u> <u>white</u> <u>Austrian</u> horses perform <u>rhythmic</u> movements in the show.
>
> An adjective usually goes before the word it describes. An adjective may, however, follow the word it describes.
>
> The children, <u>eager</u> and <u>excited</u>, waited for a turn to ride the pony.

A. Underline the descriptive adjective or adjectives in each sentence.

1. Horses have been <u>useful</u> animals for thousands of years.

2. Before the invention of the car they were an <u>important</u> means of transportation.

3. Horses' legs, <u>long</u> and <u>muscular</u>, give them the strength to pull <u>heavy</u> loads.

4. <u>Early</u> ancestors of the horse lived in Europe and the Americas.

5. These <u>prehistoric</u> horses had <u>round</u> backs and <u>pointed</u> noses.

6. They were <u>small</u> animals.

7. <u>Modern</u> horses appeared about 3 million years ago.

8. No one knows when horses became <u>tame</u> animals.

9. <u>Asian</u> peoples used horses in war and for sport thousands of years ago.

10. The disappearance of the <u>prehistoric</u> horse from the Americas has no <u>clear</u> explanation.

B. Underline the descriptive adjectives in these sentences. Write **B** above an adjective if it comes before the noun it describes. Write **A** if it comes after the noun.

1. **[B]** <u>Spanish</u> explorers brought horses back to the Americas in the 1500s.

2. **[B]** <u>New</u> types of horses, **[B]** <u>Arabian</u> horses, were introduced to Europe in the 1600s.

3. Today's Thoroughbreds, **[A]** <u>speedy</u> and **[A]** <u>powerful</u>, are their descendants.

4. Thoroughbreds are the **[B]** <u>valuable</u> horses that are used for racing.

5. Horses are even participants in **[B]** <u>Olympic</u> sports.

6. These events feature horses and riders, **[A]** <u>elegant</u> and **[A]** <u>sleek</u>.

7. Horses, **[A]** <u>obedient</u> and **[A]** <u>responsive</u>, can be trained to follow signals.

8. **[B]** <u>Good</u> riders know how to make a horse respond to a **[B]** <u>tiny</u> signal.

9. Horses are generally chosen for a **[B]** <u>specific</u> purpose.

10. **[B]** <u>Modern</u> horses vary greatly in size.

11. More on the Position of Adjectives

An adjective may come before a noun or after a linking verb. An adjective that follows a linking verb is a subject complement.

My teacher is <u>young</u>.

An adjective that follows the direct object and completes the thought expressed by the verb is an object complement.

Pretzels make me <u>thirsty</u>.

A. Above each *italicized* adjective, write **B** for before the noun, **SC** for subject complement, or **OC** for object complement.

1. Perhaps you have seen a *small, birdlike* animal at night.
   [B] **[B]**

2. It was probably a bat, one of the most *unusual* and *mysterious* creatures.
   [B] **[B]**

3. This *swift* creature is actually a *furry* mammal that flies.
   [B] **[B]**

4. It sleeps during the day and becomes *active* at night.
   [SC]

5. Contrary to *popular* belief, bats are not *blind*.
   [B] **[SC]**

6. Most possess *keen* eyesight as well as a *sonar* system.
   [B] **[B]**

7. Their ears, which are overly *large*, pick up echoes
   [SC]
   of the bat's *own* sounds.
   [B]

8. Despite some *bad* habits, these *birdlike* creatures are *useful*.
   [B] **[B]** **[SC]**

9. They make *outdoor* life *bearable* by consuming *great* numbers of insects.
   [B] **[OC]** **[B]**

10. Farmers find bats *beneficial* and depend on them to control *harmful* pests.
    [OC] **[B]**

B. Underline the adjective(s) in each sentence. On the line write **B** for before the noun, **SC** for subject complement, or **OC** for object complement.

__**[B]**__ 1. Valley Forge is a <u>historical</u> park.

__**[B]**__ 2. It is in <u>southeastern</u> Pennsylvania.

__**[SC, SC]**__ 3. Louis thought the park was <u>fun</u> and <u>informative</u>.

__**[SC]**__ 4. It was <u>important</u> during the Revolutionary War.

__**[SC]**__ 5. The location was <u>strategic</u>.

__**[B]**__ 6. It could provide many of the <u>basic</u> needs, such as water and wood.

__**[OC]**__ 7. Some of his soldiers found it <u>intolerable</u>.

__**[SC]**__ 8. The weather was <u>severe</u>.

__**[SC, SC, SC]**__ 9. Often the soldiers were <u>cold</u>, <u>hungry</u>, and <u>unfit</u> for service.

__**[B]**__ 10. It was, however, a <u>turning</u> point for the army.

12. Demonstrative, Interrogative, and Indefinite Adjectives

> **Demonstrative adjectives** point out definite persons, places, things, or ideas. The demonstrative adjectives are *this, that, these,* and *those.*
>
> **Interrogative adjectives** are used in questions. The interrogative adjectives are *what, which,* and *whose. Which* is usually used to ask about one or more of a specific set of items.
>
> **Indefinite adjectives** refer to any or all members of a group. Indefinite adjectives include *all, another, any, both, each, either, few, many, more, most, much, neither, other, several,* and *some.* Note that *another, each, every, either,* and *neither* are always singular.

A. Underline the demonstrative, interrogative, or indefinite adjective in each sentence. Identify each by writing **demonstrative, interrogative,** or **indefinite.**

[indefinite] 1. All fans of jazz music are familiar with the music of Duke Ellington.

[interrogative] 2. What songs by Duke Ellington do you know?

[indefinite] 3. Many people will name songs such as "Mood Indigo" and "Take the A Train."

[indefinite] 4. Few people probably know that his given name was Edward.

[interrogative] 5. Whose idea was it to call him Duke because of his elegant manner?

[demonstrative] 6. In the 1920s he did radio broadcasts from New York with his band, and these broadcasts made him famous throughout the country.

[indefinite] 7. Swing and jazz became popular in the 1920s and 1930s, and Ellington was a master of both styles.

[interrogative] 8. Which song is his best?

[demonstrative] 9. This question may be answered differently by different fans.

[indefinite] 10. Each fan may have a particular favorite.

B. Complete each sentence with the type of adjective asked for. **[Answers may vary. Possible answers are given.]**

interrogative 1. [Whose] CD is on the table?

demonstrative 2. [Those] jazz CDs belong to my father.

interrogative 3. [What] instrument do you play in the band?

indefinite 4. [Most] people like jazz.

indefinite 5. [Some] songs on this CD are by Duke Ellington.

13. Comparative and Superlative Adjectives

Most adjectives have three degrees of comparison: **positive, comparative,** and **superlative.** For adjectives of one syllable and some adjectives of two syllables, the comparative and superlative are formed by adding *-er* or *-est* to the positive form. For adjectives of three or more syllables and many adjectives of two syllables, the comparative and superlative are formed by adding *more* or *less* or *most* or *least* in front of the positive form.

POSITIVE	COMPARATIVE	SUPERLATIVE
new	newer	newest
sunny	sunnier	sunniest
famous	more/less famous	most/least famous

Some adjectives have irregular comparisons.

POSITIVE	COMPARATIVE	SUPERLATIVE
good	better	best
bad	worse	worst

A. Write the comparative and superlative forms of each adjective.

	COMPARATIVE	SUPERLATIVE
1. small	[smaller]	[smallest]
2. beautiful	[more beautiful, less beautiful]	[most beautiful, least beautiful]
3. cloudy	[cloudier]	[cloudiest]
4. bad	[worse]	[worst]
5. delicious	[more delicious, less delicious]	[most delicious, least delicious]

B. Write the degree of comparison for each *italicized* adjective. Use **P** for positive degree, **C** for comparative degree, and **S** for superlative degree.

[S] 1. Birds are among the *most interesting* animals.

[S] 2. Some would say that birds are *most musical* of all animals.

[C] 3. They are *lighter* than most animals because their bones are hollow.

[C] 4. Taking flight is *more difficult* for large birds than for small ones.

[S] 5. One of the *fastest* flying birds is the peregrine falcon.

[S] 6. The ostrich is the world's *most enormous* bird, but it cannot fly.

[S] 7. It is the *speediest* two-legged animal on earth.

[S] 8. Some people think it is *least attractive* of all birds.

[C] 9. The raven may be *smarter* than all other birds since it is very adaptable.

[P] 10. When it cannot find a *favorite* food, it will learn to eat something else.

14. More Comparative and Superlative Adjectives

The comparative degree is used to compare two items or two sets of items. This comparative form is often followed by *than*.

> **Towers such as the CN Tower in Toronto are <u>higher</u> structures than buildings.**

The superlative degree is used to compare three or more items.

> **For many centuries the pyramids were the <u>tallest</u> structures in the world.**

A. Circle the correct choice in parentheses.

1. The castle of Neuschwanstein is the (more romantic (most romantic)) castle in the world.

2. The (earlier (earliest)) palaces known are in Egypt and were built in the 15th century BC.

3. The Egyptian pyramids, however, are much ((more ancient) most ancient) than those.

4. Some people say that modern buildings are ((less imposing) least imposing) than those old ones.

5. The (taller (tallest)) building in the United States is the Sears Tower in Chicago, at 1,450 feet.

6. At 1,670 feet the Taipei 101 building in Taiwan is ((higher) highest) than the Sears Tower.

7. Some think that the (more unusual (most unusual)) building in the United States is one in the shape of a large duck on Long Island.

8. Do you think that it is ((stranger) strangest) than the Corn Palace in South Dakota, which is decorated with corn and other farm products?

9. Do you think that a duck-shaped building is a ((worse) worst) idea than the binocular-shaped building in Venice, California?

10. Also odd is the Winchester House in California, which has the (more complicated (most complicated)) interior of any house, with staircases that go nowhere.

B. Rewrite the sentences, correcting the errors in the use of the comparative and the superlative degrees.

1. The most interestingest thing we did in Chicago was to visit the Sears Tower.
   [The most interesting thing we did in Chicago was to visit the Sears Tower.]

2. Unfortunately, the day was cloudy, and the view was less clearer than usual.
   [Unfortunately, the day was cloudy, and the view was less clear than usual.]

3. My little brother thought that the view was least exciting than the elevator ride.
   [My little brother thought that the view was less exciting than the elevator ride.]

4. The view of the vast lake from above is one of the most magnificentest views you can see.
   [The view of the vast lake from above is one of the most magnificent views you can see.]

5. Many people think that a visit there is most interesting at night than during the day.
   [Many people think that a visit there is more interesting at night than during the day.]

15. *Few* and *Little* with Count and Noncount Nouns

> **Count nouns** name things that can be counted: *minutes, necklaces, emotions.*
> **Noncount nouns** name things that cannot be counted: *time, jewelry, confidence.*
>
> Use the adjectives *few, fewer,* and *fewest* to compare count nouns. Use the adjectives *little, less,* and *least* to compare noncount nouns.
>
> > **This book on the states has <u>fewer</u> pages.**
> >
> > **That book on the states has <u>less</u> information.**
>
> **Concrete nouns** name things you can see and touch: *arm, tree, water.*
> **Abstract nouns** name things that cannot be seen or touched: *idea, impatience, haste.*

A. Identify each *italicized* noun as count or noncount, concrete or abstract.

	COUNT OR NONCOUNT	CONCRETE OR ABSTRACT
1. Mount McKinley is the highest *mountain* in the United States.	[count]	[concrete]
2. Its *height* is 20,321 feet.	[noncount]	[abstract]
3. *Technology* is an important industry in California.	[noncount]	[abstract]
4. The *weather* on the Great Plains can be extreme.	[noncount]	[abstract]
5. It took *determination* to farm that land in the past.	[noncount]	[abstract]
6. The United States is an important producer of *sugar.*	[noncount]	[concrete]
7. *Movies* are one of the country's most important exports.	[count]	[concrete]
8. People in the United States drink a lot of *coffee.*	[noncount]	[concrete]
9. Eight *presidents* were born or lived in Ohio.	[count]	[concrete]
10. *Silver* brought many miners to Nevada in the 1860s.	[noncount]	[concrete]

B. Complete each sentence with *fewer* or *less.*

1. There is _____[less]_____ rainfall in Utah than in Oregon.

2. Connecticut has _____[less]_____ land for national parks than Nebraska does.

3. Connecticut also has _____[fewer]_____ national parks.

4. Alabama produces _____[less]_____ cotton than Texas does.

5. There are _____[fewer]_____ farmable acres in Alabama than in Texas.

6. My sister has been to _____[fewer]_____ parks than I have.

7. Rhode Island has _____[less]_____ landmass than any other state.

8. Wyoming, however, has _____[fewer]_____ people than Rhode Island has.

9. Lake Erie has _____[fewer]_____ miles of coastline than Lake Superior.

10. It also contains _____[less]_____ water.

16. Adjective Phrases

> A **prepositional phrase** is made up of a preposition, the object of the preposition, and any modifiers. A prepositional phrase can be used as an adjective. An adjective phrase describes a noun.
>
> **A bicycle is a vehicle <u>with two wheels</u>.**

A. Underline the adjective phrase or phrases in each sentence.

1. The history <u>of the bicycle</u> is a long one.

2. The idea <u>for the modern bicycle</u> did not develop quickly.

3. Cycles <u>with two wheels</u> existed some 200 years ago.

4. The force <u>behind the first bike</u> was not a pedal.

5. The feet <u>of the rider</u> were used to propel the bike and to scoot it along.

6. Bikes <u>from the 1800s</u> did not look like modern bikes.

7. There were bikes <u>with a pedal</u> <u>on the front wheel</u>.

8. The front wheel <u>of some bikes</u> was large, but the back wheel was small.

9. The result <u>of the large front wheel</u> was an increase <u>in the bike's speed</u>.

10. Tires <u>with air</u> were a later addition <u>in the development</u> <u>of the modern bike</u>.

B. Underline the adjective phrase or phrases in each sentence.
Circle the word each phrase modifies.

1. (Bikes) <u>for young children</u> have three wheels.

2. (Clowns) <u>in circuses</u> ride (bikes) <u>with one wheel</u>.

3. (Bicycles) <u>with different speeds</u> eventually became popular.

4. The (uses) <u>of bikes</u> are numerous.

5. (Bikes) <u>for mountain trails</u> are popular.

6. A (feature) <u>of mountain bikes</u> is their wide, knobby (tires) <u>for mountain roads</u>.

7. The (challenge) <u>of mountain biking</u> attracts many.

8. Today more than 50 million (people) <u>in the United States</u> cycle regularly.

9. Bicycling is considered a pleasurable (form) <u>of exercise</u>.

10. Currently more (people) <u>in China</u> cycle than in the (rest) <u>of the world</u> together.

17. Adjective Clauses

> A **clause** is a group of words that has a subject and a predicate. A dependent clause does not express a complete thought. Some dependent clauses are **adjective clauses.** They describe nouns or pronouns. Adjective clauses are introduced by *who, whom, whose, that, where,* and *when.*
>
> **Elizabeth Cady Stanton, <u>who worked tirelessly for women's rights</u>, is an American hero.**
>
> A **restrictive** adjective clause is necessary to the meaning of a sentence. A **nonrestrictive** clause is not necessary to the meaning. Nonrestrictive clauses are set off with commas.
>
> **The Nineteenth Amendment, <u>which was ratified in 1920</u>, gave women the right to vote.**
>
> **The amendment <u>that gave women the right to vote</u> was ratified in 1920.**

A. Underline the adjective clause in each sentence. Circle the noun it modifies.

1. (Elizabeth Cady Stanton,) who lived from 1815 to 1902, worked for women's suffrage.

2. This (movement,) which sought to give women the vote, gained momentum in the early 1800s.

3. At the time there were many (rights) that women did not have.

4. A (woman) whose husband had died might not be entitled to any of the family property.

5. Many were convinced that the only (role) that was suitable for women was in the home.

6. (Stanton,) whose father was a lawyer, became interested in the issue.

7. The women's rights movement was connected to the abolition (movement,) which was the effort to end slavery.

8. Stanton became acquainted with (people) who were involved in both movements.

9. Her (writings) and (speeches,) which were powerful and eloquent, encouraged others.

10. The year (1878,) when Stanton helped prompt Congress to consider an amendment for women's suffrage, marked a key date in her fight.

B. Underline the adjective clause in each sentence and decide whether it is restrictive or nonrestrictive. Write the sentences that have nonrestrictive clauses, adding commas where necessary, on the lines below.

1. Stanton <u>who was an outspoken leader</u> gained attention for the cause of women's rights.
   [Stanton, who was an outspoken leader, gained attention for women's rights.]

2. The right to vote was just one of the women's rights <u>that Stanton promoted</u>.
   _____

3. Stanton was born in New York <u>where she spent most of her life</u>.
   [Stanton was born in New York, where she spent most of her life.]

4. That amendment <u>which gave women the vote</u> was ratified 18 years after her death.
   [That amendment, which gave women the vote, was ratified 18 years after her death.]

5. Stanton's determination and energy provide an example for all <u>who fight for rights</u>.
   _____

18. Reviewing Adjectives

A. Identify the position of each *italicized* adjective by writing **B** for before the noun, **SC** for subject complement, or **OC** for object complement.

_____[B, B]_____ 1. The *hot, dry* desert has many unusual animals.

_____[SC]_____ 2. Most desert animals are *nocturnal.*

_____[B]_____ 3. They remain in *underground* burrows during the day.

_____[OC]_____ 4. The animals find the daytime heat *intolerable.*

_____[SC]_____ 5. During the night the temperature is *cooler.*

Adjectives

B. Identify each *italicized* adjective by writing **Des** for descriptive, **D** for demonstrative, **Ind** for indefinite, or **Int** for interrogative.

_____[Des]_____ 6. John Adams was described as a *political* philosopher.

_____[Ind]_____ 7. Before becoming president, he held *many* political positions.

_____[Des]_____ 8. One was the vice presidency, which he termed an *insignificant* office.

_____[Int]_____ 9. In *which* city was he inaugurated?

_____[D]_____ 10. Philadelphia was the nation's capital at *that* time.

_____[Des, Des]_____ 11. In 1800 he moved into the *damp, unfinished* rooms of the White House.

_____[Ind, Des]_____ 12. *Each* year brought new challenges to the *young* country.

_____[Ind]_____ 13. His son was elected president *several* decades later.

_____[D]_____ 14. *That* circumstance has happened only twice.

_____[Int]_____ 15. *What* other families have also produced two presidents?

C. Write the comparative and the superlative forms of each adjective.

16. green _____[greener]_____ _____[greenest]_____

17. slow _____[slower]_____ _____[slowest]_____

18. beautiful _____[more/less beautiful]_____ _____[most/least beautiful]_____

19. original _____[more/less original]_____ _____[most/least original]_____

20. full _____[fuller]_____ _____[fullest]_____

CONTINUED

D. Circle the correct adjective in parentheses.

21. The blue whale is the (larger (largest)) animal that has ever lived.

22. Its body is ((bigger) biggest) than that of any known dinosaur.

23. The blue whale also makes the (louder (loudest)) sound of any animal.

24. The female of the species is ((more talkative) most talkative) than the male.

25. Blue whales, once almost extinct, now exist in ((greater) greatest) numbers than before.

E. Complete each sentence with *fewer* or *less*.

26. If you eat poorly, you will have _____[less]_____ energy.

27. Vegetables have _____[fewer]_____ calories than junk food does.

28. Junk food also provides _____[fewer]_____ vitamins.

29. The _____[less]_____ you exercise, the _____[fewer]_____ calories you will burn.

30. The _____[less]_____ junk food you eat, the better you will feel.

F. Underline the adjective clause once and the noun it modifies twice. Write on the line whether the clause is restrictive **(R)** or nonrestrictive **(NR)**.

___[R]___ 31. A source that can provide up-to-date information is the Internet.

___[R]___ 32. There was a time when most current data came from books and newspapers.

___[R]___ 33. The sites where I found the facts for my essay are all government sites.

___[NR]___ 34. Government sites, which are very informative, cover thousands of topics.

___[NR]___ 35. Amy, who wrote about the same topic, didn't use the Internet.

Try It Yourself

On a separate sheet of paper, write five sentences that describe an exciting event in your life. Use adjectives correctly.

Check Your Own Work

Choose a piece of writing from your portfolio or journal, a work in progress, an assignment from another class, or a letter. Revise it, applying the skills you have learned in this chapter. This checklist will help you.

✔ Have you included appropriate adjectives?

✔ Have you used the comparative forms of adjectives correctly?

✔ Have you chosen adjectives that create a clear picture for your reader?

✔ Have you used your thesaurus?

Name _____

19. Personal Pronouns

> A **pronoun** is a word that takes the place of a noun. **Personal pronouns** change form depending on **person**—the speaker (*first person*); the person spoken to (*second person*); or the person, place, or thing spoken about (*third person*).
>
> FIRST PERSON **I, me, mine, we, us, ours**
> SECOND PERSON **you, yours**
> THIRD PERSON **he, she, it, him, her, his, hers, its, them, theirs**

A. Underline the personal pronouns in each sentence. Write **1** above each pronoun in the first person, **2** above each pronoun in the second person, and **3** above each pronoun in the third person.

1. Do <u>you</u> enjoy reading fables? **[2]**

2. <u>They</u> are stories that have a moral or teach a lesson. **[3]**

3. My sister and <u>I</u> went to the library to look for some fables. **[1]**

4. <u>We</u> learned that Walt Disney wrote many fables. **[1]**

5. <u>He</u> told <u>them</u> in comic strips and animated cartoons. **[3]** **[3]**

6. Animals played a large part in <u>them</u>. **[3]**

7. <u>We</u> searched the computer database for other fables. **[1]**

8. <u>We</u> borrowed books from the library for <u>her</u> and <u>me</u>. **[1]** **[3]** **[1]**

9. In "The Fox and the Lion" a fox is terrified when <u>it</u> meets a lion. **[3]**

10. <u>You</u> should try to write your own fable. **[2]**

B. Complete each sentence with the correct personal pronoun. The person and the number are given.

Third person, singular 1. The first semester started; _____[it]_____ is the term during which creative writing is taught.

First person, singular 2. The students and _____[I]_____ explored the writing process.

Third person, plural 3. _____[They]_____ would have a good chance of learning about themselves through writing.

First person, plural 4. _____[We]_____ worked to discover new ideas.

First person, plural 5. Working as a team was a worthwhile experience for _____[us]_____.

20. Personal Pronouns, Number and Gender

> A personal pronoun can be singular or plural. The singular pronouns are *I, me, mine, you, yours, he, him, she, her, it, his, hers,* and *its.* The plural pronouns are *we, us, ours, you, yours, they, them,* and *theirs.*
>
> Third person singular personal pronouns also change form, depending on the gender of what is referred to (feminine, masculine, or neuter). The feminine pronouns are *she* and *her;* the masculine pronouns are *he* and *him;* the neuter pronoun is *it.*

A. Underline the personal pronoun or pronouns in each sentence. Write **S** (for *singular*) or **P** (for *plural*) above each to tell its number. For third person singular pronouns also write **F** (for *feminine*), **M** (for *masculine*), or **N** (for *neuter*) to tell the gender.

1. Our eighth-grade teacher, Mr. Edwards, gave us [P] a fun assignment last month.

2. He [S, M] told us [P] that we [P] had to choose a book, read it [S, N], and then persuade others to read it [S, N].

3. He [S, M] gave us [P] a list of books, and we [P] had to choose ours [P] by the end of the day.

4. Mine [S] was an action mystery story because that type of book interests me [S].

5. The main character is Lily; she [S, F] is determined to be first in the class.

6. She [S, F] received a B, however, from the social studies teacher, and later he [S, M] is found dead!

7. Suspicions begin to fall on her [S, F], but she [S, F] knows she [S, F] is innocent.

8. The book kept me [S] interested, and I [S] knew that it [S, N] would interest others.

9. I [S] chose a few good passages and read them [P] to the class for my presentation.

10. I [S] asked the other students to tell what they [P] would do in Lily's circumstances.

B. Write the correct pronoun for the italicized word or phrase.

_____[theirs]_____ 1. Students chose different kinds of books; I enjoyed some of *the other students'.*

_____[We]_____ 2. *Luisa and I* selected mystery books with school settings.

_____[She]_____ 3. *Luisa* chose a book by Gordon Korman.

_____[It]_____ 4. *The book* sounded interesting.

_____[He]_____ 5. *The hero* is accused of pulling some pranks at school during a play.

_____[They]_____ 6. *Marcus and Elena* chose books in the Harry Potter series.

_____[them]_____ 7. I had already read *those books.*

_____[us]_____ 8. The reports gave *the other students and me* ideas for books to read.

_____[they]_____ 9. My favorite stories are those in which *students* solve the mysteries.

_____[he]_____ 10. In one story *a science student* uses his lab equipment to catch a thief.

Name _____

21. Pronouns as Subjects

> A personal pronoun can be used as the subject of a sentence.
> The subject pronouns are *I, we, you, he, she, it,* and *they.*

A. Circle the correct pronoun in parentheses.

1. Ellen and (**I** me) are good friends.

2. (**We** Us) should help with the packing.

3. My brother and (**I** me) read an exciting book about winter camping.

4. Have Juan and (him **he**) returned with the camp stove?

5. Was (**he** him) given the necessary camping permit?

6. (**He** Him) and (**I** me) are partners in the first aid project.

7. Leo and (him **he**) quit and joined the rock-climbing class.

8. Neither (**he** him) nor (**she** her) has ever been hiking at Starved Rock.

9. (**She** Her) and her friends have promised to go.

10. Where have Rosa and (**she** her) put the tents?

11. (**We** Us) are all going camping this weekend.

12. (Us **We**) girls have prepared the food pack.

13. You and (me **I**) will go and stay in the lodge!

14. (**She** Her) and (**I** me) are not going.

15. (**We** Us) have too much homework.

B. On the line write a pronoun that can replace the *italicized* word or words.

___[They]___ 1. *The students* began to plan a class trip.

___[He, She]___ 2. *Their teacher* suggested going to Washington, D.C.

___[We]___ 3. *"You and I* will want to see the Air and Space Museum," she said.

___[He, She]___ 4. *The class secretary* called the bus company.

___[It, They]___ 5. *The company* charged $350 for the bus rental.

___[He]___ 6. *Mr. Zimmerman* gave Sara seventy-five dollars to spend on the trip.

___[She]___ 7. *Sara* packed her own snacks to save money for souvenirs.

___[It]___ 8. *The White House* was the first stop.

___[They]___ 9. *Dana and Zeke* climbed to the top of the Washington Monument.

___[It]___ 10. *The trip* was a huge success.

22. Pronouns as Subject Complements

A subject pronoun can replace a noun used as a subject complement. A subject complement follows a linking verb and refers to the same person or thing as the subject of the sentence.

Mom thought it was I who called.

The pronoun must agree in person (*first, second,* or *third*) and number (*singular* or *plural*) with the subject. The third person singular must also agree in gender.

A. Circle the correct pronoun in parentheses.

1. Was it (**she** her) who missed the bus?

2. I am not sure if it is (her **she**).

3. Mr. Fisher said that it could have been (them **they**).

4. No one would have believed it was (**I** me).

5. Jim said it was (him **he**) who called.

6. Cheryl thinks it was (**I** me) who called her.

7. It isn't (**they** them) who go to early morning choir.

8. Mindy could not believe it was (**we** us) on the bus that early.

9. Last year the route scheduler was (**she** her).

10. Did you know that the algebra winner was (**he** him)?

B. Complete each sentence with an appropriate pronoun. Write the person, number, and gender of your pronoun on the line at the left. **[Sample answers are shown.]**

EXAMPLE:

__**[1st, pl.]**__   **The first students to enter the hall were** ____*we*____.

__**[1st , sing.]**__   1. The buyer of tickets for the entire group was ____[I]____.

__**[2nd, sing.]**__   2. The person with the aisle seat is ____[you]____.

__**[3rd, pl.]**__   3. The musicians arriving early are ____[they]____, the violists.

__**[3rd, sing., M]**__   4. The conductor may be ____[he]____ in the gray suit.

__**[3rd, sing., F]**__   5. A main attraction is ____[she]____, a 10-year-old cellist.

__**[3rd, sing., M]**__   6. Another performer appearing today will be ____[he]____.

__**[3rd, sing., F]**__   7. The last soloist to perform is ____[she]____, the vocalist.

__**[2nd, sing.]**__   8. Because of your great talent the soloist should be ____[you]____.

__**[3rd, sing., F]**__   9. Our music teacher is ____[she]____, sitting in front.

__**[3rd, sing., M]**__   10. Sometimes a substitute is ____[he]____, the principal.

23. Pronouns as Direct Objects

> A personal pronoun can be used as the direct object of a verb. The object pronouns are *me, us, you, him, her, it,* and *them.*
>
> **The bell startled <u>us</u>.**

A. **Circle the correct pronoun in parentheses.**

1. Our chemistry teacher surprised (we (us)) last week.

2. The lesson on the periodic table of the elements interested ((us) we).

3. The periodic table arranges (they (them)) in rows called periods.

4. Mr. Gonzalez, the teacher, praised Steve and ((me) I) for our report on element 104.

5. The teacher invited (she (her)) to chemistry club.

6. All the members wanted ((them) they) on the science team.

7. A science reporter interviewed (he (him)) about the atom model.

8. The newspaper will help ((them) they) with money for more study.

9. The field of chemistry excited (I (me)) after that.

10. The chemistry teacher warned (we (us)) about the work involved.

B. **Write the pronoun that correctly replaces the underlined word or words.**

___[him]___ 1. Did you meet <u>Larry</u> at the movie?

___[them]___ 2. Grace invited <u>Steve and Ben</u> to the discussion afterwards.

___[us]___ 3. The speaker informed <u>the group and me</u> about movie making.

___[him]___ 4. Have you met <u>Jeremy Black</u>, the *Tribune's* new reviewer?

___[her]___ 5. His opinions sometimes infuriate <u>Sheila</u>.

___[it]___ 6. We saw <u>the movie *Cast Away*</u> on Saturday.

___[us]___ 7. Call <u>Jean and me</u> when you are ready to see it.

___[her]___ 8. After the lecture Mom expected <u>Mai</u> to come right home.

___[them]___ 9. Instead she joined <u>our friends</u> at the coffee shop.

___[him]___ 10. They criticized <u>the speaker</u> for his latest review.

24. Pronouns as Indirect Objects or as Objects of Prepositions

> An object pronoun can be used as the indirect object of a verb.
> **The secretary read <u>them</u> the minutes.**
> An object pronoun can be used as the object of a preposition.
> **The president made copies for <u>her</u>.**

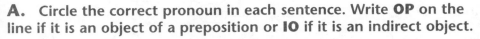

A. Circle the correct pronoun in each sentence. Write **OP** on the line if it is an object of a preposition or **IO** if it is an indirect object.

__[IO]__ 1. Jan showed (we (us)) her report about Dorothy Day.

__[IO]__ 2. It certainly gave (I (me)) something to think about.

__[OP]__ 3. One historian referred to (she (her)) as one of the most significant, interesting, and influential women in America.

__[IO]__ 4. During the Great Depression, Day established houses of hospitality for less fortunate people; she gave ((them) they) food, shelter, and hope.

__[OP]__ 5. The shelters served meals to about 5,000 of ((them) they) every day.

B. Rewrite the following sentences, substituting pronouns for the *italicized* words.

1. In 1933 Day started a newspaper for Catholic workers with *Peter Maurin*.
   [In 1933 Day started a newspaper for Catholic workers with him.]

2. This monthly newspaper gave *the workers* information on peaceful change.
   [This monthly newspaper gave them information on peaceful change.]

3. During the 1960s Day showed her support for *activists* by fasting for 10 days.
   [During the 1960s Day showed her support for them by fasting for 10 days.]

4. Mother Teresa gave *Day* a special cross.
   [Mother Teresa gave her a special cross.]

5. My mother handed *my brother* an article about *Dorothy Day*.
   [My mother handed him an article about her.]

Dorothy Day worked to improve the lives of those less fortunate. She spoke out in favor of peace and nonviolent change. Give an example of how you can work for peace and fairness in your daily life.

25. Pronouns After *Than* or *As*

The words *than* and *as* are used in comparisons. These conjunctions often join clauses. Part of the second clause, however, is sometimes omitted. Add the omitted part mentally to determine whether the pronoun needed is a subject pronoun or an object pronoun.

Bill is as tall as <u>he</u> (is). (subject pronoun)

She takes Wanda to the movies more often than (she takes) <u>me</u>.
(object pronoun)

A. Circle the pronoun in parentheses with which the *italicized* word is compared.

1. In the office *Claire* is as efficient as (⟨she⟩ her).

2. The trainer gave *Lanette* fewer pointers on phone use than (⟨me⟩ I).

3. *Luce* wrote a more realistic business plan than (⟨he⟩ him).

4. Because we took a long break, *we* received our assignment later than (⟨they⟩ them).

5. The girls had seen *Keith* more often than (she ⟨her⟩) at the copy machine.

6. More computer help-desk requests reach *me* than (he ⟨him⟩).

7. The *bosses* are as happy as (⟨we⟩ us).

8. *The owners* spend longer hours at work than (⟨they⟩ them).

9. Sam offered *Sean* as well as (he ⟨him⟩) a full-time job.

10. *Brian* was more excited at the prospect of working than (⟨I⟩ me).

B. Underline the word with which the *italicized* pronoun is compared.

1. <u>Christine</u> is older than *I.*

2. Gramps called <u>Ellen</u> more frequently than *her.*

3. My <u>Aunt Jo</u> needed him more than *I.*

4. In the final inning <u>Johann</u> played better than *he.*

5. Uncle Will threw <u>Josie</u> more curves than *me.*

6. Ed told <u>Piku</u> the secret as well as *me.*

7. In the first game <u>Dad</u> scored better than *I.*

8. Mick gave <u>Ozzie</u> a bigger piece than *me.*

9. Is <u>Jan</u> as short as *she?*

10. Do you know <u>his brother</u> better than *him?*

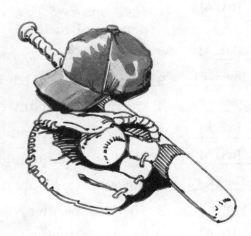

26. Possessive Pronouns and Adjectives

> Possessive pronouns and possessive adjectives show possession or ownership.
> A **possessive pronoun** takes the place of a possessive noun; it stands alone.
> The possessive pronouns are *mine, ours, yours, his, hers, its,* and *theirs.*
>
> **These gloves are Phil's. Here are mine.**
>
> A **possessive adjective** modifies a noun. The possessive adjectives are *my,*
> *our, your, his, her, its,* and *their.*
>
> **He said his hands were dirty.**

A. Circle the possessive pronouns. Underline the possessive adjectives.

1. John Greenleaf Whittier spent his boyhood with his parents in Massachusetts.

2. (Theirs) was a quiet, religious life spent farming.

3. Because his parents were Quakers, Whittier is called the Quaker poet.

4. His poems celebrated our New England country life.

5. (His) was not just a life spent dreaming about the beauties of rural life.

6. His work against slavery is well known.

7. My history book describes him as an abolitionist.

8. (Yours) might mention his term in the Massachusetts legislature.

9. Is that copy of *Snow-Bound* (ours?)

10. I'll give you (mine,) but you must return it.

B. Replace the *italicized* word(s) with a possessive. Write **A** on
the line if the possessive is an adjective or **P** if it is a pronoun.

_____[Its, A]_____ 1. *The Monterey Bay Aquarium's* otters are a popular attraction.

_____[his, A]_____ 2. Have you read *Roy Nickerson's* book on otters?

_____[hers, P]_____ 3. Much early research into otter behavior was *Dr. Edna Fisher's.*

_____[their, A]_____ 4. She described many of *the otters'* antics that viewers enjoy.

_____[Its, A]_____ 5. *California's* laws ban the use of gill nets.

_____[Its, A]_____ 6. *A gill net's* victim might include a harbor porpoise.

_____[Theirs, P]_____ 7. *Tankers' oil spills* are among the greatest dangers.

_____[hers, P]_____ 8. The idea for otter relocation was *a woman's.*

_____[its, A]_____ 9. Sharks and whales are among *this animal's* natural predators.

_____[ours, P]_____ 10. An otter's need for clean and safe water is like *our need.*

27. Intensive and Reflexive Pronouns

Intensive pronouns and reflexive pronouns end in *-self* or *-selves*. An **intensive pronoun** emphasizes a preceding noun or pronoun. A **reflexive pronoun** acts as a direct or an indirect object of a verb or as the object of a preposition.

INTENSIVE   **She herself signed the lease.**

REFLEXIVE   **She informed herself about the terms of the lease.**

A. Underline the intensive pronoun or the reflexive pronoun in each sentence. Write on the line whether it is intensive **(I)** or reflexive **(R)**.

___[I]___ 1. Bev and Wes themselves chose to do a report on Thomas Edison.

___[R]___ 2. They familiarized themselves with his many achievements.

___[I]___ 3. Bev herself wondered how one person alone

could have patented 1,093 inventions.

___[R]___ 4. Wes said that it was possible because Edison

never allowed himself to rest.

___[I]___ 5. He added, "Edison himself defined genius as

1 percent inspiration and 99 percent perspiration."

___[R]___ 6. The two decided to reenact Edison's light bulb

experiment for themselves.

___[I]___ 7. They followed the same steps that the inventor

himself had followed many years earlier.

___[I]___ 8. They also found that the filament itself was not the only important factor.

___[R]___ 9. After countless attempts and two successful lightings,

both students were proud of themselves.

___[R]___ 10. They concluded that Edison's genius spoke for itself.

B. Complete each sentence with an intensive pronoun or a reflexive pronoun. If a reflexive pronoun is needed, write **DO** on the line if it is used as a direct object, **IO** if an indirect object, or **OP** if the object of a preposition.

___[OP]___ 1. My brother bought a new jigsaw puzzle for _____[himself]_____ .

_____ 2. The puzzle's instruction sheet _____[itself]_____ was hard to figure out.

_____ 3. You _____[yourself]_____ are responsible for this puzzle, I told him.

___[DO]___ 4. I restrained _____[myself]_____ from putting in even one piece.

___[IO]___ 5. Many people buy _____[themselves]_____ very challenging puzzles.

28. Agreement of Pronouns and Antecedents

> The word to which a pronoun refers is called its **antecedent**. Pronouns agree with their antecedents in person, number, and gender.
>
> **Akhenaten** (antecedent) **is a source of endless fascination and speculation, but we really know very little about him.**

A. Underline the antecedent for each italicized pronoun. Above the pronoun write **1st**, **2nd**, or **3rd** to indicate its person and **S** or **P** for its number. If the antecedent is third person singular, also write **F**, **M**, or **N** to indicate the gender.

1. Many <u>mysteries</u> surrounded the discovery of King Tut, and *they* [3rd, P] made the boy king famous.

2. <u>Tut</u> ruled for a short time; *he* [3rd, S, M] was the son of the fascinating ruler, Akhenaten.

3. The <u>name</u> of Akhenaten was not included in Egypt's official list of pharaohs, and later people tried to remove *it* [3rd, S, N] from history.

4. One theory is that <u>priests</u> of the popular religion at that time opposed Akhenaten, so *they* [3rd, P] wanted to eliminate all traces of him.

5. The <u>Egyptians</u> worshipped many gods, but Akhenaten wanted *them* [3rd, P] to worship one god, the sun god Aten.

6. Akhenaten had moved the traditional <u>capital</u> to a different site along the Nile, where *it* [3rd, S, N] now remains a mysterious, desolate place surrounded by desert.

7. In art from the period, <u>Akhenaten and his family</u> are shown worshipping the rays of the sun; *they* [3rd, P] are also depicted conducting everyday activities.

8. <u>Nefertiti</u> was one of Akhenaten's wives, and *she* [3rd, S, F] is sometimes pictured with him.

9. The <u>couple</u> were often depicted with long, thin limbs, and *they* [3rd, P] had pear-shaped bodies.

10. One <u>sculpture</u> shows Nefertiti with an elegant, swanlike neck, and *it* [3rd, S, N] has helped establish her as one of history's most beautiful women.

B. Complete each sentence with the appropriate pronoun or pronouns. Make sure that each agrees with its antecedent in person, number, and gender.

1. Scientists continue to look for artifacts related to Akhenaten in hopes that ____[they]____ will find more clues to the mysteries surrounding ____[him]____.

2. The art of Akhenaten's time indicated a huge break from the style of earlier Egyptian monarchs, and ____[it]____ undoubtedly shocked his subjects.

3. Akhenaten encouraged changes in building methods also, including among such things as smaller stone blocks set in strong mortar.

4. After Akhenaten died, his city was abandoned, and ____[it]____ crumbled over time.

5. The temples were torn down, and stones from ____[them]____ were used in other buildings.

29. Agreement of Intensive and Reflexive Pronouns

> Intensive pronouns and reflexive pronouns must agree with their antecedents in person, number, and gender.

A. Circle the intensive pronoun or the reflexive pronoun in each sentence. Write **1st**, **2nd**, or **3rd** on the line at the left to indicate person and **S** or **P** to indicate number of the antecedent. If the pronoun is third person singular, also write **F**, **M**, or **N** to indicate its gender.

[2nd, S]   1. Did you hurt (yourself) when you fell?

[1st, P]   2. We made (ourselves) comfortable in the boat.

[1st, S]   3. I (myself) find little that is new in the navigation course.

[3rd, S, M]   4. He has no confidence in (himself.)

[3rd, S, F]   5. Jean (herself) completed the work on her small sailboat.

[3rd, S, F]   6. My sister (herself) cooked lunch in the boat's microwave.

[2nd, S]   7. You should prepare (yourself) for a storm on Monday.

[3rd, S, F]   8. She (herself) lost courage after that last outing.

[3rd, S, F]   9. She blamed nobody but (herself) for the tragedy.

[1st, P]   10. Suddenly we found (ourselves) in a beautiful harbor.

B. Rewrite each sentence, adding an intensive pronoun or a reflexive pronoun. Add additional words as necessary. Write **I** on the line at the left if the addition is intensive or **R** if it is reflexive. [Answers may vary. Sample answers are shown.]

[R]   1. Martin Luther King, Jr., and other African-American civil rights leaders found a place in history.

[Martin Luther King, Jr., and other African-American civil rights leaders found a place in history for themselves.]

[I]   2. Martin Luther King, Jr., was jailed for his nonviolent protests.

[Martin Luther King, Jr., himself was jailed for his nonviolent protests.]

[I]   3. King's supporters were often the targets of violence.

[King's supporters themselves were often the targets of violence.]

[R]   4. I recently read King's "I Have a Dream" speech.

[I recently read King's "I Have a Dream" speech for myself.]

[I]   5. The work for civil rights was carried on by Coretta Scott King.

[The work for civil rights was carried on by Coretta Scott King herself.]

30. Interrogative Pronouns

An **interrogative pronoun** is used in asking a question. *Who, whom,* and *whose* are used when asking about persons. *Who* is used when the pronoun is the subject of the question. *Whom* is used when the pronoun is the direct or indirect object of the verb or the object of a preposition. *Whose* is used when asking about possession. *Which* is used when asking about one member of a class or group of persons, places, or things. *What* is used for asking about things and seeking information.

A. Underline the interrogative pronouns. Write on the line whether each pronoun seeks information about a person, place, or thing.

____[person]____ 1. Who has driven along the coast of California?

____[thing]____ 2. What are some of the sights we can see?

____[thing]____ 3. What should you take for the climate changes?

____[place]____ 4. Which is the best park to visit in Big Sur?

____[person]____ 5. My mother asked, "Which of the authors
           lived on Cannery Row?"

____[person]____ 6. Who wants to go to the aquarium?

____[place]____ 7. Which of the state parks has the elephant seals?

____[person]____ 8. For whom was Hearst Castle named?

____[person]____ 9. Who is worried about driving on Highway 1?

____[place]____ 10. To which of the attractions do you wish to travel?

B. Circle the interrogative pronoun in each sentence. Write on the line whether it is used as the subject **(S)**, the subject complement **(SC)**, the direct object **(DO)**, the indirect object **(IO)**, or the object of a preposition **(OP)**.

__[S]__ 1. (Which) of Edison's inventions is most important?

__[S or SC]__ 2. (Who) was Jan Matzeliger?

__[S]__ 3. (Who) invented the traffic light?

__[OP]__ 4. To (whom) is industry indebted for the automatic lubricator?

__[DO]__ 5. (Which) of the problems faced by farmers in the West did Glidden solve?

__[IO]__ 6. Mrs. Swenson gave (whom) the report on Baekland's important new material?

__[S]__ 7. (Who) discovered electricity?

__[DO]__ 8. (What) do you wish to invent, Natalie?

__[OP]__ 9. In (which) of the references did you find information on Margaret Knight?

__[DO]__ 10. (Whom) do you admire?

31. Interrogative Pronouns *Who* and *Whom*

> *Who* is used as a subject pronoun in questions. *Whom* is used as the direct or indirect object of the verb or as the object of a preposition.

A. Circle the interrogative pronoun in each sentence. On the line at the left, write what its role is in the sentence—**S** for subject, **SC** for subject complement, **DO** for direct object, **IO** for indirect object, or **OP** for object of a preposition.

___[S]___ 1. (Who) directed the 1981 Academy Award–winning *Chariots of Fire?*

___[OP]___ 2. To (whom) did Dorothy turn for help in *The Wizard of Oz?*

___[S]___ 3. (Who) wrote the poems mentioned in the movie *Il Postino?*

___[S, SC]___ 4. (Who) was the lead actor in *Gladiator?*

___[OP]___ 5. By (whom) was the Ark of the Covenant stolen in the first Indiana Jones movie?

___[IO]___ 6. Shostakovich gave (whom) permission to use his musical score?

___[DO]___ 7. (Whom) did you meet at the Oscar party?

___[S]___ 8. (Who) owned the small bookshop in *You've Got Mail?*

___[S, SC]___ 9. (Who) was the oldest person to win an Oscar?

___[DO]___ 10. (Whom) did you see at the movies last night?

B. Complete each sentence with *who* or *whom*.

1. _____[Who]_____ was chained to a cliff to be devoured by a monster but was instead rescued by Perseus?

2. _____[Who]_____ slew the Minotaur and married Ariadne?

3. With _____[whom]_____ did the nymph Echo fall in love?

4. _____[Whom]_____ did Zeus kill for driving the sun chariot too close to the earth?

5. _____[Whom]_____ did Paris carry to Troy, an act that led to the Trojan War?

6. _____[Who]_____ was the Queen of Heaven and the wife of Zeus?

7. _____[Who]_____ unwittingly murdered his father and married his mother?

8. By _____[whom]_____ was Medusa, the gorgon, slain?

9. After _____[whom]_____ have we named our books of maps?

10. _____[Who]_____ threw himself into the Aegean Sea in distress?

32. Demonstrative Pronouns

A **demonstrative pronoun** points out a specific person, place, or thing. *This* and *these* are used for objects that are near. *That* and *those* are used for objects that are distant.

A. Circle the demonstrative pronoun in each sentence. Write whether it indicates near or distant objects.

_____[near]_____ 1. (This) is the painting you wanted to see.

_____[near]_____ 2. Look at the brush strokes and notice how (these) are close together.

_____[near]_____ 3. (This) is a painting far superior to the one in the brochure.

_____[distant]_____ 4. (Those) are among the paintings in the gallery on the second floor.

_____[near]_____ 5. The curator is happy that you brought (these) in today.

_____[near]_____ 6. Do you like (this?)

_____[distant]_____ 7. (Those) are similar to woodcuts we saw last year in Europe.

_____[distant]_____ 8. Unfortunately, (that) was the trip we had to cut short.

_____[near]_____ 9. (This) was painted by Rembrandt in his early years.

_____[near]_____ 10. (These) are unusual frames.

B. Complete each sentence with the correct demonstrative pronoun.

1. The softest pillows are _____[these]_____ on this couch.

2. Is _____[that]_____ your car at the end of the driveway?

3. _____[This]_____ is the first time I have seen the recipe.

4. _____[These]_____ are the only pieces left in this box.

5. _____[Those]_____ in the next room are from the Ming dynasty.

6. Was _____[that]_____ your brother on the bus?

7. The only change I could find is _____[this]_____ in my pocket.

8. Mother's flowers are _____[these]_____ at our feet.

9. _____[Those]_____ are my friends standing on the next corner.

10. What is _____[that]_____ rising over the mountain?

Pronouns

33. Relative Pronouns

A relative clause is a dependent clause that describes or gives information about a noun. A **relative pronoun** joins the dependent clause to its antecedent in the main clause. The relative pronouns are *who, whom, whose, which,* and *that. Who, whom,* and *whose* refer to persons. *Which* refers to places or things. *That* refers to persons, places, or things.

> **Hal** (antecedent), **who** (relative pronoun) **grew up in Indonesia, lives in Chicago.**

A. Underline the relative pronoun in each sentence. Circle its antecedent.

1. Mountains are (landforms) that are higher than their surroundings.

2. The (mountain) that you climb may be a hill to someone else.

3. The (Alps,) which are considered a young mountain range, are a mere 15 million years old.

4. (Sir Edmund Hillary,) who became the first person to climb Mount Everest, did so in 1953.

5. Tenzing Norgay was the Sherpa (guide) who accompanied Hillary.

6. Other (climbers) whom you may have read about have also accomplished the feat.

7. (Mount Whitney,) which is in the Sierra Nevada range, is the highest mountain in California.

8. (Ararat,) which is in Turkey, is where Noah's Ark is said to have ended up after the great flood.

9. (Mountain climbers,) whose journals are often published, can have interesting tales to tell.

10. (Into Thin Air,) which chronicled one climb, was quite popular.

B. Underline the relative pronoun in each sentence. Write on the line whether it is a subject or an object and how it is used in the sentence.

EXAMPLE:

<u>subject of is outstanding</u>   **The Newberry Library has a collection of maps that is outstanding.**

[subj. of *are used*]   1. Maps are tools <u>that</u> are used by travelers and students.

[subj. of *shows*]   2. A map <u>that</u> shows the surface of the earth is called a physical map.

[obj. of *upon*]   3. Road maps, upon <u>which</u> I depend for my job, are designed for travelers.

[obj. of *from*]   4. Scale, from <u>which</u> a user can determine real distance, is an important map feature.

[subj. of *is mounted*]   5. A globe is a map <u>that</u> is mounted on a ball.

34. The Relative Pronouns *Who* and *Whom*

> The relative pronoun *who* is used when the pronoun is the subject of the relative clause.
>
> **The girl <u>who</u> entered the room was Carrie.**
>
> The relative pronoun *whom* is used when the pronoun is the direct or indirect object or the object of a preposition in the relative clause.
>
> **The first person <u>whom</u> we will visit is Uncle Dan.**

Pronouns

A. Circle the correct relative pronoun in parentheses. Write on the line whether it is a subject or an object and how it is used in the sentence.

___[obj. of *met*]___   1. The young woman (who (whom)) you met is Augusta Reed Thomas, composer-in-residence.

___[subj. of *has received*]___   2. Bach was a composer ((who) whom) has received much study.

___[obj. of *favor*]___   3. Mozart is the composer (who (whom)) I favor.

___[subj. of *wrote*]___   4. He is the one ((who) whom) wrote *The Magic Flute.*

___[subj. of *composed*]___   5. Was it Beethoven ((who) whom) composed *Fidelio?*

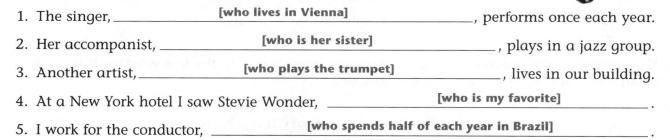

B. Complete each sentence with a dependent clause that contains the relative pronoun *who.* **[Sample answers are given.]**

1. The singer, ___[who lives in Vienna]___, performs once each year.

2. Her accompanist, ___[who is her sister]___, plays in a jazz group.

3. Another artist, ___[who plays the trumpet]___, lives in our building.

4. At a New York hotel I saw Stevie Wonder, ___[who is my favorite]___.

5. I work for the conductor, ___[who spends half of each year in Brazil]___.

C. Complete each sentence with a dependent clause that contains the relative pronoun *whom.* **[Sample answers are given.]**

1. Have you seen the oboist, ___[about whom we read]___?

2. Hugh, ___[for whom I baby-sit]___, wanted to see an opera.

3. Dr. Yurkanin, ___[with whom I study violin]___, telephoned for tickets.

4. I wrote a thank-you note to Francesca, ___[through whom I met the cellist]___.

5. The diva, ___[about whom I had heard so much]___, was a joy to hear.

35. Indefinite Pronouns

> An **indefinite pronoun** refers to any or all members of a group of persons, places, or things. Among the indefinite pronouns are *all, another, both, each, either, few, many, neither, nothing, several, some,* and pronouns that begin with *any* or *every.*
>
>   <u>Each</u> must pass the physical.
>
>   <u>Anyone</u> who is qualified can join.

A. Underline the indefinite pronouns.

1. <u>One</u> of the officials blew a whistle, and <u>each</u> of the windsurfers paddled out to sea.

2. Today was the windsurfing race, and <u>everybody</u> was on the beach.

3. The brisk wind quickly filled <u>all</u> of the sails.

4. After about 10 seconds <u>several</u> of the surfers stood up on their boards.

5. A <u>few</u> headed to the south, and <u>many</u> went to the southeast.

6. An official said that <u>either</u> of the routes would be fast because of the strong wind.

7. After an hour <u>someone</u> caught sight of two sails on the horizon.

8. <u>Neither</u> was close enough, so it was impossible for <u>anyone</u> to tell who was in the lead.

9. As the boats neared, <u>both</u> seemed to be the same distance from shore.

10. <u>Somebody</u> said that this would be a photo finish!

B. Underline the indefinite pronouns. Identify the role each plays in the sentence. Write **S** for subject, **SC** for subject complement, **DO** for direct object, **IO** for indirect object, or **OP** for object of a preposition.

[S]   1. Has <u>anybody</u> ever attended a focus group?

[IO]   2. The company sent <u>each</u> of us an invitation.

[S]   3. After the introduction <u>everybody</u> tasted the cheese spreads.

[DO]   4. One woman found <u>none</u> of them satisfactory.

[DO]   5. After the first test the moderator introduced <u>another</u>.

[DO]   6. Did the moderator give you <u>both</u> of the yogurts to try?

[SC]   7. Cheese, yogurt, and ice cream are a <u>few</u> of my favorite foods.

[IO]   8. She gave <u>each</u> of us a rating sheet to complete.

[OP]   9. I received curious looks from a <u>few</u> of the reviewers.

[S]   10. <u>Neither</u> of the reviewers next to me wanted to fill out the form.

36. Agreement with Indefinite Pronouns

An indefinite pronoun refers to any or all of a group of persons, places, or things. Some indefinite pronouns are always singular; others are always plural; and some can be either singular or plural.

SINGULAR	**anyone, anybody, anything, each, either, neither, everyone, everybody, everything, one, no one, nobody, nothing**
PLURAL	**both, few, many, others, several**
SINGULAR OR PLURAL	**all, any, more, most, none, some**

A. Circle the correct word in parentheses. Underline its antecedent.

1. <u>Each</u> of the women was satisfied with (**her**) their) booth at the bazaar.

2. <u>Neither</u> of the food booths had (**its**) their) food ready in time.

3. <u>Many</u> of the guests did not park (her (**their**) cars in the lot.

4. <u>All</u> of the people showed up for (his (**their**) free movie passes.

5. <u>Everyone</u> on the boys' team explained (**his**) their) part of the project.

B. Complete each sentence with an appropriate pronoun or possessive adjective. The pronouns and adjectives must agree in person with the *italicized* word.

1. If *anybody* wishes to study earthquakes, ___[he, she]___ can start now.

2. *Both* of my sisters liked ___[their]___ earth science classes.

3. *Everyone* is expected to do ___[his, her]___ own lab assignments.

4. *Many* of the students have read ___[their]___ assignments already.

5. A *few* of the students dropped ___[their]___ science courses this semester.

6. *Each* had ___[his, her]___ volcano model evaluated by an expert.

7. Has *anyone* completed ___[his, her]___ seismograph project?

8. *Neither* of the seismologists admitted that ___[he, she]___ had missed the warning signs.

9. *Several* of the new students wondered if ___[they]___ had the right teachers.

10. Generally, *all* of the students are satisfied with ___[their]___ courses.

37. Reviewing Pronouns

A. Circle the correct pronoun in parentheses. Identify the role each plays in the sentence. Write **S** for subject, **SC** for subject complement, **DO** for direct object, **IO** for indirect object, or **OP** for object of a preposition.

[SC] 1. It was ((they) them) who invited us to the party.

[OP] 2. Charlie made a celebratory lunch for ((her) she).

[IO] 3. He plans to send Maria and (she (her)) the leftovers.

[S] 4. Charlie and (me (I)) planned the surprise months ago.

[S] 5. Could (us (we)) keep it a secret?

[OP] 6. Charlie kept the plans with (he (him)) in his journal.

[DO] 7. Sunday we finally told ((her) she).

B. Underline the reflexive or intensive pronoun in each sentence. Write **R** if it is reflexive or **I** if it is intensive.

[I] 8. I <u>myself</u> knew his voice when I heard it.

[R] 9. She looked at <u>herself</u> in the mirror.

[R] 10. The twins made the iced tea for <u>themselves</u>.

[I] 11. He <u>himself</u> told me the story.

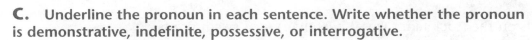

C. Underline the pronoun in each sentence. Write whether the pronoun is demonstrative, indefinite, possessive, or interrogative.

[demonstrative] 12. <u>That</u> was the movie I saw last week.

[indefinite] 13. Sam noted that <u>each</u> of the actors wore black.

[indefinite] 14. The movie gave <u>neither</u> a fair portrayal.

[interrogative] 15. <u>What</u> is the kind of story that makes the best screenplay?

[indefinite] 16. <u>Someone</u> once said real-life dramas make the best movies.

[possessive] 17. That opinion isn't <u>mine</u>.

CONTINUED

D. Complete each sentence with *who* or *whom*.

18. _____[Who]_____ wrote *The Maltese Falcon?*

19. To _____[whom]_____ was the starring role given?

20. _____[Whom]_____ did Sydney Greenstreet play in the movie?

21. Do you know _____[who]_____ played opposite Humphrey Bogart?

E. Circle the correct pronoun following *than* or *as*.

22. Jenny is as excited as (she) her) about the car trip.

23. George has planned his vacation more carefully than (they) them).

24. My dad liked the Yellowstone campsite better than (he) him).

25. Bridget didn't care as much as (we) us).

26. Fran complained more than (me (I)).

F. Circle the correct possessive adjective in parentheses.

27. Either of my brothers will give you (his) their) baseball glove.

28. Neither of my sisters remembered (her) their) workout clothes.

29. Each of the girls on the track team wore (her) their) own sweat pants.

30. Several of the girls' parents offered (his (their)) help to buy uniforms.

Try It Yourself
On a separate sheet of paper, write four sentences about something you treasure. Be sure to use pronouns correctly.

Check Your Own Work
Choose a selection from your writing portfolio, your journal, a work in progress, an assignment from another class, or a letter. Revise it, applying the skills you have learned in this chapter. This checklist will help you.

✔ Have you remembered to make pronouns and their antecedents agree?

✔ Have you used subject and object pronouns correctly?

Pronouns

38. Principal Parts of Verbs

A verb expresses action or being. The principal parts of a verb are the **base** form, the **present participle**, the **past**, and the **past participle**. The present participle is formed by adding *-ing* to the base form. The past and past participles of regular verbs are formed by adding *-d* or *-ed* to the base form. The past and past participles of irregular verbs are not formed by adding *-d* or *-ed* to the base form.

BASE	PRESENT PARTICIPLE	PAST	PAST PARTICIPLE
sharpen	sharpening	sharpened	sharpened
eat	eating	ate	eaten
go	going	went	gone

A. Write the past and the past participle of each verb. Then write whether it is regular or irregular.

		PAST	PAST PARTICIPLE	
1.	wait	[waited]	[waited]	[regular]
2.	catch	[caught]	[caught]	[irregular]
3.	choose	[chose]	[chosen]	[irregular]
4.	return	[returned]	[returned]	[regular]
5.	miss	[missed]	[missed]	[regular]
6.	steal	[stole]	[stolen]	[irregular]
7.	get	[got]	[gotten]	[irregular]
8.	haunt	[haunted]	[haunted]	[regular]
9.	feel	[felt]	[felt]	[irregular]
10.	forget	[forgot]	[forgotten]	[irregular]

B. Complete each sentence with the past or the past participle of the verb.

read   1. Have you ever ____[read]____ any of Aesop's fables?

tell   2. People have ____[told]____ fables for centuries to teach useful lessons.

feel   3. Aesop ____[felt]____ that his humorous writings would help people.

hide   4. Writers generally ____[hid]____ the lessons in fables.

write   5. Aesop ____[wrote]____ a story about a lion.

represent 6. In the story the lion ____[represented]____ the king.

grow   7. The lion ____[grew]____ old and could not hunt for food.

come   8. When visitors ____[came]____ to see him, he ate them up.

choose   9. The fox had ____[chosen]____ not to visit the lion.

come   10. The fox realized the other animals had not ____[come]____ out of the lion's den.

Name _____

39. Transitive and Intransitive Verbs

> A **transitive verb** expresses an action that passes from a doer to a receiver. The receiver of the action is the direct object.
>
> > **Frost <u>killed</u> the flowers.**
>
> An **intransitive verb** has no receiver of the action. It does not have a direct object.
>
> > **The flowers <u>died</u>.**

A. Underline the verb or verb phrase in each sentence. If the verb is transitive, write **T** on the line and circle the receiver of the action. If it is intransitive, write **I**.

[I] 1. In the early 1800s passenger pigeons <u>numbered</u> in the billions.

[T] 2. Their flocks once <u>darkened</u> the (skies.)

[I] 3. Less than 100 years later, they <u>became</u> extinct in the wild.

[T] 4. Many factors <u>caused</u> the bird's (extinction.)

[T] 5. Hunting, trapping, and loss of habitat each <u>played</u> a (role.)

[I] 6. The pigeons <u>lived</u> in the eastern United States and Canada.

[T] 7. Settlers <u>used</u> (pigeons) as a source of meat.

[I] 8. Their feathers <u>were</u> useful in pillows and mattresses.

[I] 9. Passenger pigeon populations <u>dwindled</u>.

[I] 10. By 1880 the decline in numbers <u>had become</u> irreversible.

[T] 11. Scientists <u>bred</u> the (birds) unsuccessfully in captivity.

[T] 12. Nothing <u>could prevent</u> their (extinction.)

[I] 13. The last passenger pigeon <u>died</u> in captivity in 1914.

[T] 14. Today, extinction <u>is threatening</u> many other (species.)

[T] 15. The fate of the passenger pigeon <u>teaches</u> a valuable (lesson.)

B. Some verbs may be either transitive or intransitive. Write **T** if the *italicized* verb is transitive and **I** if it is intransitive.

[I] 1. Sandy sat on the porch and *read* all afternoon.

[T] 2. Ken *read* "Jack and the Beanstalk" to the twins.

[I] 3. Today the Cooking Club *baked,* roasted, and broiled.

[T] 4. I *baked* Tom's birthday cake myself.

[I] 5. We *rode* along the lakefront bike path.

40. Troublesome Verbs

The following pairs of verbs are easy to confuse. Learning the meaning of each word is the best way to avoid mistakes.

Teach (taught, taught) means "to give knowledge."
Learn (learned, learned) means "to receive knowledge."

Take (took, taken) means "to carry from a near place to a more distant place."
Bring (brought, brought) means "to carry from a distant place to a near place."

Lend (lent, lent) means "to let someone use something of yours."
Borrow (borrowed, borrowed) means "to take something and use it as one's own with the idea of returning it."

Lie (lay, lain) means "to recline."   **Lay (laid, laid)** means "to place."

Sit (sat, sat) means "to take a seat."   **Set (set, set)** means "to put down."

Rise (rose, risen) means "to get up."   **Raise (raised, raised)** means "to lift up."

A. Circle the correct verb in each sentence.

1. Dorothy (**rises** raises) before sunrise every morning.

2. I would never (**take** bring) my camera into the pool.

3. Would you (**bring** take) my book over here when you come?

4. Every experience (learns **teaches**) us a lesson.

5. Charlene (borrowed **lent**) me her tent when I went camping.

6. Lamont (sat **set**) the pie on the counter after he baked it.

7. The hot air balloon (**rose** raised) above the treetops.

8. We can't all (**sit** set) at one table in the cafeteria.

9. Lou (**raised** rose) the flag as the parade passed by.

10. Karen (**lies** lays) on the sofa for half an hour every afternoon to watch TV.

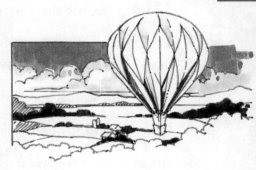

B. Complete each sentence with the correct form of the verb.

set 1. The older students _____[set]_____ a good example for the younger ones.

lay 2. Maz _____[laid]_____ his books on the table after he got home from school.

lie 3. They have _____[lain]_____ there ever since.

lie 4. The cat had _____[lain]_____ on the sunny porch all day.

take 5. The teacher asked, "Who has _____[taken]_____ Lenny's pencil?"

lend 6. I know you _____[lent]_____ me a dollar last week, but I am still broke.

teach 7. Regina has _____[taught]_____ her sister to play chess.

raise 8. Camille _____[raised]_____ her hand because she knew the answer.

rise 9. Johann _____[rose]_____ slowly after the bruising tackle.

bring 10. When Isabelle went to the bakery, she _____[brought]_____ me back a Danish.

41. Linking Verbs

> A **linking verb** joins the subject with a subject complement, which may be a noun, a pronoun, or an adjective.
>
> | NOUN | PRONOUN | ADJECTIVE |
> | :-- | :-- | :-- |
> | **Washington <u>was</u> president.** | **It <u>is</u> she.** | **I <u>became</u> hungry.** |

A. Circle the linking verb in each sentence. Underline the subject complement. Write above the complement whether it is a noun (**N**) or an adjective (**A**).

1. Most folk songs (are) <u>ballads</u> [N] that tell simple stories.

2. Many of these songs (are) an <u>expression</u> [N] of political or religious beliefs.

3. The composers of these songs often (remain) <u>anonymous</u>. [A]

4. As the songs are passed to new generations, the melodies often (become) <u>simpler</u>. [A]

5. In many songs the verses (are) a <u>story</u>, [N] and a chorus is sung between them.

6. The guitar (is) the most popular <u>instrument</u> [N] used by folksingers today.

7. Many folk songs (were) work <u>songs</u>. [N]

8. Other folk songs (became) simple <u>entertainment</u>. [N]

9. Singers today (feel) <u>sympathetic</u> [A] toward social concerns.

10. As enjoyment, folk music (remains) <u>popular</u> [A] in many countries.

B. Complete each sentence with an appropriate linking verb. [**Sample answers are given.**]

1. An opera _____[is]_____ a drama set to music.

2. The texts of operas _____[are]_____ sung.

3. Martin _____[became]_____ an opera singer last year.

4. He _____[is, was]_____ one of the lead singers in the school musical.

5. As he __[grows, becomes]__ older, his voice may get deeper.

6. Right now his voice ____[sounds, is]____ very high and clear.

7. He gets excited when he _____[is]_____ the star of the show.

8. With his costume on, he __[appears, looks]__ much older.

9. Martin's favorite composer _____[is]_____ Mozart.

10. Mozart _____[became]_____ a composer at the age of six.

42. Active and Passive Voices

> A transitive verb can be in the active voice or the passive voice. When in the **active voice**, the subject is the doer of the action. When in the **passive voice**, the subject is the receiver of the action.
>
> John Hancock <u>signed</u> the Declaration of Independence.
>
> The Declaration of Independence <u>was signed</u> by John Hancock.

Underline the verb in each sentence. Write A on the line if it is in the active voice and P if it is in the passive voice.

[P] 1. A million tons of chocolate <u>will be consumed</u> in the United States this year.

[P] 2. Much of this chocolate <u>is produced</u> by the Hershey Company.

[A] 3. In 1872, at age 15, Milton Hershey <u>started</u> a candy-making apprenticeship.

[A] 4. By 1886 he <u>had founded</u> a successful caramel company.

[P] 5. A second company <u>was</u> soon <u>created</u>.

[A] 6. This new company <u>produced</u> only chocolate.

[P] 7. The business <u>was located</u> in Derry Church, Pennsylvania.

[P] 8. Milton Hershey <u>had been born</u> there.

[P] 9. The factory <u>was completed</u> in 1905.

[A] 10. An affluent community quickly <u>grew</u> around the factory.

[P] 11. A year later the town <u>was renamed</u> Hershey.

[A] 12. Milton Hershey <u>believed</u> that advertising was unethical.

[P] 13. His factory <u>was opened</u> to the public.

[P] 14. The company's products <u>were promoted</u> through word of mouth.

[A] 15. Hershey <u>donated</u> much of his time and money to the town.

[A] 16. In 1909 Hershey <u>established</u> a school for orphans.

[P] 17. The school <u>was endowed</u> with stock from his company.

[P] 18. The school originally <u>was spread</u> over several miles.

[A] 19. The Hershey Company <u>employs</u> many of the school's graduates.

[A] 20. Today Hershey <u>produces</u> many well-known candies.

Verbs

Name _____

43. Simple Tenses

The **simple present tense** tells about an action that is repeated or that is always true. The **simple past tense** tells about an action or a condition that happened in the past. The **simple future tense** tells about an action or a condition that will happen in the future.

PRESENT | PAST | FUTURE
I <u>eat</u> hot dogs. | I <u>ate</u> a hot dog last night. | I <u>will eat</u> a hot dog for lunch tomorrow.

Verbs

A. Underline the verb in each sentence. Write its tense on the line.

__[present]__ 1. The human body <u>contains</u> more than 600 muscles.

__[past]__ 2. Scientists <u>discovered</u> three kinds of muscles in the body.

__[present]__ 3. These <u>are</u> the skeletal, the smooth, and the cardiac muscles.

__[present]__ 4. The cardiac muscles <u>are located</u> only in the heart.

__[present]__ 5. The skeletal muscles <u>hold</u> the skeleton together.

__[present]__ 6. Smooth muscles <u>are found</u> in the organs of the body.

__[present]__ 7. These muscles <u>control</u> the body processes.

__[future]__ 8. Muscle functions <u>will stop</u> under certain conditions.

__[past]__ 9. Sudden muscular contractions <u>caused</u> severe muscle cramps in many athletes.

__[future]__ 10. After repeated exercise and work, your muscles <u>will be</u> capable of strenuous work.

B. Complete each sentence with the correct form of the verb.

grow–*past* 1. Last summer Serena ___[grew]___ a vegetable garden.

eat–*past* 2. She ___[ate]___ fresh vegetables every day.

be–*present* 3. Vegetables ___[are]___ the edible products of herbaceous plants.

contain–*present* 4. Vegetables ___[contain]___ many nutrients.

water–*past* 5. Serena ___[watered]___ the plants each morning.

hope–*present* 6. She ___[hopes]___ to have a garden again next year.

plant–*past* 7. Last year she ___[planted]___ carrots, potatoes, and squash.

add–*future* 8. Next summer she ___[will add]___ tomatoes and peppers.

be–*present* 9. Tomatoes and peppers ___[are]___ actually fruit.

help–*future* 10. Her grandfather ___[will help]___ her plant the seeds.

46

44. Progressive Tenses

Progressive tenses express continuing action. The progressive tenses are formed with the present participle and a form of the auxiliary verb *be*. The **present progressive tense** tells about something that is happening right now.

The Tower of Pisa is leaning.

The **past progressive tense** tells about something that was happening in the past.

It was leaning many years ago.

The **future progressive tense** tells about something that will be happening in the future.

Engineers will be trying to stop it from leaning farther.

The **perfect progressive tenses** tell about things that happen over time.

PRESENT **I have been working in the garden all day.**

PAST **She had been working there for years when she heard the news.**

A. Complete each sentence with the progressive form of the verb.

study–*present perfect*   1. Scientists ___[have been studying]___ the Galapagos Islands for many years.

observe–*past*   2. Charles Darwin ___[was observing]___ the islands in 1835.

work–*past perfect*   3. He ___[had been working]___ as a naturalist on the *HMS Beagle*.

find–*past*   4. He ___[was finding]___ many unique species on the islands.

take–*future*   5. Students ___[will be taking]___ notes during their field trips.

B. Underline the progressive verb phrase in each sentence. Write its tense on the line.

___[present]___ 1. Today humans are causing many problems for the Galapagos.

___[past perfect]___ 2. The Galapagos tortoises had been living without natural predators.

___[past]___ 3. By the 16th century humans were visiting the islands.

___[past]___ 4. Pirates and whalers were butchering the tortoises for food.

___[past]___ 5. Settlers were also introducing foreign species to the ecosystem.

___[present]___ 6. These new species are endangering the tortoises.

___[present]___ 7. Dogs brought by settlers are attacking the defenseless animals.

___[present]___ 8. Goats are eating the plants that tortoises once fed upon.

___[future]___ 9. Until they are removed, goats will be stripping away the vegetation.

___[present]___ 10. Environmentalists are trying to preserve the Galapagos tortoise.

Verbs

45. Perfect Tenses

The perfect tenses are formed with the past participle and a form of *have*. The **present perfect tense** tells about an action that took place at an indefinite time in the past and continues into the present. The **past perfect tense** tells about a past action that happened before another past action. The **future perfect tense** tells about an action that will be completed before a specific time in the future.

PRESENT PERFECT   I <u>have eaten</u> breakfast.

PAST PERFECT   I <u>had eaten</u> before I left for school.

FUTURE PERFECT   I <u>will have eaten</u> breakfast by that time.

Progressive forms of the perfect tenses indicate ongoing actions: I <u>have been working</u> (*present perfect progressive*), I <u>had been working</u> (*past perfect progressive*), I <u>will have been working</u> (*future perfect progressive*).

A. Underline the verb in each sentence. Write its tense on the line.

___[present perfect]___ 1. It <u>has been</u> more than a century since Teddy Roosevelt succeeded President William McKinley as president.

[past perfect progressive] 2. Roosevelt <u>had been serving</u> as McKinley's vice president.

___[past perfect]___ 3. After only six months into McKinley's second term, however, someone <u>had assassinated</u> him.

___[past perfect]___ 4. At 42, Roosevelt <u>had become</u> the youngest president ever.

[past perfect progressive] 5. In 1905 he <u>had been negotiating</u> a treaty for the Russo-Japanese War.

___[past perfect]___ 6. Earlier he <u>had named</u> the Grand Canyon a national monument.

___[present perfect]___ 7. The government <u>has preserved</u> the park since 1893.

___[future perfect]___ 8. Millions of tourists <u>will have visited</u> the park by December.

___[present perfect]___ 9. Roosevelt's conservation policies <u>have influenced</u> many generations of conservationists.

___[present perfect]___ 10. He <u>has remained</u> one of our most colorful presidents.

B. Complete each sentence with form of the verb indicated.

remain–*present perfect*   1. Charlie Chaplin _____[has remained]_____ popular for nearly a century.

study–*present perfect progressive*   2. We ____[have been studying]____ his films in our history class.

star–*past perfect*   3. By 1957 he _____[had starred]_____ in more than 70 films.

see–*present perfect*   4. Our teacher _____[has seen]_____ every one of his movies.

watch–*future perfect*   5. We ____[will have watched]____ *City Lights* and one other Chaplin film by tomorrow.

Verbs

46. Indicative and Imperative Moods

Verb forms indicate *mood*. There are three moods in English: indicative, imperative, and subjunctive (covered in the next exercise).

The **indicative mood** is the form of a verb used to state a fact or ask a question.

> Scrapbooking <u>is becoming</u> more and more popular.
>
> What <u>is</u> scrapbooking?

The **imperative mood** is the form of a verb that is used to give commands.

> <u>Learn</u> more about this popular hobby and craft.

A. Underline the verb or verb phrase in each sentence. Write **IN** to identify verbs in the indicative mood or **IM** to identify verbs in the imperative mood.

___[IN]___ 1. Why <u>do</u> people <u>do</u> scrapbooking?

___[IM]___ 2. <u>Guess</u> the reasons.

___[IN]___ 3. People <u>use</u> a scrapbook as a storage place for information about many things in their lives, such as trips, school events, and parties.

___[IM]___ 4. <u>Think</u> of something in your life to use as a scrapbook topic.

___[IN]___ 5. What things <u>do</u> you <u>find</u> in a scrapbook?

___[IN]___ 6. Scrapbooks usually <u>include</u> photos as well as small objects or souvenirs, such as tickets and programs.

___[IM]___ 7. <u>List</u> other possible contents for your scrapbook.

___[IN]___ 8. An important feature of scrapbooking <u>is</u> journaling.

___[IN]___ 9. What <u>is</u> journaling?

___[IN]___ 10. People <u>describe</u> the objects in the scrapbook in captions or blocks of text.

___[IM]___ 11. <u>Look</u> for examples of scrapbooks online.

___[IN]___ 12. Some people <u>use</u> the computer as a tool in scrapbooking.

___[IN]___ 13. They even <u>create</u> scrapbook pages on the computer as webpages.

___[IN]___ 14. <u>Have</u> you <u>seen</u> any of these?

___[IM]___ 15. <u>Take</u> a look at these often beautifully styled pages.

B. Rewrite each sentence in the imperative mood. Add or delete words as necessary.

1. First you should choose an event or a theme, such as a school picnic or a hobby.

   [First choose an event or a theme such as a school picnic or a hobby.]

2. It is important to find the best photos of the event.

   [Find the best photos of the event.]

3. You need to get supplies such as paper, scissors, glue, and an album.

   [Get supplies such as paper, scissors, glue, and an album.]

4. Creating a sample page layout is essential.

   [Create a sample page layout.]

5. You should try to be creative and use your artistic sense.

   [Be creative and use your artistic sense.]

47. Subjunctive Mood

> The **subjunctive mood** of a verb can express a wish or a desire or a condition that is contrary to fact. Present wishes or desires or contrary-to-fact conditions are expressed by the past tense. *Were* is used with all subjects.
>
> WISH OR DESIRE   **I wish I <u>were</u> going to the movie with you.**
>
> CONTRARY TO FACT   **If he <u>were</u> caught up with all his chores, he could go.**
>
> Past wishes, desires, or contrary-to-fact conditions are expressed by the past perfect tense.
>
> WISH OR DESIRE   **I wished I <u>had read</u> the assignment.**
>
> CONTRARY TO FACT   **If I had read it beforehand, I <u>would have had</u> all the answers.**
>
> The subjunctive is used also to express a demand or a recommendation after *that, if,* or *whether.* The base form is used for these subjunctive verbs.
>
>   **Her teacher recommended that she <u>take</u> singing lessons.**

A. Underline the verb or verb phrase in the subjunctive mood in each sentence. On each line at the left write **W** to identify a wish or a desire, **C** to identify a contrary-to-fact condition, or **D** to identify a demand or recommendation.

__[W]__   1. I wish I <u>had</u> a mountain bike.

__[C]__   2. If I <u>had</u> more money, I would buy one.

__[C]__   3. If I <u>had saved</u> money, I would have been able to get one.

__[W]__   4. I wish I <u>hadn't spent</u> so much money on my school trip.

__[C]__   5. If I <u>had had</u> a bike last year, I would have had more fun on our vacation at the lake.

__[C]__   6. If I <u>were</u> the owner of one, I would be able to travel all around the lake area.

__[D]__   7. My mother recommends that I <u>get</u> a part-time job.

__[D]__   8. She insists, however, that I <u>take</u> piano lessons one day a week.

__[D]__   9. She also suggests that I <u>be</u> a member of the choir.

__[C]__   10. My friend says, "If I <u>were</u> you, I'd try to find work caring for people's yards."

B. Circle the correct verb to complete each sentence in the subjunctive.

1. The experts recommend that a potential bike owner (**go** goes) to a local shop.

2. So if I (was **were**) buying a mountain bike, I would go to a local shop and look at the models available.

3. If I (was **were**) you, I would buy a model from the previous year because they are usually less expensive.

4. Safety advisors insist that every biker (**get** gets) a crash helmet.

5. We wish that there (was **were**) a place to rent mountain bikes near here.

Verbs

48. Modal Auxiliaries

> Modal auxiliaries are used to express permission, possibility, ability, necessity, obligation, or intention. They are used with main verbs in the base form. Common modal auxiliaries are *may, might, can, could, must, should, will,* and *would.*
>
> **All citizens <u>may</u> exercise their right to vote.** (permission)
>
> **In some countries citizens <u>must</u> vote.** (necessity)
>
> The passive voice is formed by inserting *be, have been,* or *had been* between the modal auxiliary and the past participle.
>
> **Special elections <u>may be held</u> on special issues.** (possibility)

A. Underline the verb phrase with a modal auxiliary. Tell if the modal auxiliary expresses permission, possibility, ability, necessity, obligation, or intention. More than one description may be possible for some sentences.

[ability] 1. In a democracy voters <u>can decide</u> on their leaders.

[necessity] 2. In Australia every eligible citizen <u>must register</u> for the vote.

[possibility] 3. People in the United States <u>may register</u> if they choose to do so.

[obligation] 4. Every citizen <u>should vote</u> in elections.

[possibility] 5. Any U.S. citizen 18 years old or older <u>may participate</u> in an election.

[permission] 6. The Twentieth-Sixth Amendment says that 18-year-olds <u>may vote</u>.

[permission] 7. At one time only adult white males <u>could vote</u>.

[permission] 8. Now citizens of all races and genders <u>may vote</u>.

[permission] 9. Although the Fifteenth Amendment says that people of all races <u>could vote</u>, many African Americans were denied this right for years.

[obligation] 10. You <u>should read</u> about the history of the struggle for women's suffrage.

[intention] 11. My older brother <u>will vote</u> for the first time in the next election.

[permission] 12. People who are not at home on election day <u>may cast</u> absentee ballots.

[possibility] 13. Your life <u>may be affected</u> by the new elected leaders.

[possibility] 14. For example, the amount of the budget for education and libraries <u>might be decided</u> by them.

[obligation] 15. People <u>should take</u> their duty to vote seriously.

B. Complete each sentence with a verb phrase containing a modal auxiliary. Use the main verb and the meaning of the modal shown in parentheses. More than one answer may be correct for some sentences.

1. People born in other countries ___**[may become]**___ U.S. citizens. (become–*permission*)

2. Applicants for citizenship ___**[must be]**___ 18 years old. (be–*necessity*)

3. They ___**[must have lived]**___ in the United States for five years. (have lived–*necessity*)

4. They ___**[should agree]**___ to the principles of the Constitution. (agree–*obligation*)

5. They ___**[must take]**___ a test to show that they know basic facts about the U.S. government. (take–*necessity*)

49. Subject-Verb Agreement

A verb always agrees with its subject in person and number. The only verbs that need to change form to agree with their subjects are the verb *be* and verbs in the present tense with third person singular subjects.

The man rides a bicycle.

The men ride bicycles.

Sometimes a phrase comes between the subject and the verb. The verb must agree with the subject, not the phrase.

The dog, like many other pets, gets fleas.

A meal of potatoes and hot dogs is filling.

A. Complete each sentence with the correct form of the present tense of the verb.

bring 　 1. Olympic events ____[bring]____ together the world's finest athletes.

bear 　 2. Couriers ____[bear]____ a lighted torch from the valley of Olympia, Greece.

carry 　 3. The final runner ____[carries]____ the torch into the stadium.

light 　 4. Here the runner ____[lights]____ the Olympic Flame to open the games.

burn 　 5. This flame ____[burns]____ until the end of the games.

B. Circle the correct form of the verb in parentheses.

1. The 1936 Olympic competition, held in Berlin, (was) were) emotionally tense.

2. Imagine the year is 1936 and Adolf Hitler (lead (leads)) Germany.

3. Hitler, the leader of the Nazis, (want (wants)) his athletes to win.

4. Jesse Owens, however, ((is) are) the star of the Olympics.

5. Owens, among the first African-American U.S. Olympians, (win (wins)) three solo gold medals.

6. He and his other team members also ((triumph) triumphs) in the 100-meter relay.

7. Owens and the other Americans ((shatter) shatters) the Nazi leader's hopes.

8. The image of Owens decorated with four gold medals ((was) were) an inspiration to persecuted people everywhere.

9. After the Olympics, Owens ((was) were) active in youth athletic programs.

10. Owens, one of the world's great athletes, ((remains) remain) a source of inspiration.

Jesse Owens inspired people everywhere with his courage and determination. What inspires you? Write about how another person has inspired you.

50. *Doesn't* and *Don't*

> *Doesn't* is used when the subject of the sentence is third person singular.
>
> **Lucy <u>doesn't</u> care.**
>
> *Don't* is used with other subjects.
>
> **I <u>don't</u> care.**   **We <u>don't</u> care.**
>
> **You <u>don't</u> care.**   **Lucy's friends <u>don't</u> care.**

A. **Circle the correct form of the verb in parentheses.**

1. I (doesn't (don't)) remember who she is.

2. Most Americans (doesn't (don't)) work on Labor Day.

3. Why ((doesn't) don't) Anita drink her tea while it's hot?

4. My mother ((doesn't) don't) want me to stay up late.

5. We (doesn't (don't)) have a blender.

6. Nina ((doesn't) don't) have to practice on Saturday.

7. You (doesn't (don't)) need to read chapter seven.

8. Mr. Esposito ((doesn't) don't) have any children.

9. ((Doesn't) Don't) Jerry know he shouldn't wear his hat inside the house?

10. Those three dogs (doesn't (don't)) belong to Randy.

B. **Complete each sentence with *doesn't* or *don't*.**

1. A rainbow ____**[doesn't]**____ always appear after it rains.

2. Carmen ____**[doesn't]**____ have enough time to see a movie.

3. We ____**[don't]**____ want to spend our vacation in Antarctica.

4. Sid realized he ____**[doesn't]**____ look like Abraham Lincoln.

5. The security guard ____**[doesn't]**____ allow anyone in after six.

6. We ____**[don't]**____ care if she has ever played baseball before.

7. ____**[Don't]**____ you have any homework tonight?

8. Tina and Harriet ____**[don't]**____ want to miss the concert.

9. The dress ____**[doesn't]**____ have to be blue.

10. I ____**[don't]**____ want to miss tomorrow's football game.

Verbs

51. *There Is* and *There Are*

> When *there is* or *there are* introduces a sentence, the subject follows the verb. Use *there is (was, has been)* with singular subjects. Use *there are (were, have been)* with plural subjects.
>
> **There are about 50 million tourists to Italy every year.**

A. Circle the correct verb form in parentheses.

1. There (is (are)) many tourist attractions in Italy.
2. In Florence alone there (is (are)) many magnificent works of art.
3. During the 1400s there ((was) were) a revival of learning known as the Renaissance.
4. There (was (were)) important Renaissance artists from Florence, including Leonardo da Vinci and Michelangelo.
5. There ((was) were) interest at that time in the writings of the ancient Greeks and Romans.
6. There ((is) are) a famous museum in Florence called the Uffizi Gallery.
7. There ((was) were) once Michelangelo's original statue of David in a nearby piazza, but it is now in a museum.
8. There ((is) are) still, however, a copy of the imposing work in the piazza.
9. There ((is) are) one landmark in Rome that is the main symbol of the city—the Colosseum.
10. There ((was) were) entertainment in that arena during the time of the ancient Romans.
11. There (was (were)) once many ancient roads connecting places within the Roman Empire.
12. Throughout Europe there (is (are)) still traces of the old roads.
13. There (is (are)) many fairs in Italian towns throughout the year.
14. There (is (are)), for example, celebrations that feature local products and foods, including artichokes, asparagus, pepperoni, and gnocchi (a kind of dumpling).
15. Down the center of Italy there ((is) are) a mountain chain.
16. There (is (are)) the Alps in the north.
17. There (is (are)) also active volcanoes in Italy, including Mount Vesuvius and Mount Etna.
18. Many people know there ((was) were) a big eruption of Vesuvius in AD 79.
19. There (has been (have been)), however, other eruptions of that volcano throughout history.
20. There recently ((has been) have been) concern over the deterioration of famous landmarks such as the Leaning Tower of Pisa.

B. Complete each sentence with *is* or *are*.

1. There ___[is]___ a famous horse race in Siena, Italy.
2. There ___[are]___ horses representing the city's various *contrade,* or sections, in the race.
3. There ___[is]___ strong rivalry among these historic sections.
4. There ___[are]___ often plots to stop a rival from winning the race.
5. There ___[is]___ a prize for winning—a banner called the *Palio.*

Verbs

52. Agreement with Compound Subjects

Compound subjects connected by *and* usually require a plural verb. If, however, the subjects connected by *and* refer to the same person, place, or thing, or express a single idea, the subject is considered singular.

Chickens and ducks <u>are</u> both poultry.

Ham and eggs <u>is</u> my favorite breakfast.

A. Circle the correct form of the verb in parentheses.

1. Rock and roll (is) are) a style of music that originated in America in the 1950s.

2. Many adults and children (was (were)) shocked by this new form of music.

3. Jazz and country music (was (were)) incorporated into rock and roll.

4. Rhythm and blues ((is) are) also considered a main influence.

5. Bill Haley and the Comets ((was) were) one of the first successful acts.

6. "Shake, Rattle, and Roll" ((was) were) probably the group's biggest hit.

7. Chuck Berry and Fats Domino (was (were)) also popular singers.

8. The most famous singer and performer ((was) were) Elvis Presley.

9. This musician and actor (remain (remains)) popular today.

10. *Frankie and Johnny* ((is) are) just one of the movies Elvis starred in.

B. Complete each sentence with *is* or *are*.

1. Macaroni and cheese ____[is]____ a popular side dish.

2. Macaroni and cheese ____[are]____ the two main ingredients in the casserole.

3. "To serve and protect" ____[is]____ the motto of our police department.

4. Serving and protecting ____[are]____ worthy goals of any police officer.

5. Fox and Geese ____[is]____ an old children's game.

6. The fox and the geese ____[are]____ making a ruckus in the barnyard.

7. *Bob and Ray* ____[is]____ an old radio program inducted into the Radio Hall of Fame.

8. Bob and Ray ____[are]____ living legends in the history of radio.

9. Stars and stripes ____[are]____ painted all over Jessica's toy chest.

10. ____[Is]____ "Stars and Stripes" going to be played at the veterans' ceremony?

Verbs

53. Agreement with Compound Subjects Connected by *Or* or *Nor*

When a compound subject is joined by *or* or *nor,* the verb agrees with the subject closer to it.

Neither the dog nor the <u>cats</u> <u>are</u> inside.

Neither the cats nor the <u>dog</u> is inside.

A. Circle the correct form of the verb in parentheses.

1. Neither the lunch nor the dinner (come (comes)) with dessert.
2. ((Was) Were) either Muriel or Pedro at the wedding?
3. Neither he nor I ((work) works) on Sunday.
4. Either Mr. Anderson or you (is (are)) responsible.
5. Neither the gas bill nor the electric bill ((was) were) mailed on time.
6. Either my grandparents or my father (pick (picks)) me up from school.
7. Neither the horse's feet nor its legs (was (were)) injured in the accident.
8. Neither the pillows nor the mattress (arrive (arrives)) today.
9. Either Logan or I (has (have)) to baby-sit Veronica.
10. Neither the teacher nor the students ((know) knows) who will be selected.

B. Complete each sentence with the correct form of the present tense of the verb.

is | 1. Either the tuna or the mayonnaise _____[is]_____ rancid.

watch | 2. Neither he nor I _____[watch]_____ television on weeknights.

is | 3. Neither Madeline nor her friends _____[are]_____ going to the meeting.

feed | 4. Either Walter or his daughters _____[feed]_____ the fish when I am away.

read | 5. Neither the man nor his wife _____[reads]_____ the newspaper.

like | 6. Neither you nor my brother _____[likes]_____ taking tests.

walk | 7. Either Homer or I _____[walk]_____ the dog before school.

match | 8. Either the hat or the gloves _____[match]_____ her coat.

smell | 9. Neither the trainer nor his animals _____[smell]_____ bad.

know | 10. Neither the players nor their coach _____[knows]_____ how to get to the stadium.

54. Agreement with Subjects Preceded by *Each, Every, Many a, or No*

> When two or more subjects connected by *and* are preceded by *each, every, many a,* or *no,* the subject is considered singular.

A. Circle the correct form of the verb in parentheses.

1. Every man, woman, and child ((has) have) heard of Bigfoot.

2. Each report and piece of evidence (feed (feeds)) the public's imagination.

3. The Himalayan Yeti and the Canadian Sasquatch each ((fit) fits) the description.

4. No culture or society ((is) are) without some form of this legend.

5. Each Russian folktale, Greek myth, and Anglo-Saxon fable ((has) have) a similar figure.

6. Many a scientist and investigator (doubt (doubts)) the existence of Bigfoot.

7. Each photograph and sighting ((is) are) examined.

8. Every bird and mammal (leave (leaves)) some trace behind.

9. A family says every story and report ((was) were) false.

10. They say each footprint and sound attributed to Bigfoot ((was) were) created by a family member.

B. Complete each sentence with the correct form of the present tense of the verb.

has 1. Many a clam and oyster ___[has]___ been found in that bay.

is 2. Every mother and father ___[is]___ coming to the play.

walk 3. Each student and teacher ___[walks]___ outside when the alarm bell rings.

show 4. Every boy and girl here ___[shows]___ signs of improvement.

is 5. At the airport every bag and box ___[is]___ inspected.

has 6. Each football team and soccer team ___[has]___ a pep rally.

bring 7. Every friend and relative ___[brings]___ a present.

has 8. No child or adult ___[has]___ received a ticket to the fair.

need 9. Each lion and tiger ___[needs]___ a separate cage.

read 10. Many a teacher and student ___[reads]___ the school paper.

Verbs

55. Agreement with Indefinite Pronouns

> The indefinite pronouns *each, either, neither, one, anyone, no one, anybody, nobody, someone,* and *somebody* are always singular.
>
> **Each lives in an apartment. Nobody lives in a house.**

A. Underline the subject in each sentence. Circle the correct form of the verb in parentheses.

1. <u>Everyone</u> in Basil and Manuel's class (**is** are) going on a field trip.

2. <u>Neither</u> of the boys (**has** have) turned in his permission slip.

3. <u>Everyone</u> in the class (get **gets**) to see the Guggenheim Museum.

4. <u>Anyone</u> without a permission slip (**is** are) not allowed to go.

5. <u>Each</u> of the students (receive **receives**) a reminder.

6. <u>No one</u> (want **wants**) to miss this trip.

7. <u>One</u> of the 20th century's greatest architects (**is** are) the museum's designer.

8. <u>Everyone</u> in the class (know **knows**) that Frank Lloyd Wright designed it.

9. <u>Each</u> of his designs (remain **remains**) influential.

10. <u>Anyone</u> visiting the museum (know **knows**) it is a work of art in itself.

B. Underline the subject in each sentence. Complete each sentence with the correct form of the present tense of the verb at left.

play   1. <u>Nobody</u> ____[plays]____ as well as Diego.

bring   2. <u>Someone</u> ____[brings]____ Maria the newspaper every day.

be   3. <u>Neither</u> of the dogs ____[is]____ tired of playing.

ride   4. In Europe nearly <u>everyone</u> ____[rides]____ a bicycle.

prepare   5. <u>Someone</u> different ____[prepares]____ dinner each night.

goes   6. On the night before a test, <u>everybody</u> ____[goes]____ to bed early.

know   7. <u>Anyone</u> ____[knows]____ where that building is located.

need   8. <u>One</u> of these cakes ____[needs]____ icing.

appear   9. <u>Nobody</u> ____[appears]____ to have watered the vegetables.

want   10. <u>No one</u> ____[wants]____ to drink water from that pond.

56. Agreement with Collective Nouns

A **collective noun** names a group of persons or things: *audience, team, litter.*
A collective noun is generally thought of as a single unit and takes a singular
verb. However, when the meaning suggests that the members are being
considered as individuals, use a plural verb.

> The football team <u>practices</u> indoors when it rains.

> The football team <u>are</u> responsible for their own uniforms.

A. Circle the correct form of the verb in parentheses.

1. The choir (is are) not back from its concert tour to New England
   and Canada.

2. The faculty (was were) debating all sides of the issue.

3 The faculty (was were) unanimous in its decision.

4. The French club (meet meets) in the library
   after school on Wednesday.

5. The jury (has have) been selected by the attorneys.

6. His family (is are) currently living in Florida and Georgia.

7. Congress (was were) in session all week.

8. The flock of birds (flies fly) north
   after the summer ends.

9. The team (was were) operating as
   smoothly as a Swiss watch.

10. The audience (have has) taken their seats,
    and now the concert is about to begin.

B. Write sentences, using the collective noun as subject.
[Answers will vary. Sample answers are given.]

club   1. [The computer gaming club is less popular with the older students.]

team   2. [The team have milkshakes or root beer floats after practice.]

herd   3. [The herd of cattle grazes on the prairie.]

band   4. [Paul's band was quite famous.]

group   5. [A group of teachers meets in the library every week.]

57. Agreement with Special Nouns

Some nouns are plural in form but singular in meaning. Among them are *measles*, *mathematics*, *mumps*, *news*, *ethics*, *physics*, and *economics*. Each of these nouns requires a verb that agrees with a singular subject.

> **The <u>news</u> is terrible.**

Some nouns are used only in the plural; for example, *ashes*, *clothes*, *eaves*, *goods*, *pincers*, *pliers*, *proceeds*, *scissors*, *shears*, *suspenders*, *glasses*, *scales*, *thanks*, *tongs*, *trousers*, and *tweezers*. Each of these nouns requires a verb that agrees with a plural subject.

> **<u>Thanks</u> are in order.**

A. Underline the subject in each sentence. Circle the correct verb in parentheses.

1. The <u>tweezers</u> (go) goes) in the medicine cabinet.

2. <u>Economics</u> (is) are) sometimes taught in high school.

3. The <u>ashes</u> from the fireplace (have) has) not been removed.

4. The garden <u>shears</u> (make) makes) the job a lot easier.

5. The <u>eaves</u> on the guest house (was (were) painted last summer.

6. Bernadette's <u>clothes</u> (give) gives) her a formal appearance.

7. Diego's <u>suspenders</u> (keep) keeps) his pants from falling down.

8. <u>News</u> (spread (spreads) quickly in this modern electronic age.

9. The <u>proceeds</u> from the bake sale (was (were) used to buy new uniforms.

10. Abby's <u>glasses</u> (need) needs) to be fixed.

B. Complete each sentence with *is* or *are*.

1. The pliers _____[are]_____ in the toolbox.

2. Safety scissors _____[are]_____ better for young children.

3. Civics _____[is]_____ an interesting and important subject for children to study.

4. Rupert's slacks _____[are]_____ made out of linen.

5. Mumps _____[is]_____ a contagious disease.

6. Thanks _____[are]_____ due to our parents for their kindness and support.

7. Those rusty tongs _____[are]_____ of no use to anyone.

8. Mathematics _____[is]_____ Dejuan's favorite subject.

9. Emma's clothes _____[are]_____ in need of ironing.

10. The news _____[is]_____ coming on at six.

Verbs

Name _____

58. Reviewing Verbs

A. Underline the verb in each sentence. On the first line write **T** if the verb is transitive or **I** if it is intransitive. On the second line write **A** if the verb is active or **P** if it is passive.

__[I]__ __[A]__ 1. Some animals <u>migrate</u> every year.

__[T]__ __[P]__ 2. Monarch butterflies <u>are found</u> in Canada and the United States in the summer and in Mexico in the winter.

__[I]__ __[A]__ 3. Many birds <u>fly</u> to new homes every spring and fall.

__[T]__ __[A]__ 4. Pacific salmon <u>complete</u> their migration over their lifetimes.

__[T]__ __[P]__ 5. These migratory patterns <u>are studied</u> by U.S. and Canadian scientists

B. Underline the linking verb in each sentence. Circle the subject complement.

6. Irruption <u>is</u> an unpredictable (form) of migration.

7. Lemmings <u>are</u> an (example) of an animal that migrates in this manner.

8. Another migratory pattern <u>is</u> (remigration,) which occurs across generations.

9. Many scientists <u>are</u> (intent) on studying irruption.

10. Animal migration <u>is</u> (hard) for scientists to track.

C. Complete each sentence with the correct form of the verb.

study–*present progressive, active* 11. June's class _____[is studying]_____ animal migration.

taught–*present perfect, passive* 12. It _____[has been taught]_____ many interesting facts.

visit–*future, active* 13. The students _____[will visit]_____ the Columbia River next semester.

migrate–*future progressive, active* 14. The Chinook salmon _____[will be migrating]_____ then.

travels–*present, active* 15. This salmon _____[travels]_____ more than 2,000 miles to spawn.

place–*present perfect, passive* 16. These fish _____[have been placed]_____ on the threatened species list.

hatch–*present, active* 17. Baby salmon _____[hatch]_____ in rivers and streams.

swim–*future, active* 18. After spending their adult lives in the ocean, they _____[will swim]_____ back to the same river to spawn.

61

prevent–*present perfect, active*

19. Dams across the rivers ___[have prevented]___ some salmon from reaching their spawning grounds.

work–*present perfect progressive, active*

20. Many people ___[have been working]___ to save the salmon.

D. Write on the line the mood of the *italicized* verb. Use **A** for indicative, **B** for imperative, and **C** for subjunctive.

___[B]___ 21. *Return* these books to the library.

___[C]___ 22. Lamont wishes he *were* already on vacation.

___[A]___ 23. My sister *is reading* a scary book.

___[C]___ 24. If Emily *were* here, she would know what to do.

___[A]___ 25. Nathan *can walk* to school if he chooses.

E. Circle the correct verb in parentheses.

26. The team (is) are) meeting before the game.

27. The team (has) have) to win to advance in the tournament.

28. Each of the players (want (wants)) to do well.

29. Neither of the captains (know (knows)) which team is playing today.

30. After the game was over, everyone (raised (rose)) to leave.

Try It Yourself
On a separate sheet of paper write five sentences about something you and your friends do. Be sure to use verbs correctly.

Check Your Own Work
Choose a selection from your writing portfolio, your journal, a work in progress, an assignment from school, or a letter. Revise it, applying the skills you have learned in this chapter. This checklist will help you.

✔ Have you conveyed the meaning clearly and accurately by using the correct form of the verb?

✔ Have you written the correct form of the troublesome verbs?

✔ Have you used verb tense correctly?

Name _____

59. Participles

A participle is a verb form that is used as an adjective; it can be used to modify a noun or a pronoun. Present participles end in *-ing,* and past participles often end in *-ed.*

The cat <u>chasing</u> the mouse grew tired. (present participle)

The mouse, <u>chased</u> by the cat, ran into a small hole. (past participle)

Underline the participle used as an adjective in each sentence. Describe each by writing *present* **or** *past* **on the line at the left.**

___[present]___ 1. <u>Walking</u> at night, Kay often sees meteors.

___[present]___ 2. <u>Streaking</u> across the sky, they are a magnificent sight.

___[past]___ 3. Brilliant meteors, <u>known</u> as fireballs, are quite dramatic.

___[past]___ 4. Some, <u>called</u> bolides, have even been observed to explode like thunder.

___[present]___ 5. A meteor <u>reaching</u> a planet in one piece is called a meteorite.

___[present]___ 6. Kay, <u>listening</u> in class, learned that comets break up and form meteors.

___[present]___ 7. Asteroids and comets are small solid objects <u>orbiting</u> the sun.

___[past]___ 8. Three of the largest asteroids—<u>called</u> Ceres, Pallas, and Vesta—are found in a single asteroid belt.

___[past]___ 9. <u>Located</u> between Mars and Jupiter, they do not pose a threat to Earth.

___[present]___ 10. A giant asteroid may once have hit Earth, <u>striking</u> the Yucatan Peninsula.

___[past]___ 11. The Yucatan, <u>located</u> in Mexico, is marked by a giant crater.

___[present]___ 12. <u>Coinciding</u> with the dinosaurs' disappearance, that collision is believed to have killed them off.

___[past]___ 13. What other theories <u>offered</u> by scientists explain their disappearance?

___[past]___ 14. One, <u>proposed</u> by a health researcher, suggests that a fungus may be to blame.

___[present]___ 15. He theorizes that fungi attacked their bodies, <u>causing</u> sickness and death.

60. Placement of Participles

> A participle used as an adjective can come before or after the noun it modifies or after a linking verb.
>
> **Do not cry over spilled milk.**
>
> **The crumbs lying on the floor need to be swept up.**
>
> **His meal was very nourishing.**

A. Underline the participle in each sentence. Circle the word it modifies.

1. The (icicle,) melting rapidly, fell from the gutter.

2. It is dangerous to drive fast on the winding (road.)

3. The (news,) blaring from the TV, caught my attention.

4. It is important to watch for falling (rocks) while climbing.

5. The battle of Gettysburg was a turning (point) in the Civil War.

6. The (dog) growling in the yard scared off the hoodlums.

7. Simon had only one misspelled (word) on his paper.

8. We must repair that broken (window.)

9. The (figure) at Mabel's door was disturbing.

10. Chan threw out the chipped (plate.)

11. The baby chick emerged from the cracked (egg.)

12. The (branches) of the willow, swaying gracefully in the breeze, were a lovely sight.

13. The sound of running (water) attracted the deer to the river's edge.

14. As we listened, the (story) became more exciting.

15. The written (word) is an important link to the past.

B. Use each phrase in a sentence. Underline each participle. Circle the noun it modifies. **[Sample answers are given.]**

raging storm   1. **[The boat got caught in the raging (storm.)]** _____

retired athlete   2. **[The retired (athlete) became a used-car salesperson.]** _____

purring cat   3. **[It is nice to come home to a purring (cat.)]** _____

freezing rain   4. **[School was cancelled because of the freezing (rain.)]** _____

known facts   5. **[The detective evaluates all the known (facts) before arriving at conclusions.]**

Verbals

61. Dangling Participles

> A participle that does not modify any noun or pronoun in the sentence is called a **dangling participle**.
>
> DANGLING   **Working for days, the paper was completed.**
>
> CORRECTED   **Working for days, the student completed the paper.**

A. Write **C** to the left of each sentence in which the participle is used correctly. Underline the participle and circle the word it modifies.

[C]   1. <u>Sitting</u> at the table, (we) were served pancakes and milk.

_____   Sitting at the table, pancakes and milk were served.

_____   2. Walking along the beach, there was a beautiful sunset.

[C]   <u>Walking</u> along the beach, (I) saw a beautiful sunset.

_____   3. Nursing an injury, the performance was terrible.

[C]   <u>Nursing</u> an injury, the (dancer) performed terribly.

[C]   4. <u>Lacking</u> the money, (John) did not buy the bicycle.

_____   Lacking the money, the bicycle remained unpurchased.

_____   5. Having eaten ice cream already, the lunch remained untouched.

[C]   <u>Having</u> eaten ice cream already, (Eve) left her lunch untouched.

B. Rewrite the following sentences to avoid the dangling participle. [Sample answers are given.]

1. Climbing out of the pool, the beach chair came into view.

   [Climbing out of the pool, we saw the beach chair.]

2. Reaching into the refrigerator, the milk was taken out.

   [Reaching into the refrigerator, she took the milk out.]

3. Reading all night, the book was finished.

   [Reading all night, Leonard finished the book.]

4. Jogging early in the morning, the cool breeze is refreshing.

   [Jogging early in the morning, she found the cool breeze refreshing.]

5. Standing at the chalkboard, the lesson was presented by the teacher.

   [Standing at the chalkboard, the teacher presented the lesson.]

Verbals

62. Gerunds as Subjects

A **gerund** is a verb form ending in *-ing* that is used as a noun. A gerund may be used as the subject of a sentence. A **gerund phrase** may include a direct object and modifiers.

> **Exercising is good for your health.** (gerund)
>
> **Keeping a strict routine can be difficult.** (gerund phrase with a direct object)

A. Underline the gerund phrase. Draw an additional line under the gerund.

1. Catching fish is fun.
2. Baiting the hook is not as much fun.
3. Threading a worm on a hook requires patience.
4. Selecting a flashy lure may help catch some types of fish.
5. Making lures with exotic feathers is a popular hobby.
6. For some people, rowing the boat is the most fun.
7. Being outside is enough for others.
8. For my father, chasing a record catch is the goal.
9. Cooking and eating the fish are my mother's favorite part.
10. Identifying the fish is as close as I want to get.

B. Write sentences, using the gerund or gerund phrase as a subject. [Sentences will vary.]

walking around the track
1. [Walking around the track is good exercise.] _____

exercising
2. _____

drinking water
3. _____

listening
4. _____

eating balanced meals
5. _____

competing in organized sports
6. _____

practicing
7. _____

resting
8. _____

sleeping
9. _____

enjoying games
10. _____

63. Gerunds as Subject Complements

A gerund may be used as a subject complement. A subject complement completes the meaning of a linking verb.

Mom's hobby is <u>sewing</u>. (gerund)

Dad's is <u>building birdhouses</u>. (gerund phrase)

A. Underline the gerund phrase in each sentence. Draw an additional line under the gerund if it is used as a subject complement. Write **DO** over any word that is the direct object of a gerund.

EXAMPLE: **My job at home is <u>washing the dishes</u>.** [DO over dishes]

1. <u>Reading the newspaper</u> is a favorite Sunday activity. [DO]

2. My usual approach is <u>scanning the headlines</u>. [DO]

3. Usually, <u>poring over the sports pages</u> takes most of Dad's time.

4. My favorite thing could never be <u>scouring the want ads</u>. [DO]

5. <u>Checking the entertainment scene</u> is something the entire family enjoys. [DO]

6. My mother's response to the editorial this week was <u>writing her own letter</u>. [DO]

7. Entertainment for me is <u>laughing over the antics in my favorite comic strip</u>.

8. <u>Collecting characters from the Peanuts strip</u> has become my brother's hobby. [DO]

9. The biggest challenge now is <u>training my dog to bring me the newspaper</u>. [DO]

10. Our neighbor's favorite joke is <u>hiding the newspaper somewhere near the house</u>. [DO]

B. Complete each sentence with a phrase that contains a gerund used as the subject complement of the sentence. **[Answers will vary.]**

1. Her favorite kind of cooking is _____.

2. Her least favorite kind of cooking is _____.

3. One of her best techniques is _____.

4. Her most famous method for cooking meat is _____.

5. One source of relaxation for her is _____.

6. What upset her was _____.

7. What I don't understand is _____.

8. Her greatest joy as a chef is _____.

9. The hardest part of being a chef is _____.

10. The main job of a restaurant chef is _____.

Verbals

64. Gerunds as Direct Objects

A gerund may be used as the direct object in a sentence.
> **Sara dislikes <u>painting</u>.** (gerund)
> **Shawn enjoys <u>reviewing movies</u>.** (gerund phrase)

A. Underline the gerund phrase in each sentence.
Draw an additional line under the gerund.

EXAMPLE: **The workers began <u>laying the foundation</u>.**

1. The master carver has started <u>carving the limestone columns with a chisel and mallet</u>.

2. Carvers and workers began <u>building the Cathedral of Saint John the Divine in New York</u> more than 100 years ago.

3. Have the quarriers finished <u>cutting all the limestone</u>?

4. World War II prevented their <u>working</u>.

5. In the 1970s the Very Reverend James Parks Morton suggested <u>starting construction again</u>.

6. European stonecutters undertook <u>the training of local craftspeople</u>.

7. The plans specify <u>making templates for each block of stone</u>.

8. A special arrangement involved <u>hiring young people as apprentices</u>.

9. Laws forbid <u>working without protective gear</u>.

10. People have enjoyed <u>watching the cathedral take shape over the years</u>.

B. Use a gerund phrase from the list to complete each sentence. The gerund phrase will be the direct object in each sentence. **[Sentences will vary.]**

> **running around the track three times**
> **selling tickets for the tournament**
> **reading about the sport you like**
> **comparing our scores and the pros'**
> **going to games by car or by bus**

1. The team has started _____.

2. Do you prefer _____?

3. Try _____.

4. The bowling coach enjoys _____.

5. My workout includes _____.

Verbals

65. Gerunds as Objects of Prepositions

> A gerund may be used as the object of a preposition.
>
> **The group's assignment includes the task of <u>tutoring</u>.** (gerund)
> **The time for <u>teaching the young children</u> is after school.** (gerund phrase)

A. Underline the gerund phrase(s) in each sentence. Draw an additional line under the gerund if it is used as the object of a preposition. Circle the preposition that introduces the gerund phrase.

   Example: **Who is responsible (for) calling team members?**

1. Being kind is one way (of) helping others.

2. The sentiment (of) caring deeply affects how a person responds to others.

3. Nothing great was ever accomplished (without) working hard.

4. Working for peace helps us improve our world.

5. I'm angry with Al (for) buying violent toys.

6. Conflict resolution is a way (of) solving differences peacefully.

7. Her plan (for) negotiating a peace treaty was approved.

8. Talking exhausted her.

9. We are indebted to the group (for) supporting her efforts.

10. She impressed the president (by) describing the difficult situation in a simple way.

B. Use a phrase from the list to complete each sentence. The gerund will be the object of a preposition. Add words to fill out the sentence if you wish. **[Sentences will vary.]**

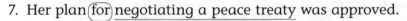

through writing	in answering	for singing
from eating	by studying	

1. He was slow _____.

2. She was known _____.

3. You can learn _____.

4. We can improve _____.

5. He was sick _____.

Verbals

66. Gerunds as Appositives

A gerund may be used as an appositive. An appositive is a word(s) that follows a noun or a pronoun and helps identify it or adds information about it.

Justin's main interest, <u>acting</u>, takes most of his spare time. (gerund)

His role, <u>playing the part of an astronaut</u>, excited him. (gerund phrase)

A. Underline the gerund phrase in each sentence. Draw an additional line under the gerund if it is used as an appositive.

1. The work of Lister, <u>introducing antiseptics into surgery</u>, was a medical breakthrough.

2. <u>Laying the Atlantic cable</u> brought fame to Cyrus Field.

3. Bell's accomplishment, <u>transmitting the human voice over the telephone</u>, took years of work.

4. Leo Hirshfield's legacy, <u>developing a sweet treat named after his daughter Tootsie</u>, is what I remember.

5. <u>Creating labor-saving devices</u> is the inventor's aim.

6. Garrett A. Morgan proposed <u>using a signal to direct traffic at intersections</u>.

7. <u>Mass-producing goods and using interchangeable parts</u> helped establish the automobile industry.

8. Strauss and Davis's idea, <u>sewing pants with rivets on the seams</u>, did work out.

9. The class assignment, <u>writing a report on a favorite inventor</u>, is due tomorrow.

10. Our teacher accomplished her goal, <u>finishing the chapter</u>.

B. Complete each sentence with one of the following gerund phrases. **[Answers will vary.]**

cleaning out the attic   **spending time with young children**
writing e-mails to friends   **becoming an astronaut**
reading romance novels

1. Juan's task, _____, was not easy.

2. That is Grandmother's latest accomplishment, _____.

3. Melanie's experience, _____, helped her get a job.

4. Donald's dream, _____, motivated him to study hard.

5. Cindy has a favorite pastime, _____.

67. Possessives with Gerunds; Using *-ing* Verb Forms

> Gerunds may be preceded by a possessive noun or a possessive adjective. These possessives describe the doer of action of the gerund.
>
> **<u>My</u> deciding to go on the camping trip surprised my family.**
>
> A verb with an *-ing* ending may be a gerund (a noun), a participle (an adjective), or a part of a verb phrase in the progressive tense.
>
> **<u>Exciting</u> adults as well as children was the aim of the trapeze artist.** (gerund)
>
> **Meanwhile, <u>exciting</u> the audience in the arena, acrobats performed their acts.** (participial adjective before a noun)
>
> **Their performances, <u>exciting</u> and courageous, left us in awe.** (participial adjective after a noun)
>
> **Every act was <u>exciting</u>.** (participial adjective after a linking verb)
>
> **Large elephants were <u>exciting</u> children in a nearby tent.** (part of a progressive verb)

A. Underline the correct form.

1. (<u>Our</u> Us) choosing a camping trip proved to be a good idea.
2. My brother agreed to (<u>my</u> me) taking his sleeping bag.
3. The scout leader was surprised at (me <u>my</u>) volunteering to put up the tent.
4. He watched (my <u>me</u>), wearing a pleased expression, as I did the job efficiently.
5. (Him <u>His</u>) praising me for my work made me feel good.
6. (Joe <u>Joe's</u>) cooking the supper was a surprise to us.
7. (Him <u>His</u>) making pioneer stew was a good idea—we loved the meal.
8. The (animals <u>animals'</u>) chattering far into the night kept us awake.
9. On the second night we again heard (<u>them</u> their), noting that they had moved closer to our camp.
10. (Them <u>Their</u>) enjoying the outdoor experience so wholeheartedly meant that the scouts would make a similar trip soon.

B. Identify each italicized word ending in *-ing* as a gerund, a participial adjective, or part of a progressive verb.

__[gerund]__ 1. *Singing* around the campfire was a fun part of the trip.

__[participial adjective]__ 2. Our *singing* voices filled the night air.

__[participial adjective]__ 3. *Singing* the entire campfire song, James proved to us that he knew all the verses.

__[part of a progressive verb]__ 4. We were *singing* old songs into the night.

__[gerund]__ 5. After the *singing* ended, we returned to our tents.

__[participial adjective]__ 6. *Hiking* in the woods, we learned to identify certain trees and wildlife.

__[part of a progressive verb]__ 7. I was *hiking* in the woods when I saw a dappled fawn.

__[gerund]__ 8. *Hiking* in the woods was the highlight of the trip for me.

__[participial adjective]__ 9. It is a good thing I had brought good *hiking* boots.

__[participial adjective]__ 10. This *hiking* experience made me appreciate the outdoors.

68. Reviewing Gerunds

A. Underline the gerund(s) in each sentence. On the line write **S** if it is the subject, **DO** if it is the direct object, **OP** if it is the object of a preposition, **SC** if it is the subject complement, and **A** if it is an appositive.

[OP] 1. The task of <u>saving</u> wildlife is crucial after an oil spill.

[S] 2. <u>Cleaning</u> the oil from sea birds is no small job.

[A] 3. In 1989 the mission of the *Exxon Valdez,* <u>hauling</u> oil off the coast of Alaska, led to disaster.

[S] 4. The <u>spilling</u> of 11 million gallons of crude oil occurred when the tanker hit a reef.

[SC] 5. One of the first tasks was <u>locating</u> oil-containment equipment.

[DO] 6. Snow did not permit rescuers' <u>getting</u> the equipment quickly.

[OP] 7. The job of <u>containing</u> the oil spill was hampered by good weather.

[DO] 8. Calm winds did not permit <u>using</u> materials to break up the oil.

[S] 9. <u>Using</u> buckets to scoop up oil produced little result.

[A, OP] 10. Crews worked at containment, <u>keeping</u> the oil from <u>spreading</u>, but their efforts weren't effective.

[A] 11. Their greatest fear, <u>removing</u> dead sea animals, became a reality.

[S] 12. <u>Seeing</u> thousands of dead birds on the beaches was heartbreaking.

[OP] 13. Rescue workers took the dying animals to centers for <u>cleaning</u>.

[A] 14. A serious consequence of the spill, <u>freezing</u> because their oil-soaked fur could not provide insulation from the cold, caused the death of many otters.

[SC, OP] 15. Our job should be <u>preventing</u> such disasters from <u>happening</u>.

B. Follow the instructions and write sentences using the following gerund phrase: *swimming in the lake.* [Sample answers are given.]

16. *(Use as a subject.)* [Swimming in the lake is great fun.]

17. *(Use as a direct object.)* [I dislike swimming in the lake.]

18. *(Use as a subject complement.)* [One thing I do enjoy is swimming in the lake.]

19. *(Use as the object of a preposition.)* [We cooled off by swimming in the lake.]

20. *(Use as an appositive.)* [My favorite pastime, swimming in the lake, is impossible in winter.]

Verbals

69. Infinitives as Subjects

An **infinitive** is a verb form, usually preceded by *to,* that can be used as a verb, a noun, an adjective, or an adverb. An **infinitive phrase** consists of the infinitive and a direct object, a complement, or modifiers. The direct object receives the action of the infinitive. An infinitive or an infinitive phrase can be used as the subject of a sentence.

To hear can be difficult in a noisy room. (infinitive)

To address an audience directly should be a speaker's main goal.
(infinitive phrase with direct object)

A. Underline the infinitive or the infinitive phrase in each sentence. Draw an additional line under each infinitive. Write **DO** over any word that is the direct object of an infinitive.

EXAMPLE:
DO   DO
To save lives and property is the work of a firefighter.

1. To solve the puzzle [DO] takes some time.

2. To hear the watchdog's bark [DO] is often frightening.

3. To have been chosen was a great honor.

4. To learn embroidery [DO] requires patient effort.

5. To drive carelessly endangers the lives of others.

6. To serve is the job of any person in the armed forces.

7. To persevere to the end demands constant effort.

8. To rescue the lost fishermen [DO] required a life raft
and two sailors.

9. To join the club [DO] was the best thing Steve did.

10. To exercise daily is an excellent habit.

B. Use an infinitive phrase from the list to complete each sentence.
The infinitive phrase will be the subject of the sentence. **[Sentences will vary.]**

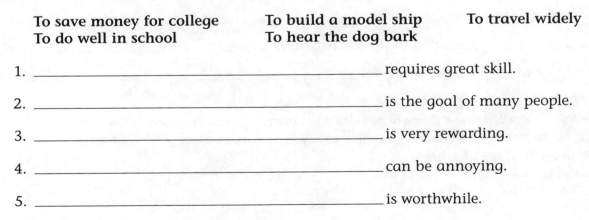

To save money for college   To build a model ship   To travel widely
To do well in school   To hear the dog bark

1. _____ requires great skill.

2. _____ is the goal of many people.

3. _____ is very rewarding.

4. _____ can be annoying.

5. _____ is worthwhile.

70. Infinitives as Subject Complements

An infinitive may be used as a subject complement. A subject complement completes the meaning of a linking verb.

> **My greatest fear is <u>to fail</u>.** (infinitive)
>
> **The recommended approach is <u>to take notes during class</u>.** (infinitive phrase)

A. Underline each infinitive phrase. Draw an additional line under the infinitive.

1. The life's work of Marie Curie was <u>to study radioactive substances</u>.

2. An early goal was <u>to learn about radioactivity in uranium ore</u>.

3. She and her husband were <u>to become a team</u>.

4. The result of their work was <u>to discover radium and polonium, highly radioactive elements</u>.

5. Another result would be <u>to win a Nobel Prize in physics</u>.

6. After her husband's death Marie Curie's distinction was <u>to earn another Nobel Prize, this time in chemistry</u>.

7. Her work was <u>to isolate radium</u> and <u>to study its properties</u>.

8. Another accomplishment was <u>to start the Radium Institute in Paris</u>.

9. Curie's idea was <u>to take X-ray machines to the battlefields</u>.

10. Her plan was <u>to use X rays for locating bullets in soldier's wounds</u>.

B. Complete each sentence with a phrase that contains an infinitive used as the subject complement. **[Sentences will vary.]**

1. A scientist's main job is _____.

2. The object of higher education has always been _____.

3. The aim of scientific study should be _____.

4. The results of experimentation in the lab generally is _____.

5. One purpose of scientific data may be _____.

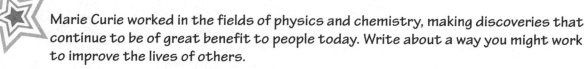

Marie Curie worked in the fields of physics and chemistry, making discoveries that continue to be of great benefit to people today. Write about a way you might work to improve the lives of others.

Verbals

74

71. More Infinitives as Subjects and as Subject Complements

An infinitive or an infinitive phrase can be used as the subject or the subject complement in a sentence. Infinitives can be active or passive, and they can also have perfect forms.

SIMPLE ACTIVE	**To do the laundry is my least favorite chore.**
SIMPLE PASSIVE	**The clothes in this hamper are to be washed.**
PERFECT ACTIVE	**To have finished the laundry will be great.**
PERFECT PASSIVE	**It was supposed to have been finished by now.**

A. Underline the infinitive phrase in each sentence. Write **A** if it is active or **P** if it is passive.

__[P]__ 1. The flag is to be raised at noon.

__[A]__ 2. To raise the flag is the privilege of the honor guard.

__[A]__ 3. The principal's role is to lead the Pledge of Allegiance.

__[A]__ 4. The students' duty is to recite it after her.

__[P]__ 5. Then the parade is to be started.

__[P]__ 6. The school song is to be played by the pep band.

__[A]__ 7. The first float is to carry the football team.

__[P]__ 8. The float is to be driven by the coach.

__[A]__ 9. To excite the crowd is the job of the cheerleaders.

__[A]__ 10. To have a lot of fun is my expectation.

B. Underline the infinitive phrase in each sentence. Write **A** if it is active or **P** if it is passive.

__[A]__ 1. Our goal was to have made dinner by six o'clock.

__[P]__ 2. The potatoes were to have been boiled earlier in the day.

__[A]__ 3. My brother's job was to have fried them with onions and celery.

__[P]__ 4. The carrots for the salad were to have been shredded by my sister.

__[P]__ 5. The lettuce was to have been washed and dried by 5:30.

__[A]__ 6. My job was to have marinated the chicken.

__[P]__ 7. The chicken was to have been baked with mushroom gravy.

__[A]__ 8. Unfortunately nothing was to have happened as it did.

__[A]__ 9. To have had a disaster like this was unprecedented.

__[A]__ 10. The worst part was to have disappointed our parents.

Verbals

72. Infinitives as Direct Objects

> An infinitive may be used as the direct object in a sentence.
>
> **My aunt plans to move.** (infinitive)
>
> **She expects to buy a little house in Utah.** (infinitive phrase)

A. Underline the infinitive phrase in each sentence. Draw an additional line under the infinitive.

EXAMPLE: **My friend never wants to carry a heavy backpack.**

1. A lobbyist is a person who tries to influence the proceedings of Congress.

2. Young people should try to think for themselves about politics.

3. Have you begun to learn the names of the new cabinet members?

4. The new president resolved to make changes immediately.

5. The president hopes to travel to Europe.

6. The vice president promised to serve the president.

7. Republicans attempted to pass tax laws quickly.

8. Democrats wanted to slow their actions.

9. We must learn to cooperate with others on important issues.

10. The work of the men and women in Congress deserves to be praised.

B. Use an infinitive phrase from the list to complete each sentence. The infinitive phrase will be the direct object of each sentence. **[Sentences will vary.]**

to drive a race car   to wrestle   to write a story
to learn all the dance steps   to prepare for tomorrow

1. Jonathan would like _____.

2. Have the children been taught _____?

3. Several teammates tried _____.

4. Before we retire, we must try _____.

5. Does she want _____?

Verbals

73. Infinitives as Appositives

An infinitive may be used as an appositive. An appositive follows a noun
or a pronoun and helps identify it or adds information about it.

Miguel had only one objective, to win. (infinitive)

We achieved our goal, to earn money for charity. (infinitive
phrase)

A. Underline the infinitive phrase in each sentence.
Draw an additional line under the infinitive.

1. John Adams fulfilled his responsibility, to serve his country loyally,
by taking on many government posts.

2. One huge task, to develop Washington, D.C., into the
nation's capital, was undertaken during his presidency.

3. His main obligation, to serve as president, came first.

4. A major challenge, to avoid war with France, was settled peacefully in 1800.

5. The goal of the Federalists, to organize a strong
government, was supported by Hamilton.

6. The Republicans' goal, to respond to the needs
of ordinary citizens, was defended by Jefferson.

7. One aim of Adams, to move into the president's house
in Washington, was accomplished.

8. The country's potential dilemma, to have a tie vote in the
electoral college, became a reality in 1800.

9. The duty of the House of Representatives, to break the
tie between Jefferson and Burr, took days.

10. Finally, after 36 ballots they fulfilled their responsibility,
to choose a president, and elected Jefferson.

B. Complete each sentence with one of the following infinitive phrases.
The sentence will have an infinitive as an appositive. [Sentences will vary.]

to study politics   to make education a priority
to run for office   to vote
to elect more minorities

1. Their hope, _____, will require time and effort.

2. The proposal, _____, was raised at the town hall meeting.

3. My plan, _____, was applauded.

4. Mrs. Hughes's decision, _____, was difficult.

5. He had one ambition, _____.

74. Infinitives as Adjectives

An infinitive can be used as an adjective to describe a noun or a pronoun.

Robert Fulton is an interesting person to read about.

Underline the infinitive phrase used as an adjective in each sentence.
Circle the noun it describes.

1. Steam has the (power) to run machinery.

2. Practical (ways) to use steam as a source of power for machinery were developed in the 1700s.

3. Robert Fulton's *Clermont* was one of the first (boats) to run on steam.

4. Even as a child in Pennsylvania, he thought of many (things) to make.

5. One (invention) to be built by Fulton was a paddlewheel, which he constructed when he was 13 years old.

6. Before starting on his steamboat invention, he took (time) to try his hand at painting.

7. His (articles) to highlight the benefits of canal transportation were sent to senior U.S. officials.

8. He invented a (machine) to dig canal channels.

9. He designed a (device) to cut marble.

10. He labored on an (invention) to travel underwater.

11. The (vehicle) to be developed was actually an early submarine, but it wasn't very successful!

12. He was working at the time on (weapons) to be used in sea warfare.

13. His (effort) to build a steamboat continued after he returned to the United States.

14. The (incentive) to make a steamboat came from several sources.

15. A (steamboat) to navigate the Hudson River was his plan.

16. The (race) to build steamboats for transport and travel had begun.

17. Other (efforts) to run a steamboat occurred before and after Fulton's.

18. However, the (person) to be remembered as the inventor of the steamboat was Fulton.

19. Fulton had not forgotten his (plan) to build a submarine.

20. He did not, however, have a (chance) to finish it before his death in 1815.

Verbals

Name _____

75. Infinitives as Adverbs

An infinitive can be used as an adverb to describe a verb, an adjective, or another adverb.

We went to the exhibit <u>to find out about future inventions</u>.
(describes the verb *went*)

We were happy <u>to see so many creative ideas</u>. (describes the adjective *happy*)

The inventors were creative enough <u>to have many surprising inventions</u>.
(describes the adverb *enough*)

Underline the infinitive phrase used as an adverb in each sentence. Circle the word(s) it describes. Identify the word(s) as a noun, an adjective, or an adverb. An infinitive that describes a verb often tells *why* or *how*.

[verb] 1. Our class (went) to the museum <u>to see student fantasy inventions</u>.

[adjective] 2. We were (eager) <u>to see the students' ideas</u>.

[verb] 3. <u>To illustrate their inventions</u>, students (drew) pictures or (made) models of them.

[verb] 4. They (stood) near the exhibits <u>to answer questions from visitors</u>.

[verb] 5. One invention, a comfy chair, (was designed) <u>to help people with disabilities</u>.

[verb] 6. <u>To operate it</u>, you (pressed) a button: it became a rocking chair or a chair with wheels.

[adjective] 7. The usefulness of that invention was (easy) <u>to see</u>.

[verb] 8. <u>To stop unwanted noise</u>, some students (had) the idea of a special hat.

[verb] 9. <u>To use it</u>, you just (put) it on your head, and then all traffic noise, music, or even people's voices were filtered out.

[verb] 10. Many students (used) their creativity <u>to help solve environmental problems</u>.

[verb] 11. One idea, a small bin, (would be installed) in apartment buildings <u>to get rid of garbage</u>.

[verb] 12. The bin (would separate) items into various piles—glass, paper, and so on—<u>to be recycled</u>.

[verb] 13. It also (would serve) <u>to compact the garbage into tiny disposable packages</u>.

[verb] 14. <u>To gain more living space</u>, some students (suggested) a city on stilts over the ocean.

[verb] 15. People (would use) solar panels <u>to supply energy for such a city</u>.

[verb] 16. <u>To clean the air</u>, a huge de-smogger (was proposed) by some students.

[verb] 17. The plant, with huge stacks, (worked) <u>to remove pollution from the air</u>.

[adverb] 18. We were in the exhibit long (enough) <u>to see most of the inventions</u>.

[adjective] 19. The exhibit was too (big) <u>to see them all</u>, however.

[verb] 20. On exiting, we (voted) <u>to choose the best invention that we'd seen</u>.

Verbals

79

76. Hidden and Split Infinitives

A **hidden infinitive**, one in which the word *to* is not used, appears after certain verbs, such as *hear, see, know, feel, let, make,* and *help,* and with the prepositions *but* and *except* and the conjunction *than.*

I heard the bird <u>sing</u>.
Her stories always make me <u>cry</u>.
She does nothing but <u>study</u> all day.
I can think of many things I'd rather do than <u>clean</u> my room.

A **split infinitive** results when an adverb is placed between *to* and the verb. Split infinitives generally should be avoided.

SPLIT INFINITIVE   **Hal decided to patiently wait his turn.**
IMPROVED   **Hal decided to wait his turn patiently.**

A. Underline the hidden infinitive in each sentence.

1. Will you let me <u>hold</u> the baby?

2. My mother does nothing but <u>work</u> all day.

3. All night I heard the rain <u>pound</u> on the roof.

4. "I thought I felt something <u>move</u>!" she whispered.

5. The patient did nothing but <u>sleep</u> after the surgery.

6. I have never seen him <u>run</u> so fast.

7. I heard the child <u>cry</u>.

8. The teacher helped the students <u>study</u> the new assignment.

9. Your performances always make me <u>laugh</u>.

10. Let not your hearts <u>be</u> troubled.

B. Each sentence contains a split infinitive. Rewrite the sentence, placing the adverb in a better position. [**Sample answers are given.**]

1. The teacher asked us to completely erase the boards.
   [The teacher asked us to erase the boards completely.]

2. Be sure to correctly answer the essay question.
   [Be sure to answer the essay question correctly.]

3. The doctor was unwilling to indefinitely postpone the surgery.
   [The doctor was unwilling to postpone the surgery indefinitely.]

4. We like to slowly stroll along the beach.
   [We like to stroll slowly along the beach.]

5. Our family is planning to immediately leave on vacation.
   [Our family is planning to leave on vacation immediately.]

Verbals

77. Reviewing Infinitives

A. Underline the infinitive in each sentence. On the line write **S** if it is the subject, **DO** if it is the direct object, **SC** if it is the subject complement, and **A** if it is an appositive.

___[DO]___ 1. My sister has never learned <u>to skate</u>.

___[A]___ 2. Your suggestion <u>to travel</u> by bus was a good idea.

___[DO]___ 3. We would prefer <u>to go</u> with you.

___[S]___ 4. <u>To write</u> well requires practice.

___[SC]___ 5. The purpose of the game is <u>to learn</u> math facts.

___[DO]___ 6. Try <u>to finish</u> the work before noon.

___[SC]___ 7. The reason she is coming is <u>to baby-sit</u>.

___[A]___ 8. Ms. Henry's motion, <u>to adjourn</u> the meeting, passed quickly.

___[S]___ 9. <u>To be</u> happy is an important goal in my life.

___[A]___ 10. My worst fear, <u>to fail</u> in school, motivates me.

B. Write on the line whether the *italicized* infinitive is used as an adjective or an adverb.

___[adverb]___ 11. Quarantine is sometimes necessary *to protect* others.

___[adverb]___ 12. My cousin is coming *to visit* us.

___[adjective]___ 13. Youth is the time *to sow* the seeds of character.

___[adverb]___ 14. Philip lunged *to tackle* the quarterback.

___[adverb]___ 15. They were afraid *to undertake* the journey.

___[adverb]___ 16. Quotation marks are used *to enclose* the words of a speaker.

___[adjective]___ 17. Efforts *to eliminate* the use of pesticides are gratifying.

___[adjective]___ 18. How did our school raise the money *to build* the gym?

___[adjective]___ 19. The power *to run* the mill comes from water.

___[adjective]___ 20. Her desire *to improve* is impressive.

CONTINUED

Verbals

C. Underline the hidden infinitive in each sentence.

21. Did you hear the dog <u>bark</u>?

22. She would rather learn to swim than <u>skate</u>.

23. Darlene does nothing but <u>giggle</u> when she is corrected.

24. All through the storm we heard the wind <u>howl</u>.

25. Watch me <u>dive</u> into the pool.

D. Rewrite each sentence. Place the adverb in a better position. [Sample answers are given.]

26. I expect you to wholeheartedly support me.
     [I expect you to support me wholeheartedly.]

27. The janitor does not expect to constantly pick up after us.
     [The janitor does not expect to pick up after us constantly.]

28. To quickly eat your lunch may give you indigestion.
     [To eat your lunch quickly may give you indigestion.]

29. To suddenly end our support would be disastrous for them.
     [To end our support suddenly would be disastrous for them.]

30. To positively respond to the questionnaire would aid the cause.
     [To respond positively to the questionnaire would aid the cause.]

E. Follow the instructions and write sentences using the following infinitive phrase: *to visit a foreign country.* [Sample answers are given.]

31. (*Use as a subject.*) [To visit a foreign country is an exciting adventure.]

32. (*Use as a direct object.*) [I would like to visit a foreign country.]

33. (*Use as a subject complement.*) [One goal is to visit a foreign country.]

34. (*Use as an appositive.*) [My desire, to visit a foreign country, pleases my grandmother.]

35. (*Use as an adverb.*) [The president goes periodically to visit a foreign country.]

Verbals

Name _____

78. Reviewing Verbals

A. Underline the participle in each sentence. Circle the word it modifies.

1. The audience applauded the (couple) skating in the competition.

2. The (trophy) won by the ice hockey team will be
   on display in the school hall.

3. Having eaten their lunch, the (students)
   went out onto the ice.

4. Spectators gathered to watch the (skaters)
   flying around the rink.

5. (Ellen,) having trained for years,
   prepared to perform.

6. The school trophy case contains the winners' (names) engraved in brass.

7. Vowing to return, our (coach) left his job temporarily.

8. (Skaters) trained in northern states are comfortable on the ice.

Verbals

B. Write a sentence, using each participial phrase. **[Sentences will vary.]**

standing on the corner   9. 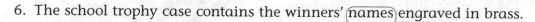 _____

_____

blown by the wind   10. _____

_____

having delivered the speech   11. _____

_____

C. Underline the gerund in each sentence. On the line write **S** if it is the subject, **DO** if it is the direct object, **OP** if it is the object of a preposition, **SC** if it is the subject complement, and **A** if it is an appositive.

___[A]___ 12. My job, working in the retirement home, gives me great satisfaction.

___[SC]___ 13. My brother's chief service is reading books for people with visual impairments.

___[OP]___ 14. We show that we care by helping others.

___[DO]___ 15. I enjoy planning activities for senior citizens.

___[S]___ 16. Working with older adults might be a career choice.

D. Follow the instructions and write sentences using the following infinitive phrase: *to attend college.* **[Sample answers are given.]**

17. *(Use as a subject.)* [To attend college is an important goal for many people.]

18. *(Use as a direct object.)* [I chose to attend college; no one influenced my decision.]

19. *(Use as an appositive.)* [My goal, to attend college, will require many sacrifices.]

E. Underline the infinitive in each sentence. On the line write **S** if it is the subject, **DO** if it is the direct object, **SC** if it is the subject complement, and **A** if it is an appositive.

[DO] 20. Most students want to attend a good college.

[A] 21. My goal, to win a scholarship, may not be realistic.

[S] 22. To afford room and board is one reason for wanting a scholarship.

[DO] 23. Most teachers try to prepare students for the future.

[A] 24. My biggest problem, to put my thoughts into writing, is something I must work on.

[SC] 25. My hope is to achieve a high score.

Try It Yourself
On a separate sheet of paper, write five or six sentences about something you would like to do in the future. Be sure to use participles, gerunds, and infinitives correctly.

Check Your Own Work
Choose a piece of writing from your portfolio or journal, a work in progress, an assignment from another class, or a letter. Revise it, applying the skills you have learned. This checklist will help you.

✔ Have you used participles, gerunds, and infinitives correctly?

✔ Have you avoided dangling participles?

✔ Have you avoided splitting the infinitives you used?

79. Types of Adverbs

An **adverb** is a word that describes a verb, an adjective, or another adverb. An adverb generally describes the time, place, manner, or degree of the word it modifies. It may also indicate affirmation (telling whether a statement is positive or giving consent or approval) or negation (expressing a negative condition or refusal).

TIME	The tide will recede <u>later</u>.	AFFIRMATION	Tides are <u>undoubtedly</u> amazing.
PLACE	The water will move <u>back</u>.		
MANNER	The water recedes <u>slowly</u>.	NEGATION	We could <u>not</u> explain the
DEGREE	The water was <u>very</u> cold.		cause of tides.

A. Underline the adverb in each sentence.

1. Have you <u>ever</u> wondered about the cause of tides?

2. The water in the ocean and other bodies of water rises and falls <u>periodically</u>.

3. Two high tides and two low tides occur <u>daily</u>.

4. Go to the ocean shore, and <u>there</u> you can see the effect of the tides.

5. You can see <u>clearly</u> the movement of the water along the shoreline.

6. At the beach you may notice that the water moves <u>up</u> over several hours.

7. <u>Soon</u> it starts to move in the other direction, receding from the shore.

8. The gravitational pull of the Moon is <u>quite</u> strong on Earth.

9. The Moon's force pulls the water toward a point <u>directly</u> below the Moon and toward a point on the exact opposite side of Earth.

10. The result is that high tide occurs <u>simultaneously</u> on both sides of Earth.

B. Underline the adverb in each sentence. On the line describe the adverb by writing **T** for time, **P** for place, **M** for manner, **D** for degree, **A** for affirmation, or **N** for negation.

__[T]__ 1. People have <u>long</u> observed the tides.

__[A]__ 2. <u>Indeed</u>, the regularity of tides was noted by ancient observers.

__[M]__ 3. They <u>carefully</u> studied the tides.

__[M]__ 4. Some ancients <u>accurately</u> theorized that a connection existed between the moon and the tides.

__[N]__ 5. The actual connection could <u>not</u> be confirmed with the knowledge people had at that time.

__[T]__ 6. <u>Then</u> Isaac Newton explained the basic laws of motion and gravity.

__[D]__ 7. Tides were recognized as <u>extremely</u> complex occurrences.

__[D]__ 8. Tides are a result of a <u>fairly</u> complicated interaction of several factors.

__[P]__ 9. Tides for any location are predicted by past observations of tides <u>there</u>.

__[M]__ 10. People work <u>meticulously</u> to produce complex tables of the tides.

80. Interrogative Adverbs

An **interrogative adverb** is used to ask a question. The interrogative adverbs are *how, when, where,* and *why.* They are used to express or to query reason, place, time, or method.

REASON	**Why did you choose the ancient Romans as a topic?**
PLACE	**Where did you get the information you needed?**
TIME	**When is the report due?**
METHOD	**How did you organize your report?**

A. Underline the interrogative adverb in each sentence. On the line describe what each adverb expresses by writing **R** for reason, **P** for place, **T** for Time, or **M** for method.

__[T]__ 1. When was the Roman Empire at the height of its power?

__[P]__ 2. Where was it located?

__[M]__ 3. How did the Romans build the empire?

__[R]__ 4. Why did the empire fall?

__[R]__ 5. Why was a wolf with two human babies the symbol of Rome?

__[T]__ 6. When was the city of Rome founded?

__[R]__ 7. Why were the aqueducts built?

__[M]__ 8. How did the aqueducts function to carry water?

__[P]__ 9. Where did the ancient Romans go for entertainment?

__[T]__ 10. When was the Colosseum built?

B. Complete each sentence with an appropriate interrogative adverb. More than one answer may be correct in some sentences.

1. ____[Where]____ is Mount Vesuvius—near Rome or near Naples?

2. ____[When]____ did the eruption of Mount Vesuvius occur—79 BC or AD 79?

3. ____[What]____ was the major result of this eruption?

4. ____[Why]____ is the eruption considered important by historians?

5. __[How, When]__ did archaeologists uncover the cities of Pompeii and Herculaneum?

6. __[How, When]__ did the volcano destroy the cities?

7. __[When, How]__ were the cities finally rediscovered?

8. ____[When]____ was the most recent eruption of Vesuvius?

9. __[Where, How]__ can you find information on volcanic eruptions?

10. ____[What]____ are some of the beneficial results of eruptions?

Adverbs

81. Adverbial Nouns

An **adverbial noun** is a noun that functions as an adverb. Generally it modifies a verb and expresses time, distance, measure, value, or direction.

The cake should bake an hour.

To Express Use Words Such As	Time hours	Distance miles	Measure pint	Value dollars	Direction north

A. Underline each adverbial noun. Write on the line what it expresses—time, distance, measure, value, or direction.

_____[time]_____ 1. Because of gold's great value, men have spent <u>years</u> searching for it.

_____[measure]_____ 2. It has been used a great <u>deal</u> for jewelry.

_____[measure]_____ 3. It can be hammered 0.000005 <u>inch</u> thick.

_____[distance]_____ 4. One ounce can be stretched 62 <u>miles</u>.

_____[measure]_____ 5. It will not melt until it reaches 1,947 <u>degrees</u> Fahrenheit.

_____[measure]_____ 6. The largest gold nugget ever found weighed 150 <u>pounds</u>.

_____[time]_____ 7. It turned up accidentally some 130 <u>years</u> ago in Australia.

_____[direction]_____ 8. Fortune hunters headed <u>west</u> during the American gold rush.

_____[time]_____ 9. Americans waited 41 <u>years</u>, until 1974, for the ban on private ownership of gold to be lifted.

_____[value]_____ 10. The gold stored at Fort Knox would cost several billion <u>dollars</u> to buy.

B. Complete each sentence with an adverbial noun that expresses the quality in italics. **[Sample answers are given.]**

time　　　1. The opera will last three _____[hours]_____.

distance　2. The theater is seven _____[miles]_____ away.

direction　3. Tell the cab driver to turn _____[left]_____ after the light.

time　　　4. We have only 15 _____[minutes]_____ till the curtain rises.

measure　5. Earlier today the ticket line stretched three _____[blocks]_____.

value　　6. The tickets cost 50 _____[dollars]_____ apiece.

distance　7. The singers traveled many _____[miles]_____ to be here.

time　　　8. The star tenor arrived just this _____[evening]_____.

measure　9. He lost 20 _____[pounds]_____ on the exercise program.

time　　　10. His last performance in America was _____[years]_____ ago.

82. Comparative and Superlative Adverbs

The comparative and superlative degrees of most adverbs that end in *-ly* are formed by adding *more* or *most* (or *less* or *least*) before the positive form of the adverb.

more sadly, most sadly   **less sadly, least sadly**

The comparative and superlative forms of adverbs that do not end in *-ly* are formed by adding *-er* or *-est*.

faster, fastest

Some adverbs, such as *well* and *much,* have irregular comparative and superlative forms.

A. Complete the chart with degrees of comparison.

Positive	Comparative	Superlative
1. slowly	less slowly	[least slowly]
2. far	[farther]	[farthest]
3. badly	[worse]	worst
4. [noisily]	more noisily	[most noisily]
5. soon	[sooner]	[soonest]
6. [playfully]	[more playfully]	most playfully
7. quickly	[more/less quickly]	[most/least quickly]
8. [clearly]	less clearly	[least clearly]
9. [highly]	more highly	[most highly]
10. well	[better]	[best]

B. Underline the adverb in each sentence. Write its degree of comparison on the line.

__[comparative]__ 1. Two people can often travel <u>more cheaply</u> than one.

__[positive]__ 2. Maggie <u>quickly</u> realized this in Europe last summer.

__[comparative]__ 3. Money stretches <u>further</u> when you can share travel accommodations.

__[positive]__ 4. She spent her money <u>mainly</u> on hotels.

__[superlative]__ 5. Deals on plane tickets can be made <u>most easily</u> when a person buys two or more.

__[comparative]__ 6. You can also travel <u>more safely</u> as a pair.

__[superlative]__ 7. Criminals <u>most often</u> target people who are by themselves.

__[superlative]__ 8. All tourists should travel <u>most cautiously</u> at night.

__[positive]__ 9. <u>Fortunately</u>, Maggie was not the victim of a pickpocket.

__[positive]__ 10. Planning a trip <u>carefully</u> will be advantageous in the long run.

83. *As . . . As, So . . . As*, and *Equally*

Adjectives and adverbs can both be used in comparisons with *as . . . as, so . . . as,* and *equally.*

When comparing persons, places, or things, use only *as . . . as* in positive statements. Use either *as . . . as* or *so . . . as* in negative statements.

> **This year's family reunion was as successful as last year's reunion. The weather was not so hot as (*or* as hot as) it was last year.**

Equally means "as" when it describes an adjective. Never use *as* between *equally* and the word it describes.

CORRECT **The first two family reunions were equally enjoyable.**
INCORRECT **The first two family reunions were equally as enjoyable.**

A. Complete each sentence by writing *as, so,* or *equally* on the line.

1. The picnic grounds were ____[as]____ crowded as they were last year.

2. The weather wasn't ____[as, so]____ cloudy last year as it was this year.

3. The food, however, was ____[as]____ wonderful this year as it was last year.

4. My dad's apple pies were ____[as]____ good as Aunt Jennie's.

5. Aunt Elaine's pies and Aunt Sally's pies were ____[equally]____ delicious.

6. My cookies, however, weren't ____[as, so]____ good as Cousin June's.

7. Cousin Kara sang ____[as]____ well as Uncle James in the karaoke contest.

8. Peter didn't sing ____[as, so]____ well as Cousin Kara, in my opinion.

9. I thought Cousin Fred and Cousin Mike sang ____[equally]____ well.

10. My pictures didn't come out ____[as, so]____ clearly as mom's.

B. Write a sentence, using each group of terms shown and *as . . . as, so . . . as,* or *equally.* Use the directions to determine the type of comparison—positive, negative, or equal.
[Sample answers are given.]

1. mystery novels, interesting, adventure stories (negative)
   [Mystery novels are not so (*or* as) interesting as adventure stories.]

2. Aunt Lila's photos, good, my mother's photos, impressive (equal)
   [Aunt Lila's photos were good, but my mother's photos were equally impressive.]

3. swimming, exciting, biking (positive)
   [Swimming is as exciting as biking.]

4. poetry, easy to read, short story (negative)
   [Poetry is not so (*or* as) easy to read as a short story.]

5. algebra, challenging, geometry (positive)
   [Algebra is as challenging as geometry.]

Adverbs

84. Adverb Phrases and Clauses

Prepositional phrases can be used as adverbs to describe verbs, adjectives, or other adverbs. These prepositional phrases are called **adverb phrases.** They tell when, where, who, and how.

A clause is a group of words that has a subject and a predicate. A dependent clause does not express a complete thought. A dependent clause that acts as an adverb is called an **adverb clause.** Some common subordinate conjunctions used to introduce adverb clauses are *after, although, as, because, if, since, so that, unless, until, when, whenever, wherever, whether,* and *while.*

A. Underline the adverb phrase in each sentence.
Circle the word(s) it describes.

1. Winston Churchill originally (trained) for a military career.
2. During his lifetime Churchill (held) numerous political offices.
3. He (led) Great Britain at a difficult time.
4. Churchill (was) prime minister during World War II.
5. Much of the European continent (had been conquered) by Hitler's German armies.
6. The island of Britain (was besieged) by enemies.
7. Through his courage and eloquence Churchill (inspired) the British people.
8. Eventually the United States and the Soviet Union (joined) with Britain.
9. They (fought) against Germany and other Axis powers.
10. The terrible war (ended) in 1945.

B. Underline the adverb clause in each sentence. Circle the verb(s) it describes.

1. As a boy, Winston Churchill (was) a poor student although he was intelligent.
2. After he served as a soldier, he (became) a politician.
3. Churchill (was serving) as prime minister when Britain faced the loss of its freedom.
4. Wherever he went during the dark days of the war, he (held) his fingers in a V formation to symbolize *victory.*
5. If he hadn't shown such courage, Britain (might have been defeated.)

Winston Churchill acted with courage and compassion during a difficult time. Not everyone will lead a country, but everyone can act with courage and compassion. Tell about a time when you have acted bravely and compassionately.

85. Reviewing Adverbs

A. Underline each adverb. On the line write its type—time, place, degree, manner, affirmation, negation.

[place]   1. Christopher Columbus sailed <u>westward</u> from Spain in 1492.

[affirmation]   2. He was <u>actually</u> looking for Asia when he landed in America.

[time]   3. Christopher Columbus is <u>often</u> credited with America's discovery.

[time]   4. But civilizations were <u>already</u> here when he arrived.

[degree]   5. Many were <u>highly</u> developed cultures.

B. Complete each question with an appropriate interrogative adverb. **[Answers may vary.]**

6. _[Where]_ did the first people to reach America come from?

7. _[Why]_ did they come to America?

8. _[How]_ did they manage to get to a continent surrounded by water?

9. _[Where]_ did they go after they got here?

10. _[What]_ was their biggest challenge?

C. Underline the adverb in each sentence. On the line write its degree of comparison—positive, comparative, or superlative.

[superlative]   11. The first Americans <u>most likely</u> came by way of the Bering Strait.

[positive]   12. The Bering Strait is <u>widely</u> believed to have been solid ice.

[positive]   13. Scholars <u>generally</u> agree that the earliest settlers were from north Asia.

[superlative]   14. These first Americans were <u>most probably</u> nomadic peoples.

[comparative]   15. Scarcity forced them to search <u>farther</u> for their food.

CONTINUED

Adverbs

D. Write on the line whether each *italicized* word is an adjective or an adverb.

___[adjective]___ 16. *Most* Native American cultures had developed agriculture by 2000 BC.

___[adverb]___ 17. Maize was the *most* commonly grown grain.

___[adverb]___ 18. Livestock was *less* important to Native American cultures.

___[adverb]___ 19. Protein was obtained *primarily* from plants.

___[adjective]___ 20. *Additional* protein was acquired through hunting and fishing.

E. Underline each adverb phrase once and each adverb clause twice. A sentence may have a phrase, a clause, or both. Circle the word(s) the phrase or the clause modifies.

21. Astronauts (float) in space, our science teacher said, because there is no gravity.

22. Gravity is what holds people down; if there wasn't any gravity, they (would float) everywhere.

23. Yesterday our class (performed) a gravity experiment in the lab.

24. Although we were careful, it (did) not (work).

25. We (should have read) the lab manual before we started.

26. I (repeated) the experiment several times by myself.

27. Unfortunately, I (failed) in every attempt.

28. Even though I didn't succeed, I (may try) again.

29. Since there is gravity everywhere on Earth, my experiments (are) probably permanently (doomed.)

30. Eventually, as an astronaut, I('ll fly) to the Moon and personally experience the lack of gravity.

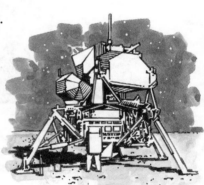

Try It Yourself

On a separate sheet of paper, write five or six sentences about something you have learned to do recently. Be sure to use adverbs correctly.

Check Your Own Work

Choose a selection from your writing portfolio or journal, a work in progress, an assignment from class, or a letter. Revise it, applying the skills you have learned in this chapter. This checklist will help you.

✔ Have you included appropriate adverbs?

✔ Have you distinguished between adjectives and adverbs?

✔ Have you used the comparison of adverbs correctly?

Name _____

86. Prepositions

A **preposition** shows the relationship between a noun or a pronoun and some other word in a sentence. A **prepositional phrase** is composed of the preposition, the object of the preposition, and words that describe the object. A **multiword preposition** is made up of more than one word but is treated as a single word. Common multiword prepositions are *according to, because of, in spite of, instead of,* and *on account of.*

Cougar is another name <u>for</u> a puma.
<u>According to</u> this article, pumas are endangered.

A. Underline the preposition or prepositions in each sentence. Circle the object of each preposition.

1. Pumas are <u>among</u> the rarest (animals) <u>in</u> the (world.)

2. Pumas are found <u>from</u> (British Columbia) <u>to</u> (Patagonia.)

3. <u>Without</u> (protection) they stand little chance <u>of</u> (survival.)

4. Their coats range <u>from</u> a reddish-brown (color) <u>to</u> a bluish-gray (hue.)

5. A puma's body can measure six feet long, even <u>without</u> its (tail.)

6. A puma has a small head <u>with</u> black (spots) <u>above</u> the (eyes.)

7. The cry <u>of</u> a (puma) often sounds <u>like</u> a person's (voice.)

8. Pumas sometimes attack cattle <u>on</u> (ranches.)

9. <u>Because of</u> such (attacks,) pumas have purposely been exterminated <u>in</u> some (areas.)

10. <u>In addition to</u> such extermination (campaigns,) encroachment <u>into</u> their (territory) <u>by</u> (humans) has also reduced their numbers.

B. Complete each sentence with one of the prepositions listed below. Use each preposition once.

against   as   because of   in   of

1. Leopards are large members _____[of]_____ the cat family.

2. They live _____[in]_____ the Eastern Hemisphere only.

3. They are known _____[as]_____ fierce hunters.

4. _____[Because of]_____ their lovely black-spotted coat, they are hunted by humans.

5. Many countries have laws _____[against]_____ this fur trading.

87. Troublesome Prepositions

You need to be careful to use certain prepositions correctly.

Beside means "at the side of or next to"; *besides* means "in addition to."

Between is used when speaking of two persons, places, or things; *among* is used in speaking of more than two.

In denotes position within; *into* denotes motion or change of position.

Differ with denotes disagreement; *differ from* denotes that two things or people are not the same.

One is *angry with* a person but *angry at* a thing.

From means "coming from the possession of someone"; *off* means "away from."

A. Circle the correct preposition in parentheses.

1. There is a pond (**beside** besides) Eva's house.
2. Many frogs lay their eggs (**in** into) this water.
3. Tadpole is a stage (among **between**) egg and frog.
4. A tadpole will later turn (in **into**) a frog.
5. Eva gets angry (with **at**) the noisy frogs when she is in bed.
6. Eva got advice (off **from**) a pet-shop owner.
7. She (**differed with** differed from) him on how to handle a pet frog.
8. Toads differ (**from** with) frogs in that toads spend most of their lives on land.
9. (Beside **Besides**) this difference, toads have warts but frogs do not.
10. Frogs are found (**in** into) a greater variety of climates than toads are.

B. Complete each sentence with a correct preposition. **[Sample answers are given.]**

1. A caterpillar will eventually turn ____[into]____ a butterfly.
2. Did you study the debate ____[between]____ Lincoln and Douglas?
3. The candy was equally distributed ____[among]____ the triplets.
4. ____[Besides]____ *Stuart Little* E. B. White also wrote *Charlotte's Web*.
5. Mr. Blair was angry ____[with]____ his son for breaking the window.
6. Mark differs ____[with]____ Jim often over who should clean the bird cage.
7. The coach was angry ____[at]____ all the errors in the news report.
8. The trees differ ____[from]____ each other in more ways than one.
9. He does not look so tall when he stands ____[beside]____ the basketball player.
10. The broom belongs ____[in]____ the closet when it's not being used.

Prepositions

88. Words Used as Adverbs and Prepositions

Some words can be used as adverbs or as prepositions. A preposition takes an object; the preposition with its object shows a relationship to another word in the sentence. An adverb tells how, when, where, why, to what extent, and under what condition. It modifies a verb, an adjective, or another adverb, and it does not have an object.

PREPOSITION   Jack fell down the hill.
ADVERB   Jack fell down.

A. On the line write **A** if the *italicized* word is an adverb or **P** if it is a preposition.

__[P]__ 1. The Eiffel Tower is one of the seven wonders *of* the modern world.

__[P]__ 2. It is located *in* Paris, France.

__[P]__ 3. The Eiffel Tower is *on* the bank of the Seine River.

__[P]__ 4. The tower was built *by* the engineer Alexandre-Gustave Eiffel.

__[A]__ 5. It tapers *upward* to a height of 984 feet.

__[A]__ 6. One may walk *up* or take an elevator.

__[A]__ 7. Every day thousands of people go to the top to look *around*.

__[P]__ 8. From the very top a person can see clear *across* Paris.

__[A]__ 9. If I were at the top, I would be afraid to look *down*.

__[P]__ 10. The uppermost platform is almost 1,000 feet *from* the ground.

B. Write sentences, using each word as an adverb. [Sentences will vary. Sample answers are given.]

away 1. [Lucy was sad when her dog ran away.]

in 2. [We watched the tides come in.]

over 3. [I skinned my knee when the bike fell over.]

before 4. [The man had been arrested before.]

around 5. [The pirate climbed the mast and looked around.]

C. Write sentences, using each word as a preposition. [Sentences will vary; sample answers are given.]

near 1. [The horse likes to run near the water.]

beyond 2. [There are some alligators beyond the rocks.]

down 3. [Her engagement ring was accidentally washed down the drain.]

between 4. [I would not want to sit between those loud gentlemen.]

off 5. [He carelessly knocked the plate off the table.]

Prepositions

95

89. Prepositional Phrases as Adjectives

> A prepositional phrase that describes a noun or a pronoun is an **adjective phrase**.
>
> **I read a book <u>about Anne Sullivan</u>.**

Underline the adjective phrase in each sentence. Circle the word it describes.

1. Anne Sullivan was the famous (teacher) <u>of Helen Keller</u>.
2. Helen was a (person) <u>without sight or hearing</u>.
3. Anne herself had (difficulty) <u>with her sight</u>.
4. This problem was the (result) <u>of a childhood illness</u>.
5. Anne went to a (school) <u>for blind students</u>.
6. She graduated at the (top) <u>of her class</u>.
7. Earlier she had lived in a (home) <u>for orphans</u>.
8. Several (operations) <u>on her eyes</u> restored some of her vision.
9. Later she accepted the (position) <u>as Helen's teacher</u>.
10. Anne used a (system) <u>of touch teaching</u>.
11. Finger movements spelled the (letters) <u>of the alphabet</u>.
12. Helen did not comprehend the (idea) <u>behind the movements</u> initially.
13. Soon, however, she grasped the (meaning) <u>of the movements</u>.
14. The (association) <u>between the letters and real-world objects</u> became clear.
15. Helen's (progress) <u>in her studies</u> was amazing.
16. She eventually became a (student) <u>at a prestigious college</u>.
17. Anne accompanied her and provided (help) <u>with her studies</u>.
18. Both Anne and Helen became (advocates) <u>for education rights</u>.
19. They strongly supported (education) <u>for blind people</u>.
20. Together, they gave (lectures) <u>about this need</u>.
21. It is said that Anne's (gift) <u>to Helen</u> was words.
22. Meanwhile, Helen gave Anne a (sense) <u>of family</u>.
23. The public's (interest) <u>in their story</u> was enormous.
24. Their story became the (topic) <u>of a well-known play</u>.
25. This story remains an (inspiration) <u>to all</u>.

Anne Sullivan persevered in teaching young Helen Keller because Anne believed in what she was doing. Give an example of something you believe in strongly. How are you working to incorporate that belief into your daily life? Write about it.

Prepositions

90. Prepositional Phrases as Adverbs

Prepositional phrases can be used as adverbs—to describe verbs, adjectives, or other adverbs. Prepositional phrases used in this way are **adverb phrases.** They answer the questions how, when, where, why, to what extent, and under what condition.

VERB **Many people season food with garlic.**
ADJECTIVE **They usually consider garlic healthful for them.**
ADVERB **The waiter talks confidently for someone who just started work.**

A. Circle the word(s) that each *italicized* adverb phrase describes. On the line write the part of speech for the circled word(s)—**V** for verb, **Adj** for adjective, or **Adv** for adverb.

__[V]__ 1. You probably (have tasted) garlic *in pasta sauce.*

__[Adj]__ 2. It is (important) *in Italian and other Mediterranean cuisines.*

__[V]__ 3. *For centuries* people (have eaten) garlic.

__[V]__ 4. They also (have used) it *in medicines.*

__[Adv]__ 5. (Early) *in history* people discovered garlic's healing properties.

B. Underline the adverb phrase(s) in each sentence. Circle the word or word phrase it describes.

1. Garlic's strong odor (protects) the plant from insects and bacteria.

2. The smell (comes) from the chemical compound allicin.

3. In recent years scientists (have studied) this compound.

4. They have found that the compound is (responsible) for garlic's healing properties.

5. It is said to be (effective) against high blood pressure, diabetes, and diarrhea.

6. Allicin may also be (useful) in cell destruction.

7. Scientists could (use) the compound against cancer cells.

8. In the future allicin (may combat) cancer and other tumors.

9. It may even prevent weight gain and (may lead) to weight loss.

10. Garlic (has been used) as a medicine for centuries.

11. The ancient Chinese (put) garlic into a solution.

12. According to folk tradition the resulting mixture (cured) dysentery.

13. From Egyptian hieroglyphics we (know) that workers who built the pyramids were given garlic.

14. It (was provided) for its strength-producing effects.

15. During World War I it (was used) to prevent gangrene if other drugs ran out.

Prepositions

91. Prepositional Phrases as Nouns

> A prepositional phrase can be used as a noun. It can be used as a subject or a subject complement.
>
> **Before bed is not a good time to eat.**

A. Underline the prepositional phrase used as a noun in each sentence. On the line write **S** if it is used as the subject or **SC** if it is used as the subject complement.

__[S]__ 1. After meals is an ideal time to brush your teeth.

__[SC]__ 2. Another good time is before bed.

__[S]__ 3. In the morning is an important time to eat something for needed energy.

__[S]__ 4. After school is when you might have a snack, like a piece of fruit.

__[S]__ 5. Without butter is the way many people prefer to eat their baked potatoes.

__[SC]__ 6. My mother's coffee preference is with sugar and cream.

__[S]__ 7. On the U.S. Department of Agriculture Web site is a good place to find the food pyramid.

__[SC]__ 8. One possible place to exercise is in a gym.

__[S]__ 9. In the park, however, seems to be the favorite exercise area for athletes in my neighborhood.

__[S]__ 10. On foot is a healthful way to get from place to place and from one floor to another.

B. Complete each sentence with a prepositional phrase used as a subject.
[Answers will vary. Samples are shown.]

1. __[In the library]__ is a good place to study.

2. __[After school]__ seems to be the right time to study.

3. __[With reference materials]__ is a good way to study.

4. __[On the Internet]__ can be an effective way to research information.

5. __[Around this bad curve]__ was where the car skidded.

C. Complete each sentence with a prepositional phrase used as a subject complement.
[Answers will vary.]

1. My favorite spot for swimming was __[in the YMCA pool]__.

2. The place to attach the label is __[on top of the box]__.

3. The best debates are __[between these two teams]__.

4. Our dog's hiding places were __[under the table and behind the couch]__.

5. My dad's next business trip may be __[to Oklahoma City]__.

Prepositions

92. Reviewing Prepositions

A. Underline the preposition(s) in each sentence. Circle the object of each.

1. The sperm whale has the heaviest brain _of_ any (animal.)
2. The brain _of_ this (type) _of_ (whale) can exceed 20 pounds.
3. The human brain has a weight _of_ less than 3 (pounds.)
4. A sperm whale's teeth can be 8 inches _in_ (length.)
5. This whale has teeth only _on_ its lower (jaw.)

B. Circle the correct preposition in parentheses.

6. There are many differences (among (between)) whales and fish.
7. Most important, whales differ ((from) with) fish in that whales are mammals.
8. (Beside (Besides)) this difference whales move their tail fins up and down, not back and forth.
9. Whales are found ((in) into) all the world's oceans and even a few rivers.
10. Most whales gather (in (into)) groups when they migrate.

C. On the line write **A** if the _italicized_ word is an adverb or **P** if it is a preposition.

__[P]__ 11. Many scientists now believe that the ancestors of whales lived _on_ land.

__[P]__ 12. These creatures foraged for food _along_ the ocean shore.

__[A]__ 13. Eighty million years passed _by_.

__[P]__ 14. The animals gradually evolved _into_ whales.

__[A]__ 15. They went through an amphibious, seal-like stage as time went _on_.

D. On the line write **Adj** if the _italicized_ prepositional phrase is used as an adjective, **Adv** if used as an adverb, of **N** if used as a noun.

__[Adv]__ 16. Sperm whales live _in social groups_.

__[Adj]__ 17. Groups _of females, calves, and young males_ live together.

__[N]__ 18. _Near the poles_ is the summer home of older males.

__[Adv]__ 19. _At six or seven_ the young males leave the group.

__[Adv]__ 20. They join _with the older males_.

__[Adv]__ 21. Sperm whales can dive _to great depths_.

CONTINUED

Prepositions

[Adj] 22. Sperm whales live on a diet *of squid.*

[Adv] 23. They may be able to capture squid more easily far *under the water.*

[Adv] 24. The movements of the squid may be more lethargic *because of less available oxygen.*

[Adj] 25. The teeth on the lower jaw of a sperm whale fit into empty sockets *in the upper jaw.*

E. Underline the prepositional phrase(s) in each sentence. Above each phrase write **Adj** if it is used as an adjective, **Adv** if used as an adverb, or **N** if used as a noun.

26. A broad term **Adj** for whales is cetacean.

27. This comes **Adv** from the Latin word **Adj** for whale.

28. Whales can be divided **Adv** into two groups.

29. Toothed whales have teeth, and baleen whales have no teeth but have jaws **Adj** with plates.

30. These baleen plates resemble the material **Adj** in human fingernails.

31. A baleen whale swims **Adv** with a wide-open mouth and gathers plankton, filtering it **Adv** through the plates.

32. **N** Under the water is the place where whales feed.

33. A whale can hold its breath a long time **Adv** because of a special chemical.

34. This chemical, called myoglobin, carries oxygen **Adv** throughout the body.

35. Whales have larger amounts **Adj** of this chemical than land mammals do.

Try It Yourself

On a separate sheet of paper, write about something that you have recently studied in school or something that you have recently learned that interests you. Use prepositions in your sentences.

Check Your Own Work

Choose a selection from your writing portfolio, a journal, a work in progress, an assignment from another class, or a letter. Revise it, applying the skills you have learned. This checklist will help you.

✔ Have you used prepositional phrases to add details to your sentences?

✔ Have you used commonly confused prepositions, such as *beside, besides; in, into; between, among; differ with,* and *differ from* correctly?

Name _____

93. Sentences

> A **sentence** is a group of words that expresses a complete thought.
> A sentence has a **subject** and a **predicate**. The subject names the person, place, or thing the sentence is about. The predicate tells what the subject is or does. Every sentence begins with a capital letter.
>
> COMPLETE SUBJECT   COMPLETE PREDICATE
> **The solar system**   **contains nine major planets.**
> **All the planets in the solar system**   **orbit the Sun.**

A. Write **S** on the line if the words form a sentence and leave the line blank if they do not. Put a period at the end of each sentence.

___[S]___ 1. All the planets move in elliptical orbits[.]

___[S]___ 2. The orbits of Earth and Venus are almost circular[.]

_____ 3. Mercury and Pluto

___[S]___ 4. Jupiter's diameter is 11 times larger than Earth's diameter[.]

_____ 5. Only a tenth the diameter of the Sun

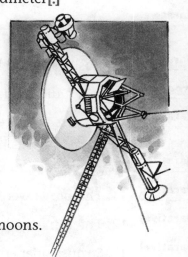

B. Read each sentence. Draw a line between the subject and the predicate.

1. Neptune | is the eighth planet from the Sun.
2. A hollowed-out Neptune | could hold nearly 60 Earths.
3. One orbit of the Sun | takes Neptune 165 years.
4. A day on Neptune | is about 16 hours long.
5. The spaceship *Voyager* | discovered six of Neptune's eight moons.
6. Methane gas | gives Neptune its blue color.
7. Several large dark spots | can be seen on the surface of Neptune.
8. The largest of these spots | is about the size of Earth.
9. *Voyager* | revealed long, bright clouds high in Neptune's atmosphere.
10. These clouds | cast shadows on the cloud decks below.
11. The strongest winds on any planet | are those on Neptune.
12. Wind speeds on Neptune | reach nearly 1,200 miles per hour.
13. Neptune | has a narrow, faint set of rings.
14. The four rings of Neptune | are made of dust particles.
15. Scientists all over the world | are studying this fascinating planet.

94. Declarative and Interrogative Sentences

A **declarative sentence** makes a statement. A declarative sentence ends with a period.

   Levi Strauss was born in Bavaria in 1829.

An **interrogative sentence** asks a question. An interrogative sentence ends with a question mark.

   What is Levi Strauss famous for?

Decide whether each sentence is declarative or interrogative. Write your answer on the line. Add the correct end punctuation.

[declarative]   1. Levi Strauss moved to San Francisco in 1850[.]

[interrogative]   2. What was his reason for moving[?]

[declarative]   3. He wanted to strike it rich during the Gold Rush[.]

[interrogative]   4. Did he look for gold[?]

[declarative]   5. Strauss had trained to be a tailor[.]

[declarative]   6. He planned to manufacture tents for the miners[.]

[declarative]   7. Business was not as good as he had hoped[.]

[interrogative]   8. What did he decide to do then[?]

[declarative]   9. Strauss had brought heavy canvas to use in making tents[.]

[declarative]   10. He decided to use the canvas to make pants for the miners[.]

[declarative]   11. The pants were very sturdy[.]

[declarative]   12. The miners found the pants perfect for their work[.]

[declarative]   13. Strauss opened a factory in San Francisco[.]

[interrogative]   14. Did he change the pants in any way[?]

[declarative]   15. He added rivets at stress points in the pants[.]

[declarative]   16. A heavy blue denim material was substituted for the canvas[.]

[declarative]   17. Levi Strauss's company is still in business[.]

[declarative]   18. The pants he made are still called Levi's[.]

[declarative]   19. Levi Strauss died in San Francisco in 1902[.]

[interrogative]   20. Have you ever worn a pair of Levi's[?]

Sentences

95. Imperative and Exclamatory Sentences

An **imperative sentence** gives a command or makes a request. An imperative sentence ends with a period.

> **Investigate the law of gravity.**

An **exclamatory sentence** expresses a strong emotion. An exclamatory sentence ends with an exclamation point.

> **That's incredible!**

A. Underline the sentences that are imperatives.

1. <u>Get some modeling clay, a marble or a ball bearing, a ruler, and a cookie sheet.</u>

2. <u>Mold the modeling clay into a flat rectangle.</u>

3. <u>Place the clay on a cookie sheet.</u>

4. <u>Drop the marble or ball bearing into the clay.</u>

5. The object will make a dent in the clay.

6. <u>Drop the object from various heights.</u>

7. <u>Measure the size of the dent each time.</u>

8. <u>Record your results.</u>

9. What happens as you drop the object from greater heights?

10. Objects that fall farther are traveling faster when they hit the ground.

B. Decide whether each sentence is imperative or exclamatory. Write your answer on the line. Add the correct end punctuation. **[Answers may vary.]**

__[imperative]__ 1. Use a heavy ball bearing, a marble, and a cookie sheet[.]

__[imperative]__ 2. Put the cookie sheet on the floor[.]

__[imperative]__ 3. Stand up very straight[.]

__[exclamatory]__ 4. Oh, how tilted you are[!]

__[imperative]__ 5. Be sure you keep your balance[.]

__[imperative]__ 6. Hold the ball bearing in one hand and the marble in the other[.]

__[imperative]__ 7. Raise your hands over your head[.]

__[imperative]__ 8. Drop the two objects at the same time[.]

__[imperative]__ 9. Listen for when they hit the cookie sheet[.]

__[exclamatory]__ 10. Yikes, they missed the cookie sheet[!]

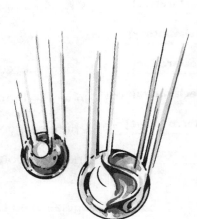

96. The Four Kinds of Sentences

> A sentence can be declarative, interrogative, imperative, or exclamatory.

Decide if each sentence is declarative, interrogative, imperative, or exclamatory.
Write your answer on the line. Add the correct end punctuation. **[Answers may vary.]**

[declarative]   1. Frederick Douglass was born into slavery in 1818[.]

[declarative]   2. As a small child, Frederick lived with his grandmother[.]

[interrogative]   3. Why didn't he live with his mother[?]

[declarative]   4. His mother had to work long hours in the corn fields[.]

[exclamatory]   5. Goodness, that's a sad situation[!]

[declarative]   6. When he was eight years old, Frederick was sent to live in Baltimore[.]

[declarative]   7. His owner's wife, Sophia Auld, taught him the alphabet[.]

[declarative]   8. Sophia's husband made her stop[.]

[declarative]   9. It was illegal to teach slaves to read[.]

[interrogative]   10. How did Frederick finally learn to read and write[?]

[declarative]   11. He had some neighborhood boys teach him[.]

[declarative]   12. As a teenager, Frederick had to work as a field hand[.]

[declarative]   13. He was whipped unmercifully[.]

[exclamatory]   14. Oh my, his life was terrible[!]

[declarative]   15. At the age of twenty, Frederick dressed up as a sailor and escaped[.]

[exclamatory]   16. What a brave young man he was[!]

[declarative]   17. Frederick became a lecturer and a newspaper publisher[.]

[declarative]   18. He worked for justice and opportunity for black people and for women[.]

[interrogative]   19. Where can you learn more about Frederick Douglass[?]

[imperative]   20. Find out about his meetings with Abraham Lincoln[.]

*Frederick Douglass used the power of language to create positive change.
Give an example of how you can use language to change things for the better.*

Sentences

97. Simple Subjects and Simple Predicates

A sentence has a subject and a predicate. The **simple subject** is the noun or pronoun that names the person, place, or thing the sentence is about. The **simple predicate** is the verb that tells what the subject does or is.

SIMPLE SUBJECT	SIMPLE PREDICATE
People	celebrate.
Native people	celebrated social occasions.
Native people of the Northwest coast	celebrated social occasions with potlatches.

A. Write each simple subject and simple predicate in the correct column.

SIMPLE SUBJECT	SIMPLE PREDICATE	
[potlatch]	[marked]	1. A potlatch often marked an event in a family's life.
[family]	[celebrated]	2. The family celebrated a birth, a marriage, or a death.
[family]	[made]	3. The host family made elaborate preparations.
[preparations]	[included]	4. The lavish preparations included huge amounts of food.
[Dishes]	[contained]	5. Dishes at a potlatch often contained fish or seal meat.
[individuals]	[ate]	6. High-ranking individuals ate the choicest dishes.
[Diners]	[dipped]	7. Diners dipped their food in seal oil.
[Guests]	[received]	8. Guests at the potlatch received extravagant gifts.
[Potlatches]	[featured]	9. Potlatches also featured speeches, singing, and dancing.
[event]	[highlighted]	10. Every event highlighted the host's wealth and status.

B. Draw one line under the simple subject of each sentence. Draw two lines under the simple predicate.

1. Parties are still important events for native peoples of the Northwest coast.
2. A family often spends a whole year planning for a family celebration.
3. Hundreds of people gather together over a weekend.
4. The host family provides food, snacks, beverages, and entertainment.
5. Honored guests receive cash and other gifts.

98. Complete Subjects and Complete Predicates

The **complete subject** is the simple subject with all the words that describe it.
The **complete predicate** is the simple predicate with all the words that describe it.

COMPLETE SUBJECT	COMPLETE PREDICATE
The city of Johnstown, Pennsylvania,	**had a population of about 30,000.**

SIMPLE SUBJECT	SIMPLE PREDICATE
city	**had**

Draw a vertical line between the complete subject and the complete predicate of each sentence. Draw one line under the simple subject. Draw two lines under the simple predicate.

1. Johnstown | was a growing and industrious community.

2. The town | lay on a flood plain between two rivers.

3. The growing community | narrowed the riverbanks to gain building space.

4. The South Fork Dam | protected the citizens of Johnstown.

5. The dam | was situated 450 feet above the town.

6. It | prevented the waters of Lake Conemaugh from flooding the city.

7. The people in town | worried about the dam.

8. Engineers | found the dam weak and unsafe.

9. Heavy rains | began to fall on May 30, 1889.

10. The dam | could not withstand the pressure.

11. The dam | burst at 4:07 p.m. on May 31.

12. Inhabitants of the city | heard a roar like thunder.

13. Twenty million tons of water | rushed through Johnstown.

14. The wall of floodwater | rose to a height of 60 feet.

15. The huge wave | crashed down the valley at 40 miles per hour.

16. The flood | destroyed most of the major buildings in the city.

17. The raging water | carried everything with it—trees, animals, and people.

18. More than 2,200 people | died.

19. Thousands of other people | suffered injuries.

20. The Johnstown Flood | was the worst flood in U.S. history.

99. Compound Subjects and Compound Predicates

A **compound subject** consists of more than one simple subject.

> <u>People</u> and <u>animals</u> eat plants.

A **compound predicate** consists of more than one simple predicate.

> Food from plants <u>satisfies</u> hunger and <u>provides</u> nutrients.

A. Each sentence has a compound subject or a compound predicate. Draw a vertical line between the subject and the predicate. Underline the compound subject or the compound predicate.

1. <u>People</u> and <u>animals</u> | have lived together for thousands of years.

2. The earliest peoples | <u>hunted</u> and <u>killed</u> animals for food.

3. Eventually they | <u>domesticated</u> some animals and <u>began</u> to raise them.

4. <u>Cattle</u>, <u>sheep</u>, and <u>goats</u> | provided people with meat and milk.

5. <u>Sheep</u> and <u>goats</u> | also provided wool for clothing.

B. Underline the simple subject(s) in each sentence. Circle the simple predicate(s).

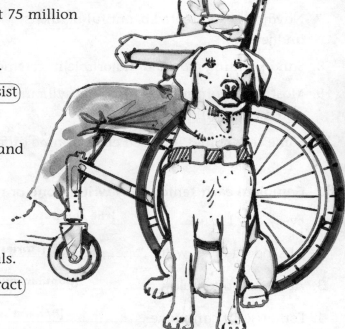

1. Today many <u>people</u> (own) and (care) for pets.

2. More than 65 million pet <u>dogs</u> and about 75 million pet <u>cats</u> (live) in the United States.

3. Some <u>dogs</u> and <u>cats</u> (care) for their owners.

4. Service <u>animals</u> and therapy <u>animals</u> (assist) people with disabilities.

5. Guide <u>dogs</u> (navigate) for sightless people and (lead) them around obstacles.

6. Signal <u>dogs</u> (listen) for sounds and (alert) their deaf owners.

7. Both <u>cats</u> and <u>dogs</u> (act) as therapy animals.

8. Therapy <u>animals</u> (visit) hospitals and (interact) with the patients.

9. The <u>patients</u> (pet) the animals and (play) with them.

10. The <u>animals</u> (amuse) the patients and (make) them feel better.

100. Direct Objects

A **direct object** is the noun or the pronoun that answers the question *whom* or *what* after an action verb. Many sentences need direct objects to complete their meaning. A direct object may be compound.

SUBJECT	VERB	DIRECT OBJECT
The children	are studying	Navajo <u>arts</u> and <u>culture</u>.
They	found	<u>information</u> on the Internet.

A. Circle the direct object(s) in each sentence.

1. The earliest Navajo used (deerskins) to make clothing.

2. Later the men wore cotton or velvet (shirts,) (breeches,) and (moccasins.)

3. Women wore (dresses) made of plain, dark cloth.

4. The Navajo built round (houses) of logs, brush, and earth.

5. Each of these hogans represented the (religion) or (philosophy) of its owner.

6. They welcomed the morning (sun.)

7. Navajo artists created beautiful (blankets) and (jewelry.)

8. Sand painting played a major (role) in ceremonies.

9. Most sand paintings required many (hours) and much (skill) to create.

10. Some ceremonies included eight or nine different sand (paintings.)

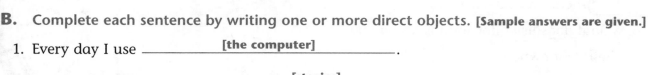

B. Complete each sentence by writing one or more direct objects. **[Sample answers are given.]**

1. Every day I use _____[the computer]_____.

2. At school I often write _____[stories]_____.

3. At home I often play _____[popular music]_____.

4. For dessert I can make _____[banana splits]_____.

5. On the weekends I sometimes buy _____[ice cream]_____.

101. Indirect Objects

Some sentences have two objects—a direct object and an indirect object. The **indirect object** is the noun or pronoun that tells to whom, for whom, to what, or for what the action is done. An indirect object may be compound.

> **The artist sold the picture.**
> **The artist sold <u>Alice</u> the picture.**
>
> **Alice bought the picture.**
> **Alice bought her <u>mother</u> and <u>father</u> the picture.**

A. Circle the indirect object(s) in each sentence. The direct object is in *italics*.

1. The principal promised the (students) a spring *party*.

2. The children sent their (parents) and (friends) *invitations*.

3. The teachers showed the (students) the *schedule* of athletic events.

4. The coach told the (athletes) the *rules*.

5. He assigned certain (players) key *positions*.

6. The music teacher taught the (orchestra) and the (chorus) a new *song*.

7. She gave each (member) a *copy* of the music.

8. The merchant sold the (girls) and (boys) *supplies* to make posters.

9. He also offered (them) his *help*.

10. The committee wrote (everyone) a thank-you *note*.

B. Underline the direct object in each sentence. Circle the indirect object(s).

1. The reporter asked the factory (owner) a <u>question</u> about pollution.

2. The owner didn't give the (reporter) a very clear <u>answer</u>.

3. The reporter showed the (men) and (women) in the audience a court <u>order</u>.

4. The order denied (observers) <u>access</u> to the property.

5. The factory owner promised (everyone) a complete <u>explanation</u>.

102. Adjective and Adverb Phrases

> A **phrase** is a group of words that is used as a single part of speech. It does not have a subject or a verb. A phrase can be one of several types.
>
> | PARTICIPIAL | The inventor, <u>thinking creatively</u>, solved the problem. |
> | INFINITIVE | <u>To win</u>, Ellen needed a solution. |
> | GERUND | The whole class enjoys <u>solving problems</u>. |
> | PREPOSITIONAL | Ms. Guerra divided the class <u>into teams</u>. |
>
> A prepositional phrase consists of a preposition and its object, which is a noun or a pronoun. A prepositional phrase is used as an adjective or an adverb.
>
> | ADJECTIVE PHRASE | The original plan <u>for the game</u> was too complicated. |
> | ADVERB PHRASE | <u>On Monday</u> we found the answer. |

On the first line identify each *italicized* phrase according to type. If it is a prepositional phrase, on the second line write how it is used—**Adj** for adjective or **Adv** for adverb. Otherwise leave the second line blank.

[prepositional] [Adv]   1. Basketball was invented *in 1891.*

[prepositional] [Adv]   2. At that time no major sport was played *during the winter months.*

[infinitive]   _____   3. James A. Naismith's ambition was *to provide an interesting sport.*

[participial] _____   4. Naismith, *having little money,* nailed up peach baskets.

[prepositional] [Adj]   5. Another piece of equipment *for the new game* was a tall ladder.

[prepositional] [Adv]   6. The players were divided *into two teams.*

[participial] _____   7. *Using an old soccer ball,* the teams began to play.

[infinitive]   _____   8. *To score,* a player would throw the ball into the opposite team's basket.

[prepositional] [Adj]   9. There was not a standard number of players *on a team.*

[gerund]   _____   10. *Watching the first game* led Naismith to draft the original 13 rules of play.

[prepositional] [Adj]   11. Changes *to the game* were soon adopted.

[prepositional] [Adj]   12. Metal hoops *with net bags* replaced the baskets.

[gerund]   _____   13. *Pulling a cord on the net* released the ball.

[prepositional] [Adv]   14. Baskets with bottomless nets came into use *about 1913.*

[prepositional] [Adv]   15. The game of basketball has spread *throughout the world.*

James Naismith used little money but a lot of imagination to develop a new sport. How can you use your imagination to teach or entertain people?

103. Adjective Clauses

A **clause** is a group of words that contains a subject and a predicate. An **independent clause** expresses a complete thought and can stand on its own as a sentence. A **dependent clause** does not express a complete thought and cannot stand alone.

DEPENDENT   INDEPENDENT
Although only the pyramids still stand, the list of wonders has survived.

A dependent clause may be an **adjective clause,** which modifies a noun or a pronoun. An adjective clause usually begins with a relative pronoun (*who, whom, whose, which, that*) or a subordinate conjunction (*when, where, why*).

The wonder that I would most like to have seen was the Colossus of Rhodes.

A. Write on the line whether each clause is independent or dependent.

[independent] 1. the Pharos of Alexandria was an ancient lighthouse

[dependent] 2. because the bonfire burned continuously

[independent] 3. the bonfire served as a beacon

[dependent] 4. when sailors saw the light

[dependent] 5. as the ships approached the rocks

B. Underline the adjective clause in each sentence. Circle the word(s) it modifies.

1. People travel to Egypt to see the (pyramids) that were built more than 4,000 years ago.

2. The pyramids are the only ancient (wonder) that is still in existence.

3. The Great Pyramid was built as a tomb for (Khufu,) who was known to the Greeks as Cheops.

4. The (pyramids,) which are made of millions of stone blocks, are an engineering marvel.

5. (Archaeologists) who have studied the pyramids think as many as 100,000 men worked 20 years or more to build the Great Pyramid.

6. The (blocks) of stone that were hauled into place each weighed about 2.5 tons.

7. The (Great Pyramid,) which rose to a finished height of about 480 feet, was built in layers of stone blocks.

8. Each (layer,) which fit atop the previous one, covered a smaller area.

9. The stones were dragged up a (ramp,) which was made higher for each layer.

10. The finished (structure,) which looked like a set of stairs, was then filled in with white limestone.

104. More Adjective Clauses

> Remember that an **adjective clause** is a dependent clause used as an adjective. It modifies a noun or a pronoun and is usually introduced by a relative pronoun.

A. Rewrite each sentence, adding an adjective clause to modify the *italicized* word.
[Answers will vary. Sample answers are given.]

1. My *neighbor* has a pizza business.
   [My neighbor who lives next door has a pizza business.]

2. The *business* intrigued me.
   [The business, which makes a lot of money, intrigued me.]

3. Each weekend I talked to *Mr. Hawkins* about the business.
   [Each weekend I talked to Mr. Hawkins, who is the owner, about the business.]

4. He offered me a part-time *position*.
   [He offered me a part-time position, which I accepted.]

5. Every weekend I worked the late *shift*.
   [Every weekend I worked the late shift, which no one else likes to do.]

6. During that time, I learned all the aspects of *pizza making*.
   [During that time, I learned all the aspects of pizza making, which involves many steps.]

7. *Working* with the customers was quite a challenge.
   [Working with the customers who became demanding was quite a challenge.]

8. My *boss* taught me that the customer is always right.
   [My boss, whose opinion I value, taught me that the customer is always right.]

9. His *patience* is amazing.
   [His patience, which seems endless, is amazing.]

10. Now we are working toward opening a pizza parlor at a second *location*. [Now we are working toward opening a pizza parlor at a second location, which is across from the high school.]

B. Write sentences, using an adjective clause to modify each noun. [Sample answers are given.]

homework   1. [Our homework, which is assigned daily, matches the class discussions.]

television   2. [Television, which broadcasts via satellite, can show images from anywhere.]

amusement park 3. [The amusement park that was under construction last year just opened.]

gift   4. [The gift that I liked best came from Mom.]

holiday   5. [Christmas, a holiday that many people celebrate, comes on Tuesday this year.]

Sentences

105. Restrictive and Nonrestrictive Clauses

Some adjective clauses are essential to the meaning of sentences. These essential clauses are called **restrictive clauses**. An adjective clause that is not essential and that can be removed without changing the meaning of the sentence is called a **nonrestrictive clause**. Nonrestrictive clauses are set off by commas.

RESTRICTIVE   **We read about a saint who was a martyr.**
NONRESTRICTIVE   **The martyr, who sacrificed his life at an early age, died for his faith.**

A. Underline the adjective clause in each sentence. On the line write **R** if it is restrictive or **N** if it is nonrestrictive.

__[N]__ 1. Maximilian Kolbe, who was a martyred Catholic priest, is considered a hero.

__[R]__ 2. He had founded a religious group whose aim was to fight evil by living a good life and praying.

__[N]__ 3. In 1939 the Germans invaded Poland, which was Kolbe's home.

__[R]__ 4. He and other friars helped people who were being persecuted by the Nazis.

__[N]__ 5. Father Kolbe, who was viewed as a threat by the Germans, was arrested in 1941.

__[R]__ 6. He was placed in a concentration camp that held Jews and enemies of the Nazis.

__[N]__ 7. Auschwitz, which was both a labor camp and a death camp, was his destination.

__[R]__ 8. Kolbe was put to work on a building in which people were to be burned to death.

__[R]__ 9. After someone escaped from the camp, the Nazis chose 10 people who would be killed in retribution.

__[R]__ 10. Kolbe offered to take the place of a young father who was chosen to die.

B. Decide whether the adjective clause in each sentence is restrictive or nonrestrictive. Rewrite the sentences that contain nonrestrictive clauses, adding commas as needed.

1. Father Kolbe who was meant to starve to death slowly was eventually killed by injection.
[Father Kolbe, who was meant to starve to death slowly, was eventually killed by injection.]

2. The men who were condemned to death sang hymns and songs of love.

_____

3. Kolbe's courage and sacrifice which were truly heroic are still remembered.
[Kolbe's courage and sacrifice, which were truly heroic, are still remembered.]

4. The man whom he replaced as a condemned prisoner attended Kolbe's beatification in 1971.

_____

5. The feast day of Kolbe who was canonized in 1982 is on August 14.
[The feast day of Kolbe, who was canonized in 1982, is on August 14.]

_____

Sentences

106. Adverb Clauses

An **adverb clause** is a dependent clause used as an adverb. An adverb clause modifies a verb, an adjective, or an adverb. It tells where, when, why, in what way, to what extent, or under what condition. An adverb clause is introduced by a subordinate conjunction, and the clause can come before or after the independent clause.

At Yellowstone National Park the mud pots, bubbling pools of mud, were formed <u>when steam and gas rose from the ground and changed rock into clay</u>.

A. Underline the adverb clause in each sentence. Circle the word(s) it modifies.

1. <u>If you visit the West</u>, you (should make) a trip to Yellowstone.

2. <u>Because there is so much to do</u>, (plan) to stay several days.

3. More and more tourists (visit) <u>as the park's popularity has grown</u>.

4. <u>Because Yellowstone sits on magma</u>, it (has) geysers and thousands of hot springs.

5. <u>When the major geysers erupt</u>, tourists (can watch) the boiling water shoot into the air.

6. Geysers (have been compared) to volcanoes <u>because they are similar</u>.

7. Geysers (shoot) boiling water, <u>while volcanoes shoot out melted rock</u>.

8. <u>After a geyser has erupted</u>, the water (seeps) back into the earth.

9. <u>When the minerals in the water dry</u>, you (can see) beautiful formations.

10. At Yellowstone, bears, elk, and bison (roam) <u>wherever they want</u>.

11. The balance of nature (is maintained) <u>even though it sometimes seems cruel</u>.

12. <u>If the park's elk population becomes too large</u>, many animals (starve) in winter.

13. Feeding animals (is prohibited) <u>because it alters their natural eating habits</u>.

14. <u>Even though black bears seem friendly</u>, people (should avoid) them.

15. <u>Before you can camp in the wilderness</u>, you (must obtain) a permit.

B. Use each adverb clause in a sentence. **[Sample answers are given.]**

1. If you stop to think about it, **[you will realize that having friends is important]** .

2. Until the rain stops, **[we can't go home]** .

3. After I finish my homework, **[I will go skating]** .

4. Although I am good in math, **[I am better in reading]** .

5. Since the computer was invented, **[shopping has never been easier]** .

107. More Adverb Clauses

Remember that an adverb clause is always introduced by a subordinate conjunction. Be careful not to confuse a subordinate conjunction with a preposition. A subordinate conjunction connects two complete clauses, but a preposition has only a noun or a pronoun as an object.

SUBORDINATE CONJUNCTION **We waited until our favorite TV show was on.**
PREPOSITION **I can hardly wait until tomorrow for Katie's visit.**

A. Complete each sentence with an adverb clause.
The subordinate conjunction is given. [Sample answers are given.]

1. We will eat dinner when ____[Mom gets home from work]____ .

2. Jason answered as soon as ____[the phone rang]____ .

3. He listened to the stereo after ____[he finished his homework]____ .

4. When ____[winter arrives]____ , the birds fly southward.

5. They return after ____[the winter has passed]____ .

6. The storm arose as soon as ____[we arrived home]____ .

7. Edward acted as though ____[he had the starring role]____ .

8. Because ____[I don't know him]____ , I cannot recommend him.

9. He waited until ____[everyone else was ready]____ .

10. The expedition struggled on while ____[the weather grew worse]____ .

B. Complete each sentence with an adverb clause.
Circle each subordinate conjunction. [Sample answers are given.]

1. The pizza finally arrived ____(after) we called again]____ .

2. School was dismissed ____(when) the fire alarm sounded]____ .

3. The car broke down on the highway ____[(after) we passed the intersection]____ .

4. [(Because) I was so hungry,] ____ I ate two hamburgers and a large pickle.

5. [(Because) we left it outside,] ____ the rain ruined the new rug.

6. [(After) we visited the Petersons,] ____ we drove home from vacation.

7. [(Because) we had been gone so long,] ____ the milk in the refrigerator was sour.

8. [(When) the time for soccer came,] ____ everyone dressed in ratty clothes.

9. [(After) I got home from practice,] ____ I opened my drawer, but there were no socks.

10. [(While) Mom slept,] ____ Dad made me a delicious club sandwich.

Name _____

108. Reviewing Adjective Clauses and Adverb Clauses

A. Underline the dependent clause in each sentence. On the line write whether it is an adjective clause or an adverb clause.

[adverb]   1. Before you visit a Florida beach, you should become familiar with its creatures.

[adverb]   2. People collect seashells because they are beautiful.

[adjective]   3. Sea urchins, whose spines are sharp, are called the porcupines of the sea.

[adjective]   4. A sea cucumber is a marine animal that looks like a cucumber.

[adverb]   5. Until Pam studied seahorses, she didn't realize that the male helps to hatch the eggs.

[adverb]   6. When the ocean tide is low, you can see a variety of sea life.

[adjective]   7. Sea turtles, which weigh up to 300 pounds, come ashore to lay eggs.

[adverb]   8. After I was stung by a Portuguese man-of-war, I became more careful.

[adjective]   9. A blue crab, whose legs really are blue, is a delicacy in the Far East.

[adverb]   10. If you're hungry, you can make a tasty broth from coquinas.

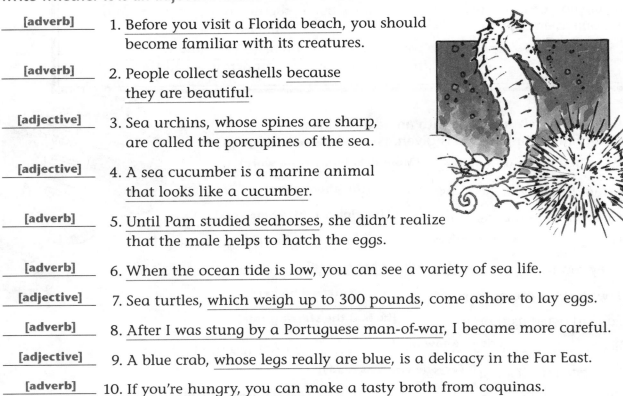

B. Complete each sentence with an adjective clause. **[Sample answers are given.]**

11. Our teacher, [whom we all respect], returned the test papers.

12. I enjoyed reading this book, [which I found buried in my drawer].

13. The players, [who were evenly matched], did not stop until noon.

14. The car, [which the mechanic had just checked over], broke down.

15. The Joneses, [who had a soccer game to attend], left the party.

C. Complete each sentence with an adverb clause. **[Sample answers are given.]**

16. [Before we went to class], we decided to play volleyball.

17. Take the train [even though the bus is more direct].

18. I ate everything in sight [before I went to the game].

19. [While I am at camp], I plan to read four novels.

20. We were stranded on the island [when everyone else went shopping].

Sentences

109. Noun Clauses as Subjects

A **noun clause** is a subordinate clause used as a noun. It can perform several functions in a sentence, including serving as the subject. A noun clause is a dependent clause even though it is an essential part of the independent clause.

That reptiles fascinate people is clearly shown in the film. (*That reptiles fascinate people* is a subordinate clause; the entire clause serves as the subject of the sentence.)

A. Underline the noun clause used as a subject in each sentence.

1. That pandas are adorable creatures is undisputed.
2. Whether pandas are endangered is also not questioned.
3. Why some pandas reproduce and others don't is being studied.
4. That female pandas can mate for only about three days each year is a biological fact.
5. That pandas are essentially solitary doesn't increase their odds of reproducing.
6. What scientists are learning about pandas in captivity may help keep pandas alive in the wild.
7. That female pandas usually give birth to twins is not new information.
8. Why the mother panda frequently rejects one twin is a puzzle.
9. Whether the female selects the stronger twin is not known.
10. Whoever solves that mystery will help increase the panda population.

B. Complete each sentence with a noun clause used as the subject. Remember that a clause has a subject and a predicate. [Answers will vary. Sample answers are given.]

1. [What we saw that November night] _____ was not clear at all.
2. [What Jane saw] _____ was perfectly evident.
3. [What he knew] _____ did not discourage him.
4. [That Grandma was from Missouri] _____ was a well-kept secret.
5. [Why Justin came home] _____ mystified everyone.
6. [How the children will be entertained] _____ will be decided by the group.
7. [That teaching is a difficult job] _____ is clear to most of us.
8. [Who will go on the trip] _____ will be announced.
9. [That I like to play word games] _____ was not a surprise to Jay.
10. [Why the temperature is often cooler by the lake] _____ is the topic of my paper.

110. Noun Clauses as Subject Complements

A noun clause may be used as a subject complement.

The question was whether the candidate had strong views on vital issues.
(*Whether the candidate had strong views on vital issues* is the subject complement; it restates the subject *question*.)

A. Underline the noun clause used as a subject complement in each sentence.

1. A qualification for the presidency is that the candidate be a native-born citizen.

2. Is this what you understood about the qualifications?

3. Constant fundraising is what can take up a candidate's time.

4. The best candidate is not always who will win.

5. Their greatest disappointment is that they don't have time to study the issues.

6. The demand of the voters was that the lottery money be spent on schools.

7. The issue was how test scores could be raised.

8. The decision of the committee was that the money would go for energy research.

9. The senator's prediction was that aid to foreign countries would decrease.

10. A requirement is that the country must improve its human rights record.

B. Complete each sentence with a noun clause used as a subject complement. Remember that a clause has a subject and a predicate. **[Answers will vary. Sample answers are given.]**

1. A safety rule of biking is ___[that you always use hand signals]___ .

2. His chief difficulty was ___[that he was not prepared]___ .

3. My main concern is ___[that someone will get lost]___ .

4. The pilot's first thought was ___[how could she land the plane safely]___ .

5. The advice of our coach is ___[that we stretch before running]___ .

6. The survivor's only hope is ___[that a boat will come by]___ .

7. The question became ___[who would win the prize]___ .

8. The student's excuse, as always, will be ___[that she didn't have enough time]___ .

9. The reason for the defeat was ___[that our best goalie couldn't play]___ .

10. Mom's greatest joy was ___[what you would expect, her children's happiness]___ .

Sentences

111. Noun Clauses as Appositives

A noun clause may be used as an appositive.

The theory that Surtsey is an island created by an underwater volcano intrigues me. *(That Surtsey is an island created by an underwater volcano is an appositive that renames the noun theory.)*

A. Underline the noun clause used as an appositive in each sentence. Circle the word it renames.

1. The (idea) that a new landform can be created seems like science fiction.

2. The (fact) that an island can be formed from an underground volcanic eruption is fantastic.

3. The people of Iceland accepted the (idea) that an island was growing off their southern coast.

4. In class we discussed the (idea) that eruptions can be divided into six groups.

5. The (classification,) how scientists identify various volcanoes, is based on violence of eruption and material erupted.

6. The (fact) that the eruption of Mount Pelee in 1902 killed more than 38,000 people is the reason that most violent eruptions are called Pelean.

7. The (promise) that we would see an Icelandic eruption came true.

8. My sister's (wish) that she see a volcano erupt is possible.

9. Dad kept his (promise) that he would take us to see Kilauea.

10. I find very odd the (thought) that people want to see something so destructive.

B. Complete each sentence with a noun clause used as an appositive. Remember that a clause has a subject and a predicate. **[Answers will vary. Sample answers are given.]**

1. Joan kept her promise ___[that she would meet us at the basketball game]___.

2. The motion ___[that we have pop machines in the cafeteria passed]___.

3. The rumor ___[that Jennifer was leaving spread quickly]___.

4. Her suggestion ___[that the dog be trained was a good one]___.

5. The fear ___[that she would not pass was groundless]___.

6. Trudy was upset by the report ___[that named her the culprit]___.

7. The thought ___[that boys are better scientists is wrong]___.

8. Dad's wish ___[that we all play nicely came true]___.

9. My idea ___[that we decorate the gym in the school colors was voted down]___.

10. Jack's assumption ___[that everyone would vote for him was incorrect]___.

Sentences

119

112. Noun Clauses as Direct Objects

> A noun clause may be used as the direct object of a verb.
>
> **Scientists know <u>that the balance in nature is easily upset</u>.**
>
> *(That the balance in nature is easily upset* is the direct object of the verb *know.)*

A. Underline the noun clause used as the direct object.

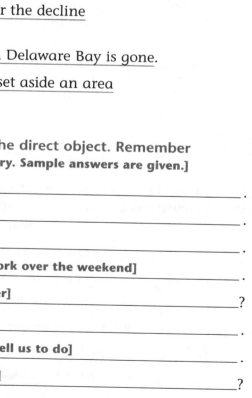

1. We know <u>that all parts of an ecosystem are important</u>.

2. Did you realize <u>that harvesting a species of crab can lead to a decline in a species of bird</u>?

3. Biologists know <u>that horseshoe crabs come ashore in Delaware Bay to spawn in May</u>.

4. They also know <u>that shorebirds arrive to eat crabs' eggs</u>.

5. The crabs' eggs provide <u>whatever energy the birds have for their migration to the Arctic</u>.

6. Lately biologists have noticed <u>that the number of red knots, a type of shorebird, has declined</u>.

7. Scientists think <u>that the birds' food supply has dwindled</u>.

8. They believe <u>that commercial fishing is responsible for the decline in the number of crabs</u>.

9. They have calculated <u>that half the crab population in Delaware Bay is gone</u>.

10. The U.S. Department of Commerce proposed <u>that we set aside an area in the ocean as a horseshoe crab reserve</u>.

B. Complete each sentence with a noun clause used as the direct object. Remember that a clause has a subject and a predicate. **[Answers will vary. Sample answers are given.]**

1. The boy said **[that his dog ate his homework]** _____.

2. She could not remember **[what she had seen]** _____.

3. We all knew **[who was at the door]** _____.

4. Our teacher promised **[that we would have no homework over the weekend]** _____.

5. Did they discover **[what group had written the letter]** _____?

6. Kim proved **[that she could pitch as well as anyone]** _____.

7. We should always do **[what our mothers and fathers tell us to do]** _____.

8. Has anyone heard **[that the dance has been canceled]** _____?

9. Jerry tried to explain **[how the accident happened]** _____.

10. All of us hope **[that the rain will not spoil the picnic]** _____.

Sentences

113. Noun Clauses as Objects of Prepositions

> A noun clause may be used as the object of a preposition.
>
> **The spectators came upon <u>what was an ancient racetrack</u>.**
>
> (*What was an ancient racetrack* is the object of the preposition *upon*.)

A. Underline the noun clause used as the object of a preposition. Circle the preposition.

1. We had an excellent view of the race (from) <u>where we stood</u>.

2. We searched (through) <u>what used to be Grandma's old chest</u>.

3. Last week the team studied (about) <u>how the previous relay teams trained</u>.

4. The group walked (around) <u>where the old town plaza had been</u>.

5. During the summer I practiced my shots (in) <u>what is the renovated recreation center</u>.

6. The bridge passes (over) <u>where the rivers meet</u>.

7. The bug crawled (under) <u>whatever was lying on the table</u>.

8. John gave every explanation (except) <u>why he was so late</u>.

9. You give the baton (to) <u>whoever is there</u>.

10. Our coach will give a pizza (to) <u>whoever wins the heat</u>.

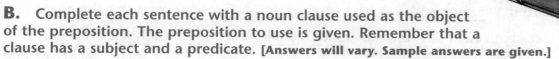

B. Complete each sentence with a noun clause used as the object of the preposition. The preposition to use is given. Remember that a clause has a subject and a predicate. **[Answers will vary. Sample answers are given.]**

1. You have no idea about __[how our ancestors survived the cold climate]__ .

2. I plan to succeed beyond __[whatever goals have been set for me]__ .

3. Give the package to __[whoever turns up]__ .

4. The park lies between __[where the golf course ends and the track begins]__ .

5. Marcy was delighted with __[what the rabbit did]__ .

6. There has been some dispute about __[who will wear the mascot costume]__ .

7. During the ride we talked about __[whatever occurred to us]__ .

8. We walked toward __[what was originally an old sawmill]__ .

9. Many books have been written about __[what the right diet should contain]__ .

10. She can give the assignment to __[whoever comes in late]__ .

114. Reviewing Noun Clauses

A. Underline the noun clause in each sentence. Write on the line how it is used. Use **S** for subject, **DO** for direct object, **OP** for object of a preposition, **SC** for subject complement, and **A** for appositive.

[DO] 1. This article says <u>that a society lived in Peru a thousand years before the Inca.</u>

[OP] 2. Such a discovery is exciting to <u>whoever is interested in archaeology.</u>

[SC] 3. The truth is <u>that the Moche state extended 220 miles along Peru's coast.</u>

[S] 4. <u>That the Moche had a highly stratified society</u> is indicated by the burial tombs.

[A] 5. Excavations, <u>where archaeologists clear away tons of rock and dirt,</u> are yielding fabulous objects of gold, silver, and copper.

[S] 6. <u>That these tombs were looted for more than four centuries</u> is unfortunate.

[DO] 7. Archaeologists say <u>that the Moche did not have a writing system.</u>

[S] 8. <u>Whatever we know about their activities</u> is recorded on ceramic pots, textiles, and murals.

[SC] 9. The fact is <u>that the Moche lived in one of the driest regions on earth.</u>

[DO] 10. Archaeologists say <u>that the Moche had a complicated irrigation system.</u>

[SC] 11. One idea is <u>that bats were important symbols to the Moche.</u>

[DO] 12. Archaeologists explain <u>that bats appear in depictions of human sacrifice.</u>

[A] 13. One find, <u>what appeared to be a headdress with bats,</u> supports this theory.

[SC] 14. A fact about each burial tomb is <u>that it contained one very tall adult male.</u>

[DO] 15. Archaeologists do not know <u>why such a man was buried with much smaller people.</u>

B. Write sentences, using each noun clause as indicated. [Sample answers are given.]

16. that those children study *(direct object)*

    [The teacher wanted primarily that those children study.]

17. when the Yankees won the World Series *(subject)*

    [When the Yankees won the World Series last year was the first time I visited New York.]

18. whether the clock is correct *(subject complement)*

    [The question is whether the clock is correct.]

19. whatever dangers threatened it *(object of a preposition)*

    [The animal escaped from whatever dangers threatened it.]

20. that she was running for mayor *(appositive)*

    [The report that she was running for mayor was true.]

Sentences

115. Reviewing Clauses

A. Underline the subordinate clause in each sentence. Write whether it is used as an adjective, an adverb, or a noun.

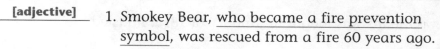

__[adjective]__   1. Smokey Bear, who became a fire prevention symbol, was rescued from a fire 60 years ago.

__[adjective]__   2. A bear cub is a creature that everybody loves.

__[adverb]__   3. After the cub was rescued from the fire in New Mexico, he was sent to a zoo.

__[adverb]__   4. As a fire raged through Montana in 2000, another cub was found.

__[adjective]__   5. The cub, which was a black bear, was found by a game warden.

__[adverb]__   6. The cub needed help because his little paws were burned.

__[noun]__   7. What the rescuers should do with this cub after bandaging his paws was not an issue.

__[noun]__   8. A wildlife official insisted that this cub go back to the forest.

__[noun]__   9. The plan was that the cub be put into a hand-dug den to hibernate.

__[adjective]__   10. The cub was in the den with another orphaned cub that rangers found.

B. Combine each set of sentences into one sentence, using an adjective or an adverb clause as directed. Use a subordinate conjunction as needed to connect clauses. [**Sample answers are given.**]

11. *(adverb)* Traffic was backed up for miles. A huge truck was on fire.

[**Because a huge truck was on fire, traffic was backed up for miles.**]

_____

12. *(adverb)* I turned the corner. A gust of wind blew my hat off.

[**Just as I turned the corner, a gust of wind blew my hat off.**]

_____

13. *(adjective)* Leonardo da Vinci made a mechanical lion. Leonardo da Vinci was an artist and inventor.

[**Leonardo da Vinci, who was an artist and inventor, made a mechanical lion.**]

_____

14. *(adverb)* I was standing in a good spot. I had an excellent view of the Grand Canyon.

[**I had an excellent view of the Grand Canyon, because I was standing in a good spot.**]

_____

Sentences

15. *(adjective)* There are magazines piled on the table. Don't take any of the magazines.

 [Don't take any of the magazines that are piled on the table.] _____

 _____

16. *(adjective)* The Battle of New Orleans was fought in January of 1815. It lasted only 20 minutes.

 [The Battle of New Orleans, which was fought in January of 1815, lasted only 20 minutes.] ___

 _____

17. *(adverb)* John and Sue did all the work. We should be grateful to John and Sue.

 [We should be grateful to John and Sue because they did all the work.] _____

 _____

18. *(adverb)* Frank was vice president of the camera club. Frank organized many interesting programs.

 [When Frank was vice president of the camera club, he organized many interesting programs.] ___

 _____

19. *(adjective)* A new supermarket is opening here soon. The supermarket will provide jobs for many people.

 [The new supermarket, which is opening here soon, will provide jobs for many people.] ___

 _____

20. *(adverb)* The skaters finally arrived home. They were cold, tired, and hungry.

 [When the skaters finally arrived home, they were cold, tired, and hungry.] _____

 _____

C. Write sentences, using these noun clauses as indicated. [Sample answers are given.]

21. where they had started *(object of a preposition)*

 [They wanted to return to where they had started.] _____

22. that the contest be held at this school *(subject complement)*

 [The teacher's expectation was that the contest be held at this school.] _____

23. whether I will arrive in time *(subject)*

 [Whether I will arrive in time is always in question.] _____

24. that we visit my aunt *(appositive)*

 [The plan that we visit my aunt fell through.] _____

25. where the game was being played *(direct object)*

 [My neighbor told us where the game was being played.] _____

Sentences

116. Simple Sentences

A **simple sentence** consists of one independent clause. Remember that an independent clause has a subject and a predicate and can stand alone as a complete thought.

A. Make sentences by matching the complete subjects in Column A with the complete predicates in Column B. Write the correct letter on the line. Use each letter once.

	COLUMN A	COLUMN B
[a]	1. A cat's skeleton	a. has about 250 bones.
[d]	2. The exact number of bones	b. aid in a soft landing.
[e]	3. The skeleton	c. helps it stay balanced.
[h]	4. A cat's ears	d. depends on tail length.
[f]	5. After eating or sleeping, a cat	e. protects internal organs.
[g]	6. Long, thin, flexible leg muscles	f. cleans itself.
[i]	7. Owners sometimes	g. enable a cat to run fast.
[j]	8. Being a carnivore, a cat	h. can lie flat on its head.
[c]	9. A cat's tail	i. remove a cat's claws.
[b]	10. Pads on its paws	j. likes to eat meat.

B. Choose the best simple predicate to complete each sentence. Use each once.

have written   **read**   **borrowed**   **describes**   **named**
imagined   **enjoy**   **saw**   **appears**   **delights**

1. Authors throughout the ages ____[have written]____ about cats.

2. *Puss in Boots* ____[delights]____ both young and old readers.

3. A favorite nursery rhyme ____[describes]____ mittenless kittens.

4. The author of *Catwings* ____[imagined]____ flying cats.

5. In *Alice in Wonderland* a Cheshire cat ____[appears]____ from time to time.

6. We ____[saw]____ a play about Dick Whittington and his cat.

7. I ____[borrowed]____ a book about a cat that saw ghosts.

8. I ____[enjoy]____ reading poetry about cats.

9. Sometimes I ____[read]____ aloud to my cat, Jake.

10. My sister ____[named]____ her black cat Ichabod Crane.

Sentences

117. Compound Sentences

> A **compound sentence** contains two or more independent clauses. The clauses may be joined in three different ways.
>
> **The day was cold, yet we decided to go.** (comma and conjunction)
> **The day was cold; we still decided to go.** (semicolon)
> **The day was cold; nevertheless, we decided to go.**
> (semicolon and adverb)

A. Create compound sentences by combining clauses from both columns. Use each clause once. On the line at the left, write the letter of your selection from Column B. On the line at the right, add the proper punctuation and, as appropriate, a conjunction or an adverb. **[Answers will vary.]**

COLUMN A

[b] 1. Cars are easy to drive __[, but]__

[j] 2. Dad bought a new SUV __[, and]__

[i] 3. We like riding in it __[; however,]__

[h] 4. The car is good for off-road driving __[, but]__

[c] 5. Mom does not drive __[, nor]__

[g] 6. She walks everywhere __[, or]__

[f] 7. Riding a bike is good exercise __[, and]__

[e] 8. My sister is 16 __[, and]__

[a] 9. Will she pay for gas __[, or]__

[d] 10. Fuel prices go up __[, but]__

COLUMN B

a. will Dad pay?

b. they are expensive to maintain.

c. does she want to.

d. people still want to drive.

e. she wants to drive.

f. it doesn't pollute.

g. she rides her bicycle.

h. we live in a suburb.

i. we don't enjoy buying gas for it.

j. it uses a lot of fuel.

B. Complete each sentence with an independent clause. **[Sample answers are given.]**

1. The girls arranged the chairs, and __[the boys set up the tables]__.

2. The assignment was difficult, but __[it was completed on time]__.

3. The crowd was silent; __[the pianist began to play]__.

4. Finally the game began, and __[we began to play our toughest opponent]__.

5. Take my advice, and __[you will succeed]__.

6. I am not a musician, but __[I could have played better]__.

7. The weeds we pulled were poison ivy; consequently, __[we all got a rash]__.

8. I did not finish my chores; therefore, __[I did not get paid]__.

9. We spent the entire afternoon at the beach, and __[I got badly sunburned]__.

10. We bought treats for the children, but __[Jason dropped his ice-cream cone in the sand]__.

Sentences

Name _____

118. Complex Sentences

> A **complex sentence** contains one independent and one or more dependent clauses.
>
> DEPENDENT CLAUSE   INDEPENDENT CLAUSE
> **If you visit Australia,**   **you can see the largest coral reef in the world.**

A. Underline the independent clause in each sentence. Write the word that begins each dependent clause on the line.

___[Although]___ 1. Although the name suggests a continuous strip, Australia's Great Barrier Reef is made up of more than 2,800 reefs.

___[when]___ 2. A coral reef forms when colonies of plant and animal skeletons pile up.

___[that]___ 3. Divers meet many sharks that seem more curious than dangerous.

___[Because]___ 4. Because the waters are clear, divers can go 150 feet deep or lower.

___[who]___ 5. Biologists, who find new species of fish every year, have already discovered more than 2,000.

B. Underline the dependent clause in each sentence. Write the word that begins each dependent clause on the line.

___[Because]___ 1. Because they look like plants, corals were originally wrongly classified.

___[After]___ 2. After corals were studied further, scientists likened them to anemones and jellyfish.

___[Because]___ 3. Because they eat other animals, corals are carnivores.

___[If]___ 4. If you dive around the Great Barrier Reef, you are likely to see sea turtles.

___[that]___ 5. Some marks on a sea turtle's shell are from sharks that bit it.

C. Complete each sentence with a dependent clause. **[Sample answers are given.]**

1. Vegetables are good for you because ___[they contain fiber]___.

2. The dog panted as if ___[it had run a long way]___.

3. July 4 is the date when ___[the band will march in the parade]___.

4. I have a suggestion that ___[she will like]___.

5. We wondered how ___[the machine worked]___.

6. Spring is the season when ___[many trees bloom]___.

7. We should honor our school because ___[we're proud of it]___.

8. Be sure to return those books if ___[you go to the library]___.

9. I will finish my paper after ___[my research is completed]___.

10. The game was forfeited because ___[the other team didn't show up]___.

Sentences

127

Name _____

119. Combining Sentences

> A simple sentence consists of a subject and a predicate, either of which may be compound.
> A compound sentence consists of two or more independent clauses.
> A complex sentence contains one independent clause and one or more dependent clauses.

Combine each pair of sentences. Write at least two simple sentences, two compound sentences, and two complex sentences. After each of your sentences, write whether it is simple, compound, or complex. [Sample answers are given.]

1. The date of the festivities was announced. I cannot attend.
   [The date of the festivities was announced, but I cannot attend. compound]

2. Books are a great source of knowledge. They can broaden people's minds.
   [Because books are a great source of knowledge, they can broaden people's minds. complex]

3. Football is an exciting sport. I like hockey more than football.
   [Football is an exciting sport, but I like hockey more. compound]

4. Snakes are unusual animals. They are often misunderstood.
   [Because snakes are unusual animals, they are often misunderstood. complex]

5. The car sped around the corner. It skidded into a ditch.
   [The car sped around the corner and skidded into a ditch. simple]

6. Study in a quiet place. You will be able to concentrate.
   [If you study in a quiet place, you will be able to concentrate. complex]

7. The students assemble in the yard. They assemble there every morning.
   [The students assemble in the yard every morning. simple]

8. The aircraft carrier entered the harbor. People on the dock cheered.
   [As the aircraft carrier entered the harbor, people on the dock cheered. complex]

9. The students were cooperative all year. The class went on a trip to a theme park.
   [The students were cooperative all year; consequently, the class went on a trip to a theme park.

   compound]

10. The story is quite interesting. It was written by Walter Dean Myers.
    [The story written by Walter Dean Myers is quite interesting. simple]

Name _____

120. Reviewing Sentences

A. Tell how each underlined phrase is used. Write **Prep** if it is a prepositional phrase, **Part** if a participle, **Inf** if an infinitive, or **Ger** if a gerund.

_____[Part]_____ 1. *Mary Rose,* an English ship built in the early 1500s, sank in 1545 near the southern coast of England.

_____[Prep]_____ 2. The story of this famous shipwreck is fascinating.

_____[Ger]_____ 3. Recovering the ship was a painstaking task.

_____[Inf]_____ 4. The effort to raise the ship was successful in 1982.

_____[Prep]_____ 5. It was watched on TV by some 60 million people.

B. Underline the dependent clause in each sentence.

6. When the *Mary Rose* was built, it was one of the first warships with cannons on its sides.

7. People of the time said that it was a favorite ship of King Henry VIII.

8. The king was actually present as the ship went out to sea in 1545.

9. A storm that arose very suddenly sank the ship.

10. Although most of the crew was lost, some of them did survive.

11. The *Mary Rose* settled into the silt on the ocean floor, which helped preserve it over the centuries.

12. That the ship remained intact for so many years was truly amazing.

13. The objects that were recovered from the ship present a view into the world of the 1500s.

14. From the remains historians have learned about what sailors at that time ate.

15. Archaeologists have even found leather shoes that survived all those years in the water.

C. Underline the dependent clause in each sentence. Write **Adj** if it is used as an adjective, **Adv** if used as an adverb, or **N** if used as a noun.

[Adv] 16. Because the ship contained so many artifacts, historians have learned a lot about its crew.

[Adj] 17. The games that were found include a backgammon board with pieces.

_[N]_ 18. That music was important in a sailor's life is obvious from the number of musical instruments on board.

_[N]_ 19. The amount of fishing equipment found indicates that fishing was a major pastime for the sailors.

Sentences

__[Adv]__ 20. The leather covers of some books survived <u>although the pages of the books had deteriorated</u>.

__[Adj]__ 21. A chest <u>that had containers in it</u> belonged to the ship's surgeon-barber.

__[Adj]__ 22. It contained peppercorns, <u>which were used as a medicine at the time</u>.

__[Adv]__ 23. <u>When crew members were injured</u>, the surgeon tended to them.

__[Adj]__ 24. At other times he groomed sailors <u>who wished to be shaved</u>.

__[N]__ 25. <u>That there was little gold aboard the warship</u> was not surprising.

D. Identify the type of each sentence by writing **Simple**, **Compound**, or **Complex**.

__[Simple]__ 26. The *Mary Rose* is now in a museum in Portsmouth, England.

__[Complex]__ 27. Visitors may actually touch a piece of rope that was under the sea for more than 400 years.

__[Complex]__ 28. For a period of time after the wooden ship was raised, it was preserved by a constant spray of water.

__[Simple]__ 29. The ship is now being coated with a water-soluble wax polyethylene to help preserve it.

__[Compound]__ 30. This process will be completed in several years, and the ship will then go through a drying process.

Try It Yourself

On a separate sheet of paper, write five or six sentences about an animal you would like to study. Vary your writing by including different kinds of sentences.

Check Your Own Work

Choose a selection from your writing portfolio, a journal, a work in progress, an assignment from class, or a letter. Revise it, applying the skills you have learned in this section. This checklist will help you.

✔ Have you varied your sentences, using simple, compound, and complex sentences when appropriate?

✔ Have you combined sentence parts correctly?

Name _____

121. Coordinating Conjunctions

> A **coordinating conjunction** joins words or groups of words that are similar. It can also connect independent clauses to form compound sentences. The coordinating conjunctions are *and, but, or, nor, so,* and *yet.*
>
> **Elizabeth I ruled England and Ireland.** (words)
> **Her reign was troubled by religious unrest at home and by tensions with continental powers.** (phrases)
> **The political achievements during her reign were impressive, but the artistic achievements also were impressive.** (clauses)

Circle the coordinating conjunction in each sentence. Underline the words or groups of words it joins. On the line write **W** to tell if it joins words, **P** if it joins phrases, and **C** if it joins clauses.

[C]   1. Elizabeth's reign lasted more than four decades, (and) she is considered one of England's most famous rulers.

[W]   2. There were great achievements (and) prosperity during her reign.

[C]   3. She ruled England from 1558 to 1603, (so) this period is commonly referred to as the Elizabethan Age.

[P]   4. This was a time for the English nation (and) for English arts to flourish.

[W]   5. Elizabethan dramatists include Shakespeare (and) Christopher Marlowe.

[C]   6. Elizabeth became queen, (but) she had had a difficult childhood.

[C]   7. She was locked in the Tower of London for two months, (and) she was threatened with execution.

[C]   8. Elizabeth earlier had supported her sister Mary's becoming queen, (yet) Mary had her imprisoned.

[C]   9. Elizabeth was young at the start of her reign, (but) she ruled with great intelligence.

[P]   10. She had grown into a striking young lady who did not use cosmetics (or) wear fancy clothes.

[C]   11. During her reign the English navy defeated the Spanish Armada, (so) England became a great sea power.

[W]   12. This helped the nation's merchants (and) its economy.

[P]   13. England prospered despite foreign threats (and) despite religious unrest.

[P]   14. Elizabeth was dedicated to her country (and) to her people.

[W]   15. Her reign is noted for its poets (and) dramatists.

Queen Elizabeth I was a supporter of writers, artists, and musicians. Describe a way you can encourage the creativity of others.

131

122. Correlative Conjunctions

> **Correlative conjunctions** are conjunctions that are used in pairs to connect words or groups of words that have parallel structure in a sentence. The most commonly used correlative conjunctions are *both . . . and, either . . . or, neither . . . nor, not only . . . but also,* and *whether . . . or.*

Circle the correlative conjunctions in each sentence. Underline the words or phrases they connect.

1. Historians think Native Americans crossed over from Asia (either) as late as 12,000 years ago (or) as early as 40,000 years ago.

2. (Whether) at the earlier date (or) at the later date, they probably came from Siberia.

3. Early Americans were (both) hunters (and) farmers.

4. Native Americans lived (either) in permanent houses (or) in portable ones.

5. Some had (not only) winter homes (but also) summer homes.

6. Many lived in (either) towns (or) small villages.

7. Native Americans wore clothes of (either) animal skin (or) plant fiber.

8. Because these Native Americans had (neither) horses (nor) oxen, they often traveled by water in canoes.

9. (Both) corn (and) beans, which could be stored and dried, were important in the diet of Native Americans in the East.

10. These crops were rich (not only) in protein (but also) in essential vitamins.

11. (Both) beans (and) squash were often planted in the same field as corn.

12. The squash served (both) to choke weeds (and) to keep the ground moist.

13. Different groups of Native Americans worshiped different gods, some of which were (either) the sun (or) animals like buffalo.

14. Religious leaders called shamans had the power (not only) to contact the spirit world (but also) to help in healing.

15. A shaman might use (both) spiritual power (and) herbal medicines in treating an illness.

16. (Both) men (and) women were usually involved in providing food, but they would likely have had different tasks.

17. Europeans had (neither) corn (nor) tomatoes before their arrival in the Americas.

18. (Neither) horses (nor) sheep were known to Native Americans before Europeans arrived.

19. (Both) the Native Americans (and) the Europeans changed because of their contact with each other in North America.

20. Some regional cultures embrace (not only) European (but also) Native American ways.

Name _____

123. Conjunctive Adverbs

> A **conjunctive adverb** connects independent clauses and helps to make their relationship clear. Some common conjunctive adverbs are *also, besides, consequently, however, in fact, later, moreover, nevertheless, otherwise, still,* and *therefore.* When a conjunctive adverb connects clauses, a semicolon is used before it and a comma after it.

A. Underline the conjunctive adverb in each sentence.

1. One of the most famous diamonds in the world is a large blue diamond with a reddish tint called the Hope Diamond; <u>indeed</u>, it has a fascinating history.

2. A merchant bought a 112-carat diamond in India; <u>later</u>, he sold it to King Louis XIV.

3. The diamond became part of the French crown jewels; <u>in fact</u>, the king himself wore it.

4. During the French Revolution King Louis XVI tried to flee with the jewels; <u>consequently</u>, the revolutionary government seized them.

5. Later the jewels were stolen, and people thought they had been lost forever; <u>however</u>, in 1812 a 45-carat blue diamond appeared on the English market.

B. Combine each pair of sentences into a single compound sentence. Choose the correct conjunctive adverb in parentheses. Add semicolons and commas as needed.

1. The thieves would not have wanted to get caught. (Therefore Moreover) they would likely have had the diamond cut again to alter its appearance.
[The thieves would not have wanted to get caught; therefore, they would likely have had the diamond cut again to alter its appearance.]

2. The Hope Diamond is smaller than the original diamond. (Still Moreover) it is striking.
[The Hope Diamond is smaller than the original diamond; still, it is striking.]

3. One of its owners was named Hope. (Nevertheless Consequently) it was given that name.
[One of its owners was named Hope; consequently, it was given that name.]

4. The Hope Diamond had several other owners. (Finally Therefore) it became part of a collection at the Smithsonian Institution in Washington, D.C.
[The Hope Diamond had several other owners; finally, it became part of a collection at the Smithsonian Institution in Washington, D.C.]

5. Recent research seems to confirm that the Hope Diamond was cut from the lost French diamond. (However In fact) some of its sides may even be the same.
[Recent research seems to confirm that the Hope Diamond was cut from the lost French diamond; in fact, some of its sides may even be the same.]

124. Subordinate Conjunctions

> A **subordinate conjunction** is used to join an independent clause and a dependent clause and to indicate their relationship. Subordinate conjunctions generally introduce adverb clauses. Common subordinate conjunctions are *after, although, because, before, even though, if, in order that, since, so that, than, when,* and *while.*
>
> INDEPENDENT CLAUSE   SUBORDINATE CONJUNCTION IN THE DEPENDENT CLAUSE
> **Ludwig wanted to practice**   **even though** his elbow ached.

A. Circle each subordinate conjunction. Underline each dependent clause.

1. (Although) she is fictitious, Rosie the Riveter played an important role in World War II.

2. (Before) the war started, most American women did not work outside their homes.

3. Many jobs were left vacant, however, (when) men began enlisting in the army.

4. (Because) a war was being fought, production of certain goods had to be increased.

5. Something had to be done (so that) America's productivity did not decline during the war.

6. (Since) help was needed to maintain production, an ad campaign was designed to recruit women.

7. Rosie the Riveter was created (in order that) women would view factory work as patriotic.

8. (Before) the war was over, more than six million women had joined the workforce.

9. The needs of Americans would not have been met (if) it had not been for their help.

10. (Although) many lost their jobs after the war, these women helped make working outside the home acceptable.

B. Write sentences, using the following dependent clauses. [Sample answers are given.]

because it was cold inside   1. [Sara wore a jacket because it was cold inside.]

if we are going   2. [If we are going, we need to leave now.]

unless we hear otherwise   3. [The dance is in the auditorium unless we hear otherwise.]

although it was raining   4. [Although it was raining, we stood in line for tickets.]

so that everyone gets a turn   5. [Make a single-file line so that everyone gets a turn.]

125. Troublesome Conjunctions

> Some conjunctions are frequently confused with prepositions. *Without* is a preposition; it helps form a prepositional phrase. *Unless* is a subordinate conjunction; it introduces an adverb clause.
>
> **They will be lost <u>without</u> a map.**
> **They will get lost <u>unless</u> you go with them.**
>
> *Like* is a preposition. *As if* is a subordinate conjunction used to introduce an adverb clause. *As* can function as a preposition or a conjunction.
>
> **Animals <u>like</u> zebras and cheetahs appear in my favorite nature films.**
> **Sometimes I act <u>as if</u> I am on a safari, preparing to shoot a movie.**
> **My brother, <u>as</u> the movie's director, likes to order me around.**
> **<u>As</u> we move across the jungle in our backyard, I can just see the wild animals.**

A. Circle the correct word in parentheses.

1. You won't see a camel in America ((unless) without) you go to a zoo.

2. Camels have been introduced to America but (unless (without)) success.

3. They can bear severe heat (like (as if)) it were nothing.

4. Camels can go ((without) unless) water for several days.

5. They can also drink salt water ((without) unless) getting sick.

6. Many people think a camel's hump acts ((as) as if) a storage area.

7. The hump actually contains fat that is absorbed (like (as)) the camel needs energy.

8. During sandstorms a camel's nostrils can close (like (as)) shutters do.

9. A camel, (as (like)) a giraffe, runs with both legs on one side moving at the same time.

10. I would not want to cross a desert (without (unless)) I had a camel.

B. Complete each sentence with the correct word: *without, unless, as,* or *like.*

1. _____[As]_____ a fire moves across land, it usually kills the vegetation in its path.

2. One type of protea flower cannot survive, however, _____[without]_____ fire.

3. Seeds _____[like]_____ large nuts remain in the flower head for a year.

4. _____[Unless]_____ the plant is scorched by fire, it will not release its seeds.

5. _____[As]_____ the fire passes, the bracts open, and the protea seeds are released.

6. The plant will retain the seeds until it dies _____[unless]_____ there is a fire.

7. Fire permits sunlight to reach small plants _____[as]_____ it destroys large shade trees.

8. The ashes also act _____[as]_____ fertilizer for the soil.

9. _____[Without]_____ these advantages the protea would have difficulty surviving.

10. So the fire, _____[like]_____ a sign, tells the plant it is okay to release its seeds.

126. Interjections

> An **interjection** is a word that expresses a strong or sudden emotion, such as delight, anger, surprise, anticipation, warning, impatience, pain, or wonder. An interjection may be set off from the rest of a sentence by an exclamation point. It may also function as part of an exclamatory sentence; if so, it is followed by a comma.
>
> **Ouch! The sand is hot.**
> **Wow, the view from here is incredible!**

A. Underline the interjection. Write on the line what emotion it expresses. **[Sample answers are given.]**

[wonder]	1. Listen! You can hear the waves crashing on the beach.
[anticipation]	2. Hello! Is anyone at home?
[warning]	3. Careful! The lifeguard said there is an undertow.
[anger]	4. Goodness! This mattress must be filled with rocks.
[impatience]	5. Quiet! The baby is sleeping.
[impatience]	6. See, that is what happens when you leave milk out overnight!
[wonder]	7. Look! There are dolphins playing in the water.
[surprise]	8. Oh! I did not know anyone was in here.
[pain]	9. Enough, that really hurts!
[anger]	10. Hey! No pets are allowed in the museum.

B. Write a sentence, using an interjection to express each emotion. **[Sample answers given.]**

pain	1.	**[Ouch! The water is hot.]**
joy	2.	**[Yes! Tomorrow is a holiday.]**
assent	3.	**[Okay, I admit you were right!]**
disgust	4.	**[Whew! It must be 100 degrees in here.]**
wonder	5.	**[Wow! It's amazing the way the sun sets over the lake.]**
impatience	6.	**[Quiet! I can't hear myself think.]**
surprise	7.	**[What! You still haven't finished your homework?]**
sorrow	8.	**[Gee, our basketball team won only two games this year!]**
warning	9.	**[Beware! That ice is really slippery.]**
delight	10.	**[Oh my! German chocolate is my favorite.]**

Conjunctions and Interjections

127. Reviewing Conjunctions and Interjections

A. On the line describe the *italicized* word(s) by writing **A** for a coordinating conjunction, **B** for correlative conjunctions, **C** for a subordinate conjunction, or **D** for a conjunctive adverb.

__[C]__ 1. *Although* its name implies something else, the Dead Sea is actually a lake.

__[D]__ 2. It does sustain life forms; *therefore*, it is not really dead.

__[D]__ 3. Fish cannot live in its salty water; *however*, some salt-loving microorganisms thrive there.

__[B]__ 4. Scientists have discovered that these microorganisms *not only* cope *but also* become addicted to the salt.

__[C]__ 5. The Dead Sea contains seven times more salt *than* seawater contains.

__[A]__ 6. Nearly a third of the lake consists of salt *and* other solid minerals.

__[C]__ 7. *Because* the water is so dense, a human body can float easily on its surface.

__[A]__ 8. The Dead Sea is fed by the Jordan River *and* several smaller streams.

__[D]__ 9. The lake has no outlet; *consequently*, water is carried off solely by evaporation.

__[B]__ 10. The ruins of *both* Sodom *and* Gomorrah, ancient Biblical cities, are believed to lie beneath the lake.

B. Underline the coordinating conjunction, correlative conjunctions, subordinate conjunction, or conjunctive adverb in each sentence. On the line describe the words you underline, using the letters from Exercise A.

__[D]__ 11. Lake Baikal was formed about 25 million years ago; therefore, it is believed to be the world's oldest lake.

__[C]__ 12. Because the lake lies far north in Siberia, it is frozen from January to May.

__[A]__ 13. About 335 rivers and streams flow into Lake Baikal, but only one flows out.

__[B]__ 14. Both parks and nature reserves lie along the lake's shore.

__[D]__ 15. Lake Baikal is the deepest lake in the world; in fact, it contains about 20 percent of the world's unfrozen fresh water.

__[D]__ 16. Lake Baikal has about 15,000 species unique to it; therefore, it has been compared to the Galapagos Islands off South America.

__[A]__ 17. Lake Baikal is visited and studied by many scientists.

__[A]__ 18. The unusual wildlife of the lake includes a fish called golomyanka and a freshwater seal called the Baikal seal.

__[C]__ 19. Although attempts are being made to preserve the lake, there is increasing pollution.

__[B]__ 20. Neither the water nor the air in the area has retained the degree of cleanliness it had in the recent past.

C. Circle the coordinating conjunction or the correlative conjunctions. Underline the word or groups of words that are connected.

21. (Both) the Dead Sea (and) the Great Salt Lake are very salty.

22. (Neither) the Dead Sea (nor) the Great Salt Lake has any outflowing streams.

23. The Great Salt Lake is fed by three major rivers (and) rainfall.

24. Several minor streams flow into the Great Salt Lake, (but) none flows out.

25. The lake is enjoyed (not only) by swimmers (but also) by boaters.

D. Circle each subordinate conjunction. Underline each dependent clause.

26. The Great Salt Lake has been divided into north and south sections (since) a railroad causeway was constructed through it in 1959.

27. (After) I read about the lake, I wanted to visit it.

28. The salt remains in the Great Salt Lake (when) evaporation occurs.

E. Complete each sentence with an appropriate conjunctive adverb. **[Answers may vary.]**

29. Visitors can swim or boat on the lake; _____**[in addition]**_____, they can visit a state park.

30. The waters in the northern part of the lake are extremely salty; _____**[therefore]**_____, only salt-loving algae and bacteria live there.

31. Few organisms exist in the northern part of the lake; _____**[however]**_____, the southern part has shrimp and flies on which birds feed.

F. Add an appropriate interjection to each item. **[Answers may vary.]**

32. _____**[Great!]**_____ You finally got to visit the Great Salt Lake.

33. _____**[Horrors!]**_____ What happened to all your photos?

34. _____**[Wonderful!]**_____ You got to see buffalo on the island.

35. _____**[Oh no!]**_____ You didn't get to float on the lake.

Try It Yourself
On a separate sheet of paper, write about some places that you would like to visit and what you would do in each.

Check Your Own Work
Choose a selection from your writing portfolio, your journal, a work in progress, an assignment from another class, or a letter. Revise it, applying the skills you have learned. This checklist will help you.

✔ Have you used conjunctions correctly?

✔ Do the coordinating conjunctions and correlative conjunctions connect words or phrases that are parallel in form?

128. Periods

> A **period** is used
> - at the end of a declarative or an imperative sentence
>
>   **You read** *The Golden Compass*.
>   **Tell me about the book.**
> - after most abbreviations, such as titles and standard measurements (but not metric measurements)
>
> | | | | |
> |---|---|---|---|
> | Gov. | Governor | a.m. | before noon |
> | St. | Street | Feb. | February |
> | Inc. | Incorporated | pt. | pint |
>
> - after the initials in a name
>
>   F. D. Roosevelt   Franklin Delano Roosevelt
>   T. A. Edison   Thomas Alva Edison

A. Rewrite the following phrases, substituting abbreviations and adding periods as appropriate.

1. Patricia A Vogel, MD   [Patricia A. Vogel, M.D.]

2. 4 yards   [4 yd.]

3. Tuesday, January 11, 2006   [Tues., Jan. 11, 2006]

4. Doctor Martin Luther King, Junior   [Dr. Martin Luther King, Jr.]

5. 147 East Lincoln Avenue   [174 E. Lincoln Ave.]

B. Add periods where needed in the following sentences.

1. Janet S. Anderson's *Going Through the Gate* is a suspenseful fantasy with an unusual teacher as a main character.

2. Everyone in my class has read at least one of J.K. Rowling's Harry Potter books.

3. S.E. Hinton's *The Outsiders* is the story of three children trying to stay together after their parents' death.

4. Ernest J. Gaines's *The Autobiography of Miss Jane Pittman* tells the story of an African-American woman and the US. civil rights movement from the time of the Civil War to the 1960s.

5. *Don't Sweat the Small Stuff* by Richard Carlson, PhD, is a self-help book.

6. Our librarian, Mr. Robertson, recommended that we read J.R.R. Tolkien's *The Lord of the Rings*.

7. Dr. Seuss was the pen name of Theodor Seuss Geisel, who wrote many popular books for young children.

8. Robert C. O'Brien's *The Silver Crown* is a book I've read several times.

9. There are several poems in English and in Spanish by Francisco X. Alarcon in our literature anthology.

10. Mrs. Harding assigned us to read two of O. Henry's short stories.

129. Commas–Part I

Commas are used to separate words in a series of three or more and to separate adjectives of equal importance in front of a noun.

> **Yellowstone National Park, the Grand Canyon, and Niagara Falls are a few of America's natural wonders.**
> **A tall, powerful, steamy gush of water in the air means a geyser is erupting.**

A. Add commas where needed.

1. Yellowstone National Park is located in Idaho, Montana, and Wyoming.

2. The geology of the area was affected by an ancient volcanic eruption that sent ash over all of the western United States, much of the Midwest, and northern Mexico.

3. The volcanic magma under the surface of the earth is the cause of the geysers, hot springs, and muddy pools that rise to the surface of the land.

4. In 1871 an expedition that included the geologist Ferdinand Hayden, the artist Thomas Moran, and the photographer William Henry Jackson helped convince Congress to make Yellowstone a national park.

5. A special program teaches students about the history of the park, investigates issues related to the park's ecosystem, and promotes preservation of the park.

6. Old Faithful, Castle, and Giantess are three of the geysers in the park.

7. The bubbly, steamy, muddy pools in the park are called mudpots.

8. A mountain of black glass formed by lava, a petrified forest, and terraces of falling water are among the unusual features of the park.

9. Trumpeter swans, white pelicans, and blue herons feed in its lakes and rivers.

10. The park has canyons, mountains, forests, and meadows.

B. Rewrite the following sentences to show correct use of commas. Not all of the sentences are incorrect.

1. Visitors can ride horses, hike and even ski at Yellowstone.
   [Visitors can ride horses, hike, and even ski at Yellowstone.]

2. Waterfalls, lakes, and geysers are some of the attractions of the park.

   _____

3. Wildlife in the park includes bears, elk and buffalo.
   [Wildlife in the park includes bears, elk, and buffalo.]

4. Buffalo live, roam and graze, in the park.
   [Buffalo live, roam, and graze in the park.]

5. Rangers naturalists, and a maintenance staff work in the park.
   [Rangers, naturalists, and a maintenance staff work in the park.]

   _____

Name _____

130. Commas—Part II

> A comma is used
> - to set off words in direct address
>   **Have you ever experienced a tropical storm, Rita?**
> - to set off parts of addresses, place names, and dates
>   **The concert was held at Madison Square Garden in New York, New York.**
>   **October 15, 2003, was a memorable day in Justin's life.**
> - after the salutation in a friendly letter and after the complimentary close in all letters
>   **Dear Ginny,**   **Very truly yours,**

A. Add commas where needed in this e-mail.

January 8, 20—

Dear Elena,

   My cousin works at the National Hurricane Center in Miami, Florida. When we visit there, she's going to arrange for us to tour the center. Do you want to come with me and my family? Our tour is scheduled for February 11, 20—, unless there is a change of date.
   Write soon and let me know!

Your friend,
Arianna

B. Add commas where they are needed.

1. Can you tell me what a hurricane is, class?

2. Did you know that one of the worst weather disasters in U.S. history was a hurricane that hit Galveston, Texas?

3. The hurricane struck on September 8, 1900.

4. Frederick, more than 6,000 people died in the terrible storm and the huge wave that followed it.

5. Another fierce hurricane took place in 1969, Jackie.

6. It was a hurricane named Camille that struck land on August 17, 1969.

7. Louis, more than 27 inches of rain fell on parts of Virginia in less than 24 hours in the aftermath of that hurricane.

8. The World Meteorological Organization in Geneva, Switzerland, names hurricanes.

9. The National Hurricane Center, which gives tours, is located at the following:
National Hurricane Center
11691 S. W. 17th Street
Miami, FL 33165

10. Camp Springs, Maryland, is the home office of the National Weather Service.

131. Commas–Part III

> Commas are used to set off nonrestrictive phrases and clauses. Nonrestrictive phrases are not necessary to the meaning of a sentence; they provide additional information.
>
> **Washington, D.C., the nation's capital, has many famous monuments. The Washington Monument, which stands on the Mall, is perhaps the most famous monument in the capital.**

A. Add commas to set off nonrestrictive phrases and clauses.

1. One of the most powerful of all monuments in Washington, D.C., is the Vietnam Memorial, which honors the dead U.S. military personnel from the Vietnam War.

2. The war, which took place in the 1960s and 1970s, divided the American public.

3. In 1981 a committee, which consisted of architects and designers, selected the best plan for the monument from many entries.

4. The winning entry was from Maya Lin, a 21-year-old student at Yale.

5. The design, which is basically a polished black granite slab, has the names of more than 58,000 men and women carved into it.

6. The Vietnam Memorial, now one of the most frequently visited memorials in the United States, is considered striking by most people.

7. Lin, today a respected architect, has her own design studio in New York.

8. Lin, who has designed structures in many cities, continues to produce original works.

9. Her designs, which include buildings and memorials, are much sought after.

10. The Civil Rights Memorial, a monument in Alabama honoring those who died in the struggle for civil rights, was designed by Lin.

B. Rewrite the following sentences, adding commas where necessary. Not all sentences are incorrect.

1. Maya Lin a famous architect and designer was born in Ohio in 1960.
   [Maya Lin, a famous architect and designer, was born in Ohio in 1960.]

2. Lin a Chinese American, takes inspiration from many sources.
   [Lin, a Chinese American, takes inspiration from many sources.]

3. These sources, which include Japanese gardens and Native American tombs, are varied.

   _____

4. Her buildings and monuments which are usually specific to a given site are often dramatic.
   [Her buildings and monuments, which are usually specific to a given site, are often dramatic.]

5. My family's next vacation a trip to one of Lin's recent monuments was my suggestion.
   [My family's next vacation, a trip to one of Lin's recent monuments, was my suggestion.]

132. Commas–Part IV

> Commas are used before coordinating conjunctions when they are used to connect clauses in a sentence and after conjunctive adverbs in compound sentences.
>
> **Petra is an ancient city, and it is now a World Heritage Site.**
> **Petra was long abandoned; therefore, its monuments lay undisturbed for centuries.**

A. Add commas where needed.

1. Petra is an ancient city in Jordan, but it has long been abandoned.

2. The city was carved from rose-colored rock; consequently, its site is quite beautiful.

3. Petra was in a central location in the Middle East; therefore, it became a trading center.

4. Petra prospered from farming; moreover, it was on a main caravan route.

5. The city could be reached only through a narrow pass; consequently, it was easy to defend.

6. Petra was noted for its complex irrigation system, and its builders are considered geniuses for how they made the most of an average yearly rainfall of only six inches.

7. Petra flourished from 400 to 100 BC, but it was conquered by Roman troops in AD 106.

8. Many of the buildings in Petra are tombs; however, no bodies have been found in them.

9. The walls of the tombs at Petra are dramatically colored magenta and blue, and their interiors are truly works of art.

10. These colorful walls were not painted by humans; in fact, their dramatic colors result from the natural colors of the rocks.

B. Combine each pair of sentences into a compound sentence. Use the coordinating conjunction or the semicolon and conjunctive adverb given. Add commas where needed.

1. Many tourists visit Petra. They represent a danger to its conservation. (and)
   [Many tourists visit Petra, and they represent a danger to its conservation.]

2. The site of Petra is extensive. Its ruins spread over 400 square miles. (; in fact)
   [The site of Petra is extensive; in fact, its ruins spread over 400 square miles.]

3. You have to walk a mile to enter the city. You can ride a horse or a horse-drawn cart. (or)
   [You have to walk a mile to enter the city, or you can ride a horse or a horse-drawn cart.]

4. Petra's most famous monument is the Treasury. The building has an elaborate, carved facade. (and)
   [Petra's most famous monument is the Treasury, and the building has an elaborate, carved facade.]

5. Petra's tombs and temples are magnificent. The pottery found there is of high artistic quality. (; in addition)
   [Petra's tombs and temples are magnificent; in addition, the pottery found there is of high

   artistic quality.]

133. Exclamation Points and Question Marks

An **exclamation point** is used after an interjection or to end an exclamatory sentence.

> **Wow! You have a great bike.**
> **What a sleek-looking bike you have!**

A **question mark** is used to end an interrogative sentence.

> **Are you interested in bike racing?**

Add exclamation points and question marks where needed.
Also add periods as end marks where needed. **[Some answers may vary.]**

1. Do you know the story of Lance Armstrong?

2. Incredible! He won the Tour de France seven times.

3. What is the Tour de France?

4. Isn't it the most famous bicycle race in the world?

5. What a grueling bicycle race it is!

6. It usually lasts three weeks.

7. Wow! The riders even have to race up mountains.

8. What do you know about racing bikes?

9. I read that this type of bike is very lightweight, with a frame weighing only three pounds.

10. Lance's feat is so impressive!

11. Only one previous racer had won the race as many as five times.

12. Did you know that Lance won all these races after he had treatments for cancer?

13. He had to undergo chemotherapy and surgeries.

14. He was determined, however, that he would race again.

15. What a great athlete he is!

16. Amazing! Lance won the event for the first time in 1999, a few years after his treatments.

17. Tremendous! He formed a foundation to help cancer patients.

18. Have you seen people wearing yellow wristbands to show their support for the foundation?

19. Where can I find out more about this splendid athlete?

20. Wait a minute! I need more information on the next bike race.

134. Semicolons and Colons

A **semicolon** is used
- to separate independent clauses in a compound sentence when the clauses are not joined by a conjunction

  Albert Schweitzer was first a musician and then a theologian; he eventually studied medicine also.

- to separate independent clauses in a compound sentence when the clauses are joined by a conjunctive adverb

  Albert Schweitzer first lived in France and Germany; however, he spent most of his life in Africa.

- to separate phrases or clauses of the same type that include internal punctuation

  Eventually he and his work received international recognition: honorary degrees; the Goethe Prize from Frankfurt, Germany; and the Nobel Peace Prize.

- before expressions such as *for example* and *namely* when they are used to introduce examples

  Schweitzer decided on his life's mission; namely, to serve the poor in Africa directly as a doctor.

A **colon** is used
- before a list of terms. A color never follows a verb.

  Schweitzer excelled in the following areas: music, theology, and humanitarianism.

- after the salutation of a business letter

  Dear Sir or Madam:

Insert semicolons and colons where needed.

1. An act of heroism can last a moment;for Albert Schweitzer it lasted a lifetime.

2. By age 28 Schweitzer had tried the following occupations:pastor, musician, author, and professor.

3. He felt that his life was empty;however, he eventually found his life's mission.

4. Schweitzer learned of the appalling problems in Africa:poverty;war;and diseases such as malaria, leprosy, and sleeping sickness.

5. He decided what he would do;namely, become a doctor and run a hospital in Africa.

6. His first year was full of the following activities:gaining hospital experience, learning about Africa, and raising funds.

7. French Equatorial Africa became Schweitzer's home;he set up a clinic in the city of Lambaréné.

8. His wife became his assistant;she was a trained nurse.

9. The hospital became famous;in fact, Schweitzer became known around the world.

10. In 1952 he was awarded a Nobel Peace Prize;it was a fitting tribute to a man who had nobly served so many people who needed help.

135. Quotation Marks and Italics

Quotation marks are used
- to enclose dialogue and direct quotations. Single quotation marks set off a quotation within a quotation.

    "When," asked my father, "did an American soldier say, 'Lafayette, we are here'?"
- to set off the titles of stories, poems, songs, magazine articles, episodes in a TV series, and radio programs

Italics are used for titles of books, movies, plays, newspapers, magazines, and works of art. In handwritten material, underlining is used to indicate italics.

A. Insert quotation marks and underlining where necessary.

1. "Be quiet!" said Olive, "I'm reading the <u>Tribune</u>."

2. Joseph's favorite poem is "The Charge of the Light Brigade."

3. Thoreau wrote the book <u>Walden</u> and the essay "Civil Disobedience."

4. "I lost my copy of <u>Great Expectations</u>," Oswald said.

5. "How long does <u>Sixty Minutes</u> last?" Jacob asked jokingly.

6. "I thought it was fun," Al said, "when we sang 'Hail to the Chief.'"

7. "What time," asked Marge, "does the movie <u>My Fair Lady</u> start?"

8. The teacher asked, "Have any of you read <u>Lord of the Flies</u>?"

9. Have you ever heard of the <u>Inner Sanctum</u> radio program?

10. For his birthday Noam got a subscription to <u>National Geographic</u>.

B. Rewrite each sentence, adding punctuation where needed.

1. The monkeys said Josephine are my favorite animals at the zoo
   ["The monkeys," said Josephine, "are my favorite animals at the zoo."]

2. Twain wrote the novel Tom Sawyer and the short story The War Prayer
   [Twain wrote the novel <u>Tom Sawyer</u> and the short story "The War Prayer."]

3. Look exclaimed Mr Donahue my picture is in the Chicago Tribune
   ["Look," exclaimed Mr. Donahue, "my picture is in the <u>Chicago Tribune</u>!"]

4. Buzz Lightyear said Jane is my favorite character in Toy Story
   ["Buzz Lightyear," said Jane, "is my favorite character in <u>Toy Story</u>."]

5. The last time I saw him Harper told me he said I want to be a dancer
   ["The last time I saw him," Harper told me, "he said, 'I want to be a dancer.'"]

Name _____

136. Apostrophes, Hyphens, and Dashes

An apostrophe is used
- to show possession: **Ed's car, the Caseys' house**
- to show omission of letters or numbers: **isn't, '20s**
- to show the plural of small letters but not capital letters unless the plural could be mistaken for a word: **r's, Rs, I's**

A hyphen is used
- to connect the parts of a compound number: **eighty-five, ninety-three**
- to separate the parts of some compound words: **run-through**
- to divide a word between syllables at the end of a line

A dash indicates a sudden change of thought.
> **The test—it covers three chapters—is next week.**

A. Insert apostrophes, hyphens, dashes, and other punctuation as needed.

1. Dont think that just anyone can run for the U.S. presidency!

2. The president and the vice president must be at least 35 years old.

3. They must also be natural-born citizens of the United States.

4. The first seven presidents werent born U.S. citizens.

5. They were born subjects of England the United States didnt exist yet.

6. Presidents whove been elected to two terms are rare.

7. Few presidents only 17 out of 44 have done so.

8. Franklin Roosevelt he was Teddy Roosevelts cousin was elected four times.

9. But Roosevelts long tenure 12 years prompted new legislation.

10. Now presidents may serve only two four-year terms.

B. Rewrite the following sentences, adding apostrophes, hyphens, dashes, and other punctuation as needed.

1. Youre still going to Dr. Salks house, arent you
   [You're still going to Dr. Salk's house, aren't you?]

2. Herberts keyboard it doesnt have any is or us is broken
   [Herbert's keyboard—it doesn't have any i's or u's—is broken.]

3. By midJanuary all of Jurgens relatives had gone back to Germany
   [By mid-January all of Jurgen's relatives had gone back to Germany.]

4. Julias birthday she will be 38 years old is tomorrow
   [Julia's birthday—she will be 38 years old—is tomorrow.]

5. I didnt see the display of womens clothing
   [I didn't see the display of women's clothing.]

147

Name _____

137. Capital Letters

Use a capital letter for the following:

- the first word in a sentence
- the first word of a direct quotation
- the first word of most lines of poetry
- the titles of books, plays, poems, and works of art
- proper names and adjectives
- a title when it precedes a person's name

- the names of deities and of sacred books
- the pronoun *I*
- North, East, South, and West when referring to sections of the country
- abbreviations when capital letters would be used if the words were written out

A. Rewrite each item, capitalizing letters where necessary.

1. eva l. sloan, ph.d. _____ [Eva L. Sloan, Ph.D.]

2. republican party _____ [Republican Party]

3. ohio river _____ [Ohio River]

4. private college _____ [private college]

5. professor reiss _____ [Professor Reiss]

6. fourth of july _____ [Fourth of July]

7. jesus christ _____ [Jesus Christ]

8. friday, may 3 _____ [Friday, May 3]

9. doctor _____ [doctor]

10. george w. bush _____ [George W. Bush]

B. Circle all letters that should be capitalized.

1. (b)enjamin (f)ranklin was an (a)merican author, scientist, and statesman.

2. (h)e helped draft the (d)eclaration of (i)ndependence.

3. (o)f this, he said, "(w)e must all hang together, or assuredly we will all hang separately."

4. (h)e was a member of the (p)ennsylvania (a)ssembly for 12 years.

5. (a)fter the (r)evolutionary (w)ar (f)ranklin helped to negotiate the treaty with (g)reat (b)ritain.

6. (t)he treaty was signed at (v)ersailles, (f)rance, on (s)eptember 3, 1783.

7. (i)n 1732 he published (p)oor (r)ichard's (a)lmanac.

8. (i)n it he coined many phrases, such as, "(p)ractice makes perfect."

9. (h)e also wrote (t)he (a)utobiography of (b)enjamin (f)ranklin.

10. (a)s president of the (p)ennsylvania (a)bolition (s)ociety, he urged the abolition of slavery.

138. Reviewing Punctuation and Capitalization

A. Insert commas, periods, question marks, and exclamation points where needed.

1. Have you ever read *The War of the Worlds*?

2. It is about Martians attacking Earth.

3. How scary!

4. It was written by H.G.Wells.

5. He is well known for his stories of fantasy, technology, and science fiction.

6. H.G.Wells also wrote *The Time Machine*, *The Invisible Man*, and *Ann Veronica*.

7. *The War of the Worlds* was adapted and performed on the radio by Orson Welles in 1938.

8. What happened?

9. Many people, believing the radio program was a news broadcast, thought Earth was really being attacked.

10. That's frightening!

B. Insert colons, semicolons, and quotation marks where needed.

11. Brook's father told her to do the following: mow, rake, and weed the lawn.

12. "But I'm tired," she pleaded.

13. Her father said, "Then you should not have stayed up all night."

14. She had rented some movies the night before; therefore, she was up very late.

15. Brook watched three movies: *Casablanca, Gigi,* and *Ben-Hur.*

16. "If you get started now," her father said, "you can finish by nightfall."

17. She was exhausted; nevertheless, she would do what he asked.

18. "When I was a boy," her father said, "we worked all day, or we didn't eat."

19. "Here we go again," she thought to herself.

20. Brook worked all afternoon; she finished just before dark.

C. Insert hyphens, apostrophes, and dashes where needed.

21. The fastest-growing tree on Earth is a member of the pea family.

22. One specimen grew thirty-five feet in a year.

23. The tallest tree—though not the largest—is the sequoia.

CONTINUED

24. Some oldgrowth specimens are more than 300 feet high.

25. The worlds largest tree is the redwood.

26. A redwoods weight can be more than 200 tons.

27. Its not the oldest tree, however.

28. One species of pine the worlds oldest tree can live 5,000 years.

29. These trees arent necessarily the oldest living things on Earth.

30. Lichens plants made up of algae and fungus are also thousands of years old.

D. Circle the example of correct capitalization in each row.

31. (Harvard University)	world war II	Mexican Silver
32. Mathematics	(East Coast)	Sears tower
33. (Tuesday)	Third avenue	asian
34. republicans	(Lutherans)	aunt Helga
35. *Of Mice And Men*	memorial day	(spring in Paris)
36. Nile river	sir Isaac Newton	(October)
37. (Canadian border)	Pacific ocean	Lakeview high school
38. Dictionary	middle East	(Buddha)
39. bible	Gettysburg address	(*The Time Machine*)
40. Frederick the great	(Russian history)	Dentist

Try It Yourself

On a separate sheet of paper, write six or seven sentences about what you will do after you have completed eighth grade. Be sure to punctuate your sentences carefully and correctly.

Check Your Own Work

Choose a selection from your writing portfolio. Revise it, applying the skills you have learned in this chapter. This checklist will help you.

✔ Do your sentences end with the correct punctuation?

✔ Have you used commas correctly?

✔ Have you used quotation marks before and after every quotation and around certain titles?

✔ Have you capitalized all proper nouns and adjectives?

✔ Have you used semicolons, colons, hyphens, and dashes where needed?

139. Simple Sentences

A **diagram** is a visual outline of a sentence. It shows the relationship between the words in a sentence.

- The subject, the verb, the direct object, the subject complement, and the object complement go on the main horizontal line.

- A vertical line that cuts through the main line separates the subject from the verb, and a vertical line that does not cut through the main line separates the direct object from the verb.

- A line that slants left separates a subject complement from the verb, and a line that slants right separates an object complement from the direct object.

- Indirect objects, adjectives, and adverbs are placed under the words to which they relate. Prepositional phrases, which usually act as adjectives or adverbs, go under the words they describe.

SENTENCE: **Richard gave Will advice.**

Richard | gave | advice
                \ Will

SENTENCE: **The cookies are chewy.**

cookies | are \ chewy
The

SENTENCE: **We elected Elaine secretary.**

We | elected | Elaine / secretary

SENTENCE: **The sleek horse ran swiftly.**

horse | ran
The sleek swiftly

SENTENCE: **The horse with the shiny black coat ran around the track.**

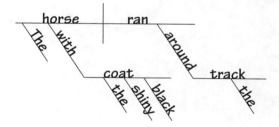

horse | ran
The with around
coat track
the shiny black the

Diagram each sentence.

1. My favorite subject is science.

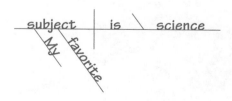

subject | is \ science
My favorite

2. Sugar gives your body quick energy.

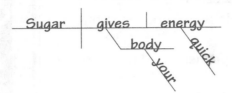

3. They named their dog Jake.

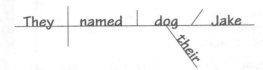

4. The movers pushed the heavy piano up the ramp.

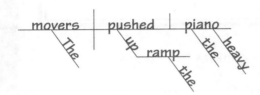

5. A veranda is a big porch with a roof.

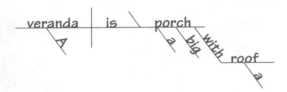

6. The sky was dark before the storm.

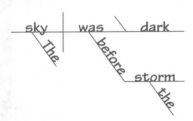

7. Peter's aunt sent him a red homemade scarf.

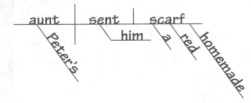

140. Appositives

> • An appositive is placed in parentheses to the right of the word it identifies.
> • Words that describe the appositive go under it.

SENTENCE: **I read *A Christmas Carol,* a famous book by Charles Dickens.**

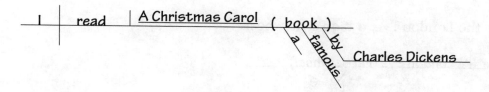

Diagram each sentence.

1. My sister is taking a class in botany, the study of plants.

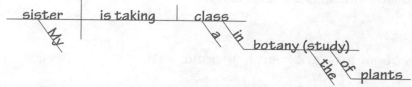

2. James Cook, a British sailor, explored the Pacific in the 1760s.

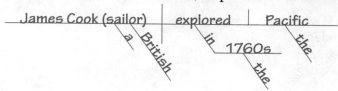

3. My brother Robert is studying Chinese.

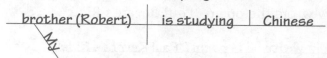

4. Ramadan, a month in the Muslim calendar, is a time of fasting.

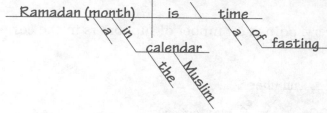

CONTINUED

5. Chicle, juice from a tropical tree, is the main ingredient in chewing gum.

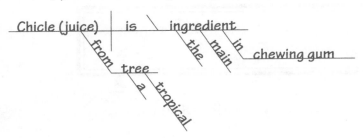

6. Many tourists ride the London Eye, a big Ferris wheel.

7. The dog Snoopy was created by Charles M. Schulz , a cartoonist.

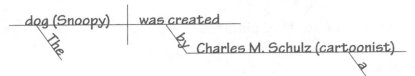

8. The poet James Berry writes about his Caribbean homeland.

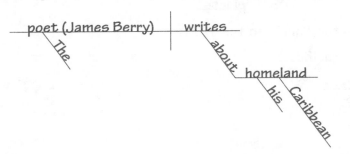

9. The writer Henry Wadsworth Longfellow wrote the poem "Paul Revere's Ride."

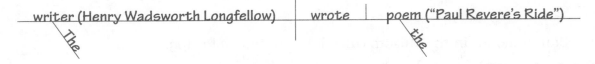

10. Abolitionism, a movement against slavery, gained a number of supporters in the early 1800s.

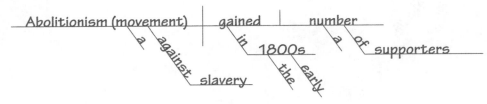

141. Compound Sentences

- Each independent clause of a compound sentence has its own horizontal line, with its subject, verb, objects, and complements in their usual positions.
- The coordinating conjunction or conjunctive adverb that connects the clauses is placed on a vertical dashed line that touches the left edges of the main horizontal lines.

SENTENCE: **I bought a blank book, and I used it for a diary.**

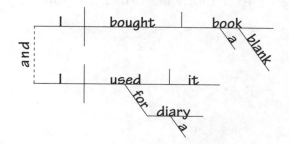

SENTENCE: **The novel was short; consequently, I finished it in one day.**

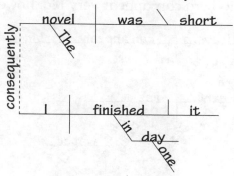

Diagram each sentence.

1. Sharks have a good sense of smell, but their eyesight is poor.

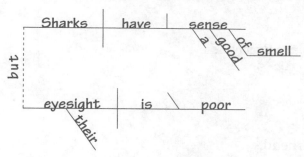

2. Sally Ride was the first American female astronaut; therefore, many people admire her.

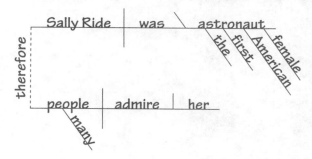

3. The campers sat around the fire, and they told scary stories.

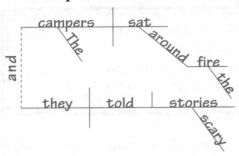

4. An iceberg can appear very big; however, its largest part actually lies under the water.

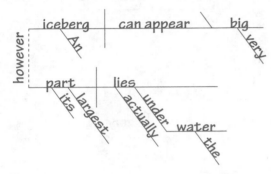

5. South Dakota was part of the Louisiana Purchase, and it became a state in 1889.

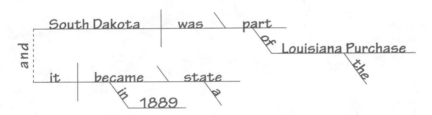

6. Waves hit the beach, and seagulls flew overhead.

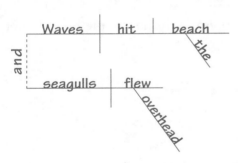

7. I can read my book, or I can watch TV.

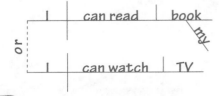

142. Compound Sentence Elements

- Compound subjects and compound predicates are placed on two separate horizontal lines that are joined to the main horizontal line.
- The conjunction connecting the compound parts is placed on a vertical line between them.
- Each subject may have its own modifiers, and each verb may have its own objects, complements, and modifiers.
- Words other than subjects and verbs may also be compound. They are diagrammed in a similar way.

SENTENCE: **Alison and I saw the concert and got autographs from a band member.**

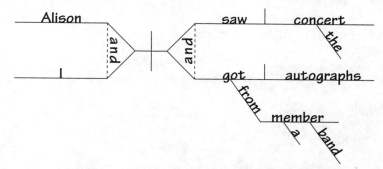

SENTENCE: **Her stories are always funny and creative.**

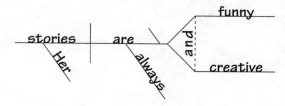

Diagram each sentence.

1. My collage contains beans and beads.

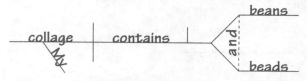

2. Similes and metaphors are figures of speech.

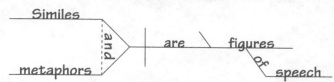

Diagramming

3. The water froze and solidified.

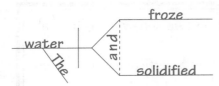

4. The ship entered the harbor and docked at a pier.

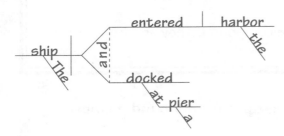

5. Lettuce and sunflowers are in the same family of plants.

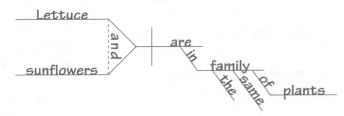

6. In ancient Greece, chariot races were a popular sport and an Olympic event.

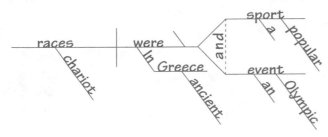

7. German shepherds are famous for their intelligence and loyalty.

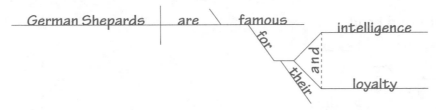

8. I dug holes in the ground and planted the pumpkin seeds.

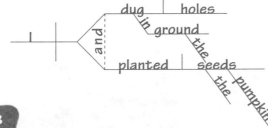

143. Participles

- The participle in a participial phrase starts on a slanted line under the noun or pronoun it describes and extends onto a horizontal line.
- Any direct object or complement is placed on the horizontal line after the participle.
- Modifiers of the participle, its object, or its complement go on slanted lines under the word being described.
- A participle that precedes the noun it describes is positioned as other adjectives are.

SENTENCE: **Cleaning the closet, I found my old skates.**

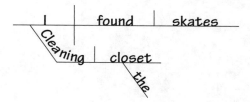

SENTENCE: **An unopened letter lay on the desk.**

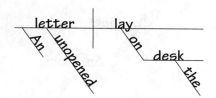

Diagram each sentence.

1. In 1872 President Grant signed a bill creating Yellowstone Park.

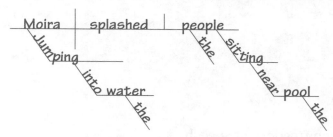

2. Jumping into the water, Moira splashed the people sitting near the pool.

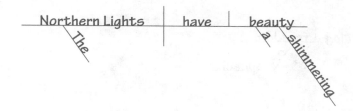

3. The Northern Lights have a shimmering beauty.

CONTINUED

159

4. Walking down the beach, the child gathered seashells.

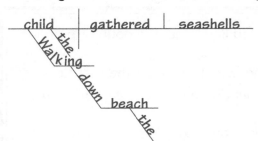

5. Spanish galleons carrying gold from the Americas crossed the Atlantic in the 1500s.

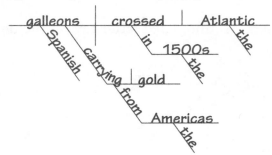

6. The doctor knelt over the injured boy.

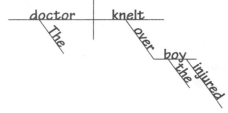

7. Fran gazed at the pictures hanging on the walls.

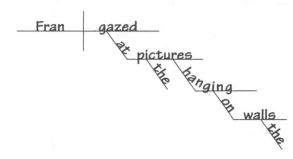

8. Congress must not make laws prohibiting freedom of speech.

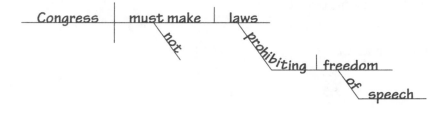

144. Gerunds

- A gerund is placed according to its function in a sentence—as a subject, a subject complement, an object of a verb, an object of a preposition, or an appositive.
- The gerund is placed on a stepped line that extends onto a horizontal line.
- A direct object or a complement is placed after the gerund. Modifiers are placed as usual.
- When used as the object of a preposition, a gerund goes on a stepped line but is not raised.

SENTENCE: **Making supper on Friday evening is my job.**

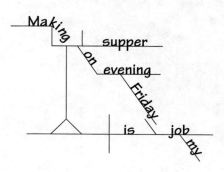

SENTENCE: **Looms are used for weaving cloth.**

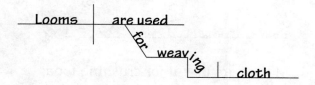

Diagram each sentence.

1. Having friends is important.

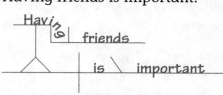

2. The plants need watering.

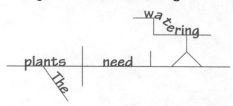

3. Writing a poem is making music.

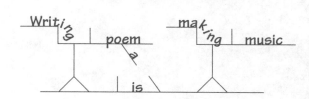

4. My mother's hobby, singing in the choir, requires weekly rehearsals.

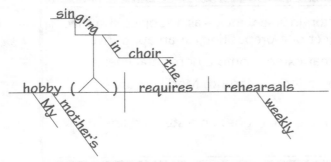

5. We started gathering seashells on the beach.

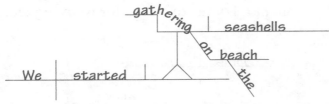

6. Molars are useful for crushing food.

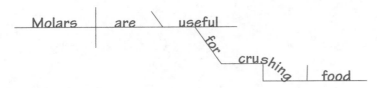

7. An important industry in Australia is raising sheep.

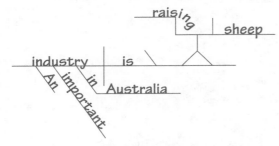

8. The idea of protecting land for wildlife originated in the 1800s.

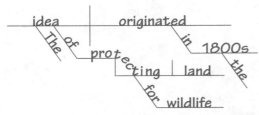

9. We started doing research for our science project.

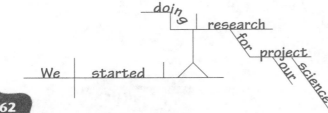

145. Infinitives

> - An infinitive is placed according to its function in a sentence—as a noun, an adjective, or an adverb. When used as a subject, a direct object, a subject complement, or an appositive, an infinitive is placed in the appropriate position over a stem above the main line.
> - As in a prepositional phrase, the word *to* is placed on a slanted line; the verb is on a horizontal line.
> - A direct object or a complement of the infinitive follows the verb on the horizontal line. Modifiers are placed in their usual positions.
> - When used as an adjective or an adverb, an infinitive is placed under the word it describes.

SENTENCE: **We decided to order pizza for supper.**

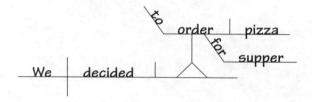

SENTENCE: **I was surprised to get a big package in the mail.**

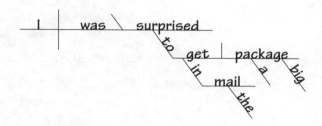

Diagram each sentence.

1. To speak Spanish well is my goal.

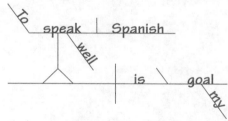

2. Jackson is saving to buy a new bicycle.

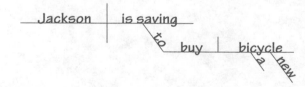

3. Chess seems difficult to play.

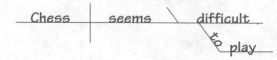

4. People first began to keep records on clay tablets.

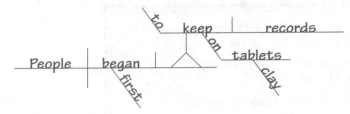

5. The best place to see the Northern Lights is located in the northern part of Alaska.

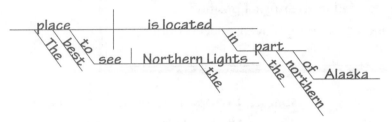

6. My brother wants to learn skiing.

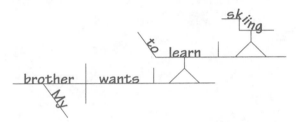

7. My suggestion, to organize a bake sale, was accepted.

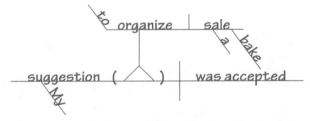

8. To consider bills for passage is Congress's job.

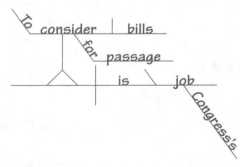

9. The park is a good place to have a picnic.

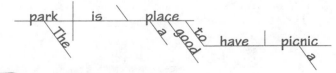

146. Adjective Clauses

- An adjective clause is placed on a horizontal line parallel to and under the horizontal line of the independent clause.
- A dashed line connects the relative pronoun or the subordinate conjunction in the adjective clause to the word in the independent clause that the clause describes. *Whose,* like other possessives, goes under the noun it is associated with.
- A relative pronoun is placed according to its function within the adjective clause.

SENTENCE: **I have some relatives who live in Japan.**

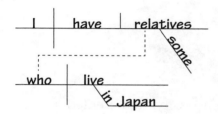

SENTENCE: **The author whose books I really like is Madeleine L'Engle.**

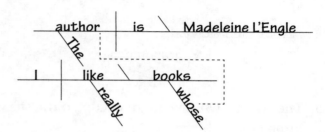

Diagram each sentence.

1. Silkworms, which are really caterpillars, feed on mulberry leaves.

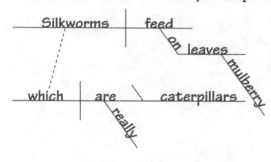

2. Lightning is electricity that people can see.

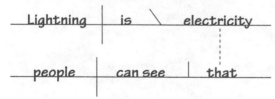

165

3. The Newbery Medal, which is awarded yearly, honors the best children's book.

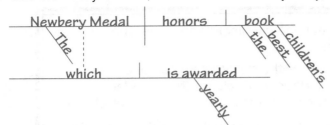

4. In the attic my mother found some antiques that belonged to my grandmother.

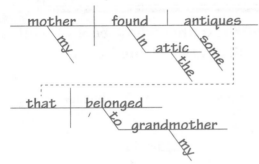

5. The Aztecs, whose capital occupied the site of present-day Mexico City, had created a large empire by the 1400s.

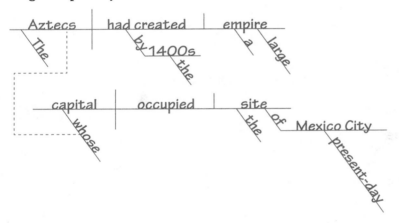

6. People who are good swimmers generally enjoy sailing also.

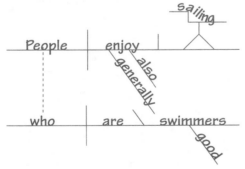

7. My brother got the job that he wanted.

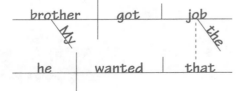

147. Adverb Clauses

> • An adverb clause goes on a horizontal line under the independent clause.
> • The subordinate conjunction is placed on a slanting dashed line that connects the verb in the adverb clause with the word in the independent clause described by the adverb clause.

SENTENCE: **After I learn Spanish, I want to visit Spain.**

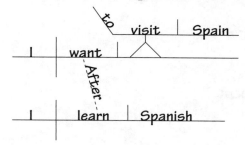

Diagram each sentence.

1. If you follow the directions carefully, you can easily make bread.

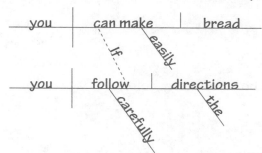

2. Few outsiders visited the Himalayas until the airplane was invented.

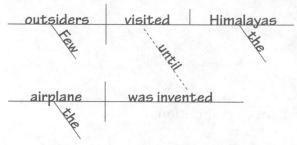

3. Although most grasshoppers can fly, they usually move by jumping.

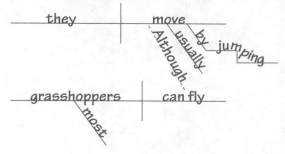

4. After several Southern states left the Union at the time of the Civil War, they formed the Confederacy.

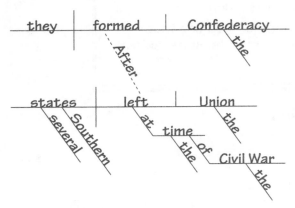

5. I started doing research as soon as I got the assignment.

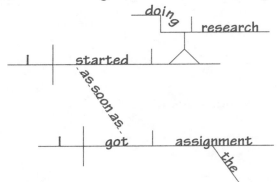

6. When light passes through a prism, it becomes a band of many colors.

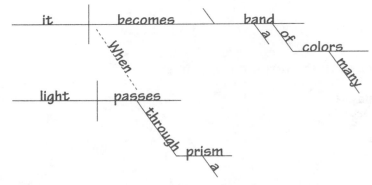

7. Dandelions spread rapidly because they do not need pollination.

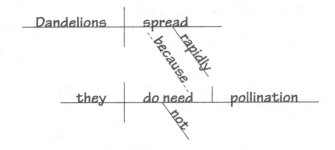

148. Noun Clauses

- A noun clause is placed according to its function in the sentence. It has its own horizontal line that rests on a stem connecting it to the horizontal line of the independent clause.

- Noun clauses, with the exception of those used as objects of prepositions, are placed above the main clause.

- If the word introducing the noun clause has a specific function in the noun clause, it is placed according to that function. If it has no specific function, it is placed on the vertical line that connects the noun clause to the independent clause.

SENTENCE: **I decided that I need a new bike.**

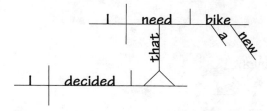

SENTENCE: **The teacher promised extra points to whoever could name all of the presidents.**

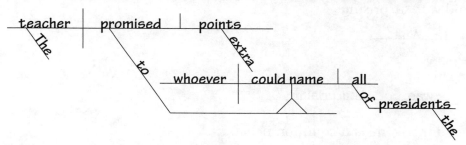

Diagram each sentence.

1. Some people believe that the Northern Lights are spirits in the sky.

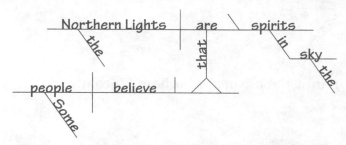

2. I could not believe what my friend told me.

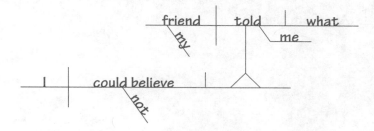

169

3. With an experiment in 1804, Thomas Young showed that light is waves.

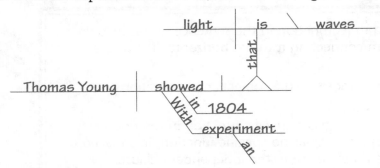

4. That Shakespeare was the greatest writer in English is an opinion held by many.

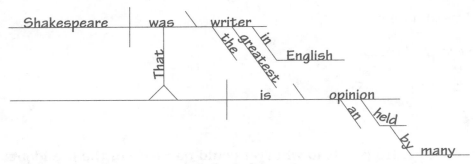

5. What the teacher said was surprising.

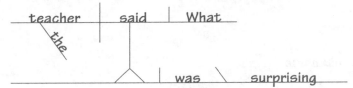

6. That laughter is a good medicine is a common belief.

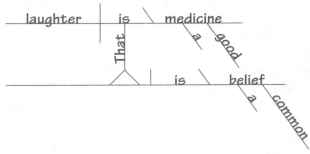

7. The idea that the nation should remain united motivated Abraham Lincoln.

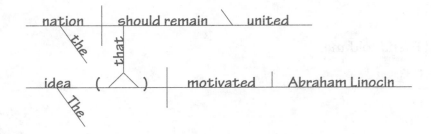

149. Diagramming Review

- Subjects, verbs, direct objects, and complements go on the main horizontal line. Adjectives, adverbs, prepositional phrases, and participles go under the words they describe.

- Gerunds and infinitives may go above or below the main line depending on how they are used in a sentence.

- Compound sentences and sentences with adjective clauses, adverb clauses, and noun clauses have two horizontal lines connected by dashed lines. An adjective clause or an adverb clause is placed on its own horizontal line under the line for the main clause. The line for a noun clause may go above the main horizontal line.

SENTENCE: **Having eaten my entire lunch at ten, I was very hungry again by noon.**

SENTENCE: **Our plan is to travel west by car.**

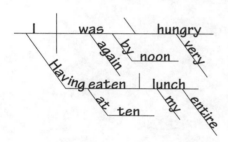
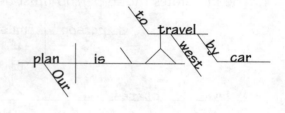

SENTENCE: **Sarah arranged the flowers that she picked from the garden.**

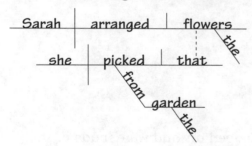

Diagram each sentence.

1. Solving crossword puzzles is fun.

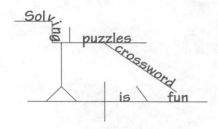

2. Paula described what she did on her trip.

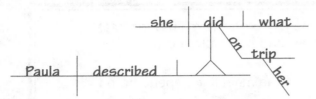

3. When we eat peas and corn, we are eating seeds.

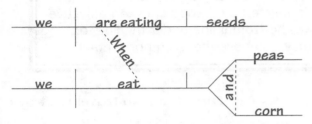

4. The law states that a person must be a citizen to vote.

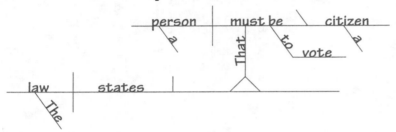

5. Cotton plants are annuals and are planted in the spring.

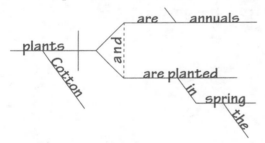

6. The theaters of the ancient Greeks were built in the open air and were made of stone.

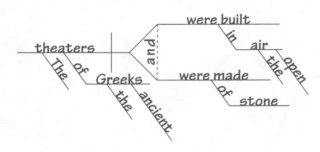

Handbook of Terms

ADJECTIVES

An **adjective** points out or describes a noun.

An **article** points out a noun. *A, an,* and *the* are articles: *a* game, *an* apple, *the* rules.

A **demonstrative adjective** points out a specific person, place, or thing. *This, that, these,* and *those* are demonstrative adjectives: *this* book, *those* pencils.

A **descriptive adjective** tells about age, size, shape, color, origin, or another quality of a noun. A descriptive adjective usually comes before the noun it describes, but it may follow the noun. It may also follow a linking verb: It was a *sunny* morning. The popcorn, *crunchy* and *salty,* tasted *great.*

An **indefinite adjective** refers to any or all members of a group. Indefinite adjectives include *all, another, any, both, each, either, few, many, more, most, much, neither, other, several,* and *some: both* boys, *either* girl.

An **interrogative adjective** is used in questions. *What, which,* and *whose* are interrogative adjectives: *Whose* book is this?

A **possessive adjective** shows possession or ownership. The possessive adjectives are *my, your, his, her, its, our, your,* and *their: my* car, *your* motorcycle.

A **proper adjective** is formed from a proper noun. A proper adjective begins with a capital letter: *American* history.

See also **antecedents, clauses, comparisons, participles, prepositions, sentences, subject-verb agreement.**

ADVERBS

An **adverb** modifies a verb, an adjective, or another adverb.

- An **adverb of affirmation** tells that something is positive or gives consent or approval: The music is *certainly* beautiful.

- An **adverb of degree** answers the question *how much* or *how little:* The boy is *very* tall.

- An **adverb of manner** answers the question *how,* or *in what manner:* Jason draws *well.*

- An **adverb of negation** expresses a negative condition or refusal: The door is *not* locked.

- An **adverb of place** answers the question *where:* Sit *here* by the gate.

- An **adverb of time** answers the question *when* or *how often:* It rained *yesterday.*

An **adverbial noun** is a noun that functions as an adverb. An adverbial noun expresses time, measure, value, or direction: Every *Sunday* we attend church. He ran six *miles.*

A **conjunctive adverb** is used to connect two independent clauses. The principal conjunctive adverbs are *consequently, however, moreover, nevertheless, therefore,* and *thus:* Jill had studied journalism; *therefore,* the newspaper editor hired her.

An **interrogative adverb** is used in asking questions. *Why, where, when,* and *how* are interrogative adverbs: *When* did you do that?

See also **clauses, comparisons, prepositions.**

ANTECEDENTS

The noun to which a pronoun or a possessive adjective refers is its **antecedent.** A pronoun or a possessive adjective must agree with its antecedent in person and number. A third person singular pronoun or possessive adjective must also agree in gender.

See also **adjectives, pronouns.**

CAPITALIZATION

Capital letters are used for many purposes, including the following:

- The first word of a sentence: The bell rang.

- Proper nouns and proper adjectives: Betsy Ross, American flag

- An abbreviation if the word it stands for begins with a capital letter: Rev. for Reverend

- The first word and the name of a person addressed in the salutation of a letter and the first word in the complimentary close of a letter: Dear Marie, Yours truly,

- The principal words in the titles of books, plays, works of art, and poems: *A Tale of Two Cities, Romeo and Juliet, Mona Lisa,* "Fire and Ice"

- The first word of a direct quotation: Mother said, "It's time for my favorite television program."

- Titles when used in direct address as substitutes for the names of persons: Thank you, Professor.

- North, East, South, West when they refer to sections of the country or the world. They are not capitalized when they refer to directions: the old West. He drove west on Main Street.
- The pronoun *I*
- Names referring to the deity or to sacred books: God, the Bible
- Two-letter state postal abbreviations: MA, NY, CA

CLAUSES

A **clause** is a group of related words that contains a subject and predicate.

A **dependent clause** does not express a complete thought and cannot stand alone. A dependent clause, together with an independent clause, forms a complex sentence.

- An **adjective clause** is a dependent clause used as an adjective. An adjective clause is usually introduced by a relative pronoun, such as *who, whom, which, whose,* or *that:* The roses *that he bought* were yellow.

- An **adverb clause** is a dependent clause used as an adverb. An adverb clause is usually introduced by a subordinate conjunction such as *after, although, as, because, before, for, since, that, though, unless, until, when, where,* or *while: After we had canoed down the river,* we went to a clambake on the beach.

- A **noun clause** is a dependent clause used as a noun. Most noun clauses begin with an introductory word such as *that, who, whom, whoever, whomever, how, why, when, whether, what, where,* or *whatever: That he was late* disappointed me.

An **independent clause** expresses a complete thought. An independent clause can stand alone as a sentence.

A **nonrestrictive clause** is a dependent clause that adds information about a person, place, or thing, but it is not necessary to the meaning of the sentence. A nonrestrictive clause is separated from the rest of the sentence by commas: New York City, *which is located on the eastern seaboard,* contains many skyscrapers.

A **restrictive clause** is a dependent clause that points out or identifies a certain person, place, or thing. A restrictive clause cannot be omitted without changing the meaning of a sentence: The girl *who runs fastest* will win the prize.

See also **sentences.**

COMPARISONS

Many adjectives and adverbs can be used to compare two or more persons, places, things, or actions.

- The **positive degree** describes one or more persons, places, things, or actions: The *tall* boy ran *fast.*

- The **comparative degree** compares two persons, places, things, or actions. Form comparatives by adding -er to the positive degree or by putting *more* or *less* before the positive degree: The *younger* child cried *more sadly.*

- The **superlative degree** compares three or more persons, places, things, or actions. Form superlatives by adding -est to the positive degree or by putting *most* or *least* before the positive degree: The *tallest* boy ran *most quickly.*

Few, fewer, and *fewest* are used to compare count nouns. *Little, less,* and *least* are used to compare noncount nouns: *few* dimes, *little* money.

Farther and *further* are used both as adverbs and as adjectives. *Farther* refers to distance; *further* denotes an addition: She went *farther* into the forest. *Further* research is necessary.

Comparisons with *as . . . as* may be made in positive or negative sentences. Comparisons with *so . . . as* may be made only in negative sentences. *As* is never used with *equally* in a comparison: Bill is *as* tall *as* Kelly. John cannot run *so* fast *as* Mike.

The conjunctions *than* and *as* are used to join clauses to make comparisons. Often part of the second clause is omitted. The omitted part must be added mentally to determine whether the pronoun needed is a subject pronoun or an object pronoun: Gary was *as* surprised *as she* (was surprised). Laura gave Tom more candy *than* (she gave) *me.*

CONJUNCTIONS

A conjunction is used to connect words, phrases, or clauses in a sentence.

A **coordinating conjunction** connects words, phrases, or clauses of the same rank and function. *And, or, but, so, nor,* or *yet* are coordinating conjunctions: Todd *or* Cindy will come early to help us.

Correlative conjunctions are conjunctions used in pairs: *Neither* Tom *nor* Laurie came to the party.

A **conjunctive adverb** connects two independent clauses. It is preceded by a semicolon and followed by a comma: The meal was expensive; *however,* I wasn't surprised.

A **subordinate conjunction** introduces a dependent clause and connects it to an independent clause: He missed gym class *because* he was sick.

See also **adverbs, clauses, sentences.**

GERUNDS

A **gerund** is a verb form ending in *-ing* that is used as a noun. A **gerund phrase** is a gerund along with any direct object, complement, and/or modifiers. A gerund or a gerund phrase can be used as a subject, a subject complement, a direct object, an object of a preposition, or an appositive: *Swimming* is good exercise. She enjoys *cooking elaborate meals*.

A gerund may be preceded by a possessive noun or a possessive adjective. The possessive describes the doer of the action of the gerund: *My* arriving early was a surprise.

INFINITIVES

An **infinitive** is a verb form, usually preceded by *to,* that can be used as a noun, an adjective, or an adverb. An **infinitive phrase** is an infinitive and its direct object, complement, and/or modifiers. An infinitive or an infinitive phrase used as a noun can be a subject, a subject complement, a direct object, an object of a preposition, or an appositive: *To win* was our goal. He wanted *to earn some money*.

A **hidden infinitive,** one in which the word *to* is not used, appears after verbs such as *hear, see, know, feel, let, make,* and *help* and with the prepositions *but* and *except* and the conjunction *than:* I helped her *construct* the framework.

A **split infinitive** results when an adverb is placed between *to* and the verb. Split infinitives generally should be avoided.

INTERJECTIONS

An **interjection** expresses a strong or sudden emotion, such as delight, disgust, pain, agreement, impatience, surprise, sorrow, or wonder. An interjection is grammatically distinct from the rest of the sentence: *Oh! Shh! Ouch! Wow!*

MOOD

Mood shows the manner in which the action or state of being of a verb is expressed.

- The **imperative mood** is used to give commands: Please *call* me.

- The **indicative mood** is used to state a fact or ask a question: Where *are* you?

- The **subjunctive mood** is used to express a wish or a desire or a condition that is contrary to fact. The subjunctive is also used to express a demand or a recommendation after *that:* She wishes she *were coming* with us. If she *had* more money, she would come. Her mother recommended that she *get* a job.

NOUNS

A **noun** is the name of a person, place, or thing.

An **abstract noun** names a quality, a condition, or a state of mind. An abstract noun names something that cannot be seen or touched: *anger, idea, spirit.*

A **collective noun** names a group of persons, places, or things considered as a unit. A collective noun usually takes a verb that agrees with a singular noun: The *crew* is tired. The *herd* is resting.

A **common noun** names any one member of a group of persons, places, or things: *queen, city, church.*

A **concrete noun** names a thing that can be seen or touched: *brother, river, tree.*

A **count noun** names something that can be counted: *nickels, bags, emotions.*

A **noncount noun** names something that cannot be counted: *money, luggage, fear.*

A **plural noun** names more than one person, place, or thing: *boys, berries, geese.*

A **possessive noun** expresses possession or ownership.

- To form the possessive of a singular noun, add -'s to the singular form: *architect's.*

- To form the possessive of a plural noun that ends in *s*, add an apostrophe to the plural form: *farmers'.*

- To form the possessive of a plural noun that does not end in *s,* add -'s to the plural form: *children's.*

- To show separate possession, add -'s to each noun: *Meg's* and *Mike's* dogs.

- To show joint possession, add -'s to the last noun only: *Jack* and *Jill's* pail.

A **proper noun** names a particular person, place, or thing. A proper noun is capitalized: *Queen Elizabeth, London, Westminster Abbey.*

A **singular noun** names one person, place, or thing: *boy, river, berry.*

See also **clauses, gerunds, infinitives, prepositions, sentences, subject-verb agreement.**

PARTICIPLES

A **participle** is a verb form that can be used as an adjective. Present participles end in *-ing,* and past participles often end in *-ed.* A participle used as an adjective can come before or after the noun it modifies or after a linking verb: The *broiled* chicken tasted great. The cake *baking* in the oven smelled delicious. The lemonade was *refreshing.*

A participial adjective that does not modify any noun or pronoun in a sentence is called a **dangling participle.** Sentences with dangling participles must be rewritten.

PREPOSITIONS

A **preposition** is a word that shows the relationship between a noun or a pronoun and some other word in the sentence. The **object of a preposition** is the noun or pronoun that follows the preposition: The huge mountain lion leaped *through* (preposition) the tall *grass* (object of the preposition).

A **prepositional phrase** is a phrase that is introduced by a preposition.

- An **adjective phrase** is used as an adjective and modifies a noun or a pronoun: The cabin *in the woods* burned down.

- An **adverb phrase** is used as an adverb and usually modifies a verb: The river flows *into the sea.*

- A **noun phrase** is used as a noun. It can be used as a subject or a subject complement: *Before dinner* is a good time to do your homework.

PRONOUNS

A **pronoun** is a word that takes the place of a noun or nouns.

A **demonstrative pronoun** points out a definite person, place, or thing. *This, that, these,* and *those* are demonstrative pronouns: *This* is mine. *Those* are yours.

An **indefinite pronoun** refers to any or all of a group of persons, places, or things. Among the indefinite pronouns are *all, another, both, each, either, few, many, neither, nothing, several, some,* and pronouns beginning with *any* or *every: Each* wants to be on the team. *Both* must pass physicals.

An **intensive pronoun** is used to show emphasis. The intensive pronouns are *myself, yourself, himself, herself, itself, ourselves, yourselves,* and *themselves:* I *myself* cooked the entire dinner.

An **interrogative pronoun** is used to ask a question. The interrogative pronouns are *who, whom, which, what,* and *whose:* To *whom* does this belong?

An **object pronoun** is used as the direct or indirect object of a verb or as the object of a preposition. The object pronouns are *me, you, him, her, it, us,* and *them.*

Personal pronouns have different forms.

- A personal pronoun shows **person:** the speaker **(first person),** the person spoken to **(second person),** or the person, place, or thing spoken about **(third person).** The first person pronouns are *I, me, mine, we, us,* and *ours.* The second person pronouns are *you* and *yours.* The third person pronouns are *he, him, his, she, her, hers, it, its, they, them,* and *theirs.*

- A personal pronoun shows **number.** It is **singular** when it refers to one person, place, or thing. The singular pronouns are *I, me, mine, you, yours, he, him, his, she, her, hers, it,* and *its.* A personal pronoun is **plural** when it refers to more than one person, place, or thing. The plural pronouns are *we, us, ours, you, yours, they, their,* and *theirs.*

- The third person singular pronoun shows **gender.** It can be **masculine** (*he, him, his*), **feminine** (*she, her, hers*), or **neuter** (*it, its*).

A **possessive pronoun** shows possession or ownership. The possessive pronouns are *mine, yours, his, hers, its, ours,* and *theirs.* A possessive pronoun takes the place of a noun and its possessive adjective. Although possessive pronouns show ownership, they do not contain apostrophes: The new skates are *hers.*

A **reflexive pronoun** can be used as a direct or an indirect object or as the object of a preposition. The reflexive pronouns are *myself, yourself, himself, herself, itself, ourselves, yourselves,* and *themselves:* She made *herself* a sandwich.

A **relative pronoun** connects a noun clause to the person, place, or thing it modifies. The relative pronouns are *who, whom, whose, which,* and *that:* Hal, *who* grew up in Indonesia, now lives in Boston.

A **subject pronoun** is used as a subject or a subject complement. The subject pronouns are *I, you, he, she, it, we,* and *they: We* played soccer. The goalie was *he.*

See also **antecedents, clauses, comparisons, gerunds, sentences, subject-verb agreement.**

PUNCTUATION

An **apostrophe** (') is used as follows:

- To show ownership: the *cook's* hat, the *girls'* horses

- To replace letters or numbers that are omitted: *wasn't, '76*

- With *s* to show the plural of small letters but not capital letters unless the plural could be mistaken for a word: *p's* and *q's, Rs* and *A's*

A **colon** (:) is used as follows:

- After the salutation in a business letter: Dear Sir:

- Before a list when terms such as *follows* or *the following* are used: We bought the following: eggs, limes, bread.

A **comma** (,) is used to make reading clearer. Among the comma's uses are the following:

- To separate words or groups of words in a series and adjectives of equal importance before nouns: On a hot, sunny day we saw elephants, giraffes, hyenas, and monkeys.

- To set off parts of dates, addresses, or geographical names: January 1, 2003; 321 Spring Road, Atlanta, Georgia

- To set off a word in direct address: Josie, I'm so pleased that you called me this morning.

- After the word *yes* or *no* when it introduces a sentence: Yes, I agree with you completely.

- To set off a direct quotation, unless a question mark or exclamation point is required: "We have only vanilla and chocolate today," he said in an apologetic tone.

- Before a coordinating conjunction or after a conjunctive adverb in a compound sentence: She called his name, but he didn't answer her. She became angry; however, she soon got over it.

- After the salutation of a friendly letter and after the closing of a letter: Dear Ben, Sincerely yours,

- To set off a parenthetical expression—a word or a group of words that is inserted into a sentence as a comment or explanatory remark but is not necessary to the thought of the sentence: The time, I think, is up.

- After a long introductory phrase or after an introductory clause: As the band marched down the street, the class cheered and applauded.

- To separate nonrestrictive phrases and clauses from the rest of the sentence: Chicago, which is the largest city in Illinois, is not the state capital.

A **dash** (—) is used to indicate a sudden change of thought: The boy jumped—indeed soared—over the hurdle.

An **exclamation point** (!) is used after an interjection and after an exclamatory sentence: Wow! What a celebration that was!

A **hyphen** (-) is used as follows:

- To divide a word at the end of a line whenever one or more syllables are carried to the next line.

- In the words for numbers from twenty-one to ninety-nine and between the parts of some compound words: *soldier-statesman, half-baked* plan.

A **period** (.) is used at the end of a declarative or an imperative sentence and after initials and some abbreviations: Pres. J. F. Kennedy was from Massachusetts.

A **question mark** (?) is used at the end of an interrogative sentence: What time is it?

Quotation marks (". . .") are used as follows:

- Before and after every direct quotation and every part of a divided quotation: "Let's go shopping," said Michiko. "I can go with you," Father said, "after I have eaten lunch."

- To enclose titles of short stories, poems, and magazine articles. Titles of books, magazines, newspapers, movies, TV shows, and works of art are usually printed in *italics* or are underlined: I read "The Lost City" in *Newsweek.*

A **semicolon** (;) is used as follows:

- To separate the clauses of a compound sentence when they are not separated by a conjunction: I can't ride my bike; the wheel is damaged.

- To separate the clauses of a compound sentence that are connected by a conjunctive adverb: Helga plays the violin; however, she can barely read music.

- To separate phrases or clauses that have internal punctuation: We went to Paris, France; Rome, Italy; and London, England.

- Before expressions such as *for example* or *namely* when they are used to introduce examples: He achieved his goals; namely, acceptance into college and a scholarship.

SENTENCES

A sentence is a group of words that expresses a complete thought. A sentence must have a subject and a predicate and may contain other elements.

- An **appositive** is a word or group of words that follows a noun or a pronoun in a sentence and renames it: Kanisha Taylor, the *president* of our class, will make the first speech.

- A **direct object** is the receiver of the action of a verb. A noun or an object pronoun can be used as a direct object: Nat helped *him* with his homework.

- An **indirect object** is a noun or an object pronoun that tells *to whom, to what, for whom,* or *for what* the action in a sentence is done: I gave *him* a present.

- A **predicate** tells something about the subject. The **simple predicate** is a verb or verb phrase: Teresa *waved.* The **complete predicate** is the verb with all its modifiers, objects, and complements: Teresa *waved to the child from the window.*

- An **object complement** follows a direct object and completes the thought expressed by the verb. An object complement can be a noun or an adjective: They elected Jim *president.* He found the job *difficult.*

- A **subject** names the person, place, or thing a sentence is about. The **simple subject** is a noun or a pronoun: The *man* is riding his bike. The **complete subject** is the simple subject with all its modifiers: *The tall, athletic, young man* is riding his bike.

- A **subject complement** is a word that completes the meaning of a sentence that has a linking verb. A subject complement may be a noun, a pronoun, or an adjective: Broccoli is a green *vegetable.* The winner was *she.* The sea will be *cold.*

A **complex sentence** contains one independent clause and one or more dependent clauses: *If you want to win, you must jump higher.*

- A **dependent clause** does not express a complete thought and cannot stand alone: *If you want to win*

- An **independent clause** expresses a complete thought: *You must jump higher.*

A **compound sentence** contains two or more independent clauses.

- The clauses in a compound sentence are usually connected by a conjunction or by a conjunctive adverb: Usually Jane drives to work, *but* today she took the train. She left early; *nevertheless,* she was late for work.

- A semicolon may be used to separate the clauses in a compound sentence: She left on time; the train was late.

A **declarative sentence** makes a statement. A declarative sentence is followed by a period: The sun is shining.

An **exclamatory sentence** expresses strong or sudden emotion. An exclamatory sentence is followed by an exclamation point: What a loud noise that was!

An **imperative sentence** gives a command or makes a request. An imperative sentence is followed by a period: Go to the store. Please pick up the papers.

An **interrogative sentence** asks a question. An interrogative sentence is followed by a question mark: Where is my pen?

A **simple sentence** contains one subject and one predicate. Either or both may be compound. Any objects and/or complements may also be compound: *Ivan* and *John* argued with the grocer. The baby *walks* and *talks* well. Wear your *hat, scarf,* and *gloves.*

See also **clauses, subject-verb agreement.**

SUBJECT-VERB AGREEMENT

A subject and a verb must always agree.

- A phrase or a parenthetical expression between the subject and the verb does not affect the verb: A *crate* of bananas *was* hoisted off the boat.

- Indefinite pronouns such as *anyone, anything, everybody, no one, nobody, nothing, one, somebody,* and *something* and indefinite adjectives such as *another, each, either, neither,* and *other* always require the verb that agrees with the third person singular. Possessive adjectives and pronouns that refer to these words must be singular: *Everyone* in this class *works* hard for *his* or *her* grades. *Neither* girl *was doing her* homework on the bus.

- Indefinite pronouns and indefinite adjectives such as *both, few,* and *many* and indefinite pronouns and indefinite adjectives such as *all, any, most,* and *some* generally require the verb that agrees with the third person plural. Possessive adjectives and pronouns that refer to these words must be plural: *Few look* to *their* left before turning. *Most* puppies *enjoy their* treats.

- A collective noun is singular if the idea expressed by the subject is thought of as a unit: The orchestra *plays* tomorrow. A collective noun is plural if the idea expressed by the subject is thought of as individuals: The family *are* living in Georgia, Virginia, and the Carolinas.

- In sentences beginning with *there,* use *there is* or *there was* when the subject that follows is singular. Use *there are* or *there were* when the subject is plural: *There is* no cause for alarm. *There were* many passengers on the bus.

- Compound subjects connected by *and* are generally plural. If, however, the subjects connected by *and* refer to the same person, place, or thing or express a single idea, the subject is considered singular: Bob and Ted *are* making breakfast. Ham and eggs *is* their favorite meal.

- When compound subjects are connected by *or* or *nor,* the verb agrees with the subject closer to it: *Neither* Ken *nor* the twins *are* here. *Neither* the twins *nor* Ken *is* here.

- When two or more subjects connected by *and* are preceded by *each, every, many a,* or *no,* the subject is considered singular: *Every* teacher and student *has heard* the news.

TENSES

The tense of a verb shows the time of its action.

- The **simple present tense** tells about something that is true or about an action that happens again and again: I *play* the piano every afternoon.

- The **simple past tense** tells about an action that happened in the past: I *played* the piano yesterday afternoon.

- The **future tense** tells about an action that will happen in the future. The future is formed with the present and the auxiliary verb *will* or the verb phrase *be going to:* The piano recital *will be* on Sunday. I *am going to play* two songs.

- The **present progressive tense** tells what is happening now. The present progressive tense is formed with the present participle and a form of the verb *be:* He *is eating* his lunch now.

- The **past progressive tense** tells what was happening in the past. The past progressive tense is formed with the present participle and a past form of the verb *be:* He *was eating* his lunch when I saw him.

- The **present perfect tense** tells about a past action that is relevant to the present. The present perfect tense is formed with *have* or *has* and the past participle: I *have lived* here for six years now.

- The **past perfect tense** tells about a past action that happened before another past action. The past perfect tense is formed with *had* and the past participle: I *had lived* in Memphis for a year before I moved here.

- The **future perfect tense** tells about an action that will be completed by a specific time in the future. The future perfect tense is formed with *will have* and the past participle: I *will have finished* dinner by the time you get here.

VERBALS

A **verbal** is a verb form used as a noun, an adjective, or an adverb. *See* **gerunds, infinitives, participles.**

VERBS

A **verb** is a word that expresses action or state of being.

An **intransitive verb** has no receiver of the action. It does not have a direct object: The sun *shone* on the lake.

A **linking verb** links a subject with a subject complement (a noun, a pronoun, or an adjective).

- The verb *be* in its many forms *(is, are, was, will be, have been,* etc.) is the most common linking verb: He *is* happy. They *are* students.

- The verbs *appear, become, continue, feel, grow, look, remain, seem, smell, sound,* and *taste* are also considered linking verbs: This *tastes* good. She *became* president.

Modal auxiliary verbs such as *may, might, can, could, must, should,* and *would* are used to express permission, possibility, ability, necessity, and obligation: You *should* hurry. We *might be* late.

A verb has four **principal parts:** the present, the present participle, the past, and the past participle.

- The present participle is formed by adding *-ing* to the present: *walking, running.*

- The simple past and the past participle of **regular verbs** are formed by adding *-d* or *-ed* to the present: *skate, skated; walked, walked.*

- The simple past and the past participle of **irregular verbs** are not formed by adding *-ed* to the present: *ran, run.*

A **transitive verb** expresses an action that passes from a doer to a receiver. The receiver is the direct object of the verb: The dog *chewed* the bone.

A **verb phrase** is a group of words that does the work of a single verb. A verb phrase contains one or more **auxiliary verbs** *(is, are, has, have, will, can, could, do, would, should,* and so forth) and a **main verb:** She *had forgotten* her hat.

VOICE

In the **active voice** the subject is the doer of the action: Betty *wrote* a poem.

In the **passive voice** the subject is the receiver of the action. Only transitive verbs can be used in the passive voice: The poem *was written* by Betty.